I0709662

reverie
Laurent Castellani

COLLECTIVE SHORTS
by NHP PUBLISHING

To my wife and my son

À ma femme et mon fils

It was in L'île de Ré, in August 1991. I could hear in
the distance the sound of the waves crashing into
the sand. A dream of freedom crossed my mind
where what I called "the hut from the very top of
the summit" (a child's phrase, with the wrong syntax).
In fact, a hut made of ferns and placed on top of a
pine tree, the smell of which comes easily to me as
I write these lines. I was 11 years old, and since then,
a lifetime of making this dream come true.

C'était dans L'île de Ré, en Août 1991. J'entendais au
loin le bruit que faisaient les vagues en s'écrasant
sur le sable. Un rêve de liberté traversait mon esprit
dans ce que j'appelais « la cabane du très haut du
sommet » (phrase d'enfant à la syntaxe fausse). En
réalité, une cahute faite de fougères et érigée en haut
d'un pin dont l'odeur me revient aisément en écrivant
ces lignes. J'avais 11 ans, et depuis, une vie passée à
réaliser ce rêve.

– Laurent Castellani

Castle Rock

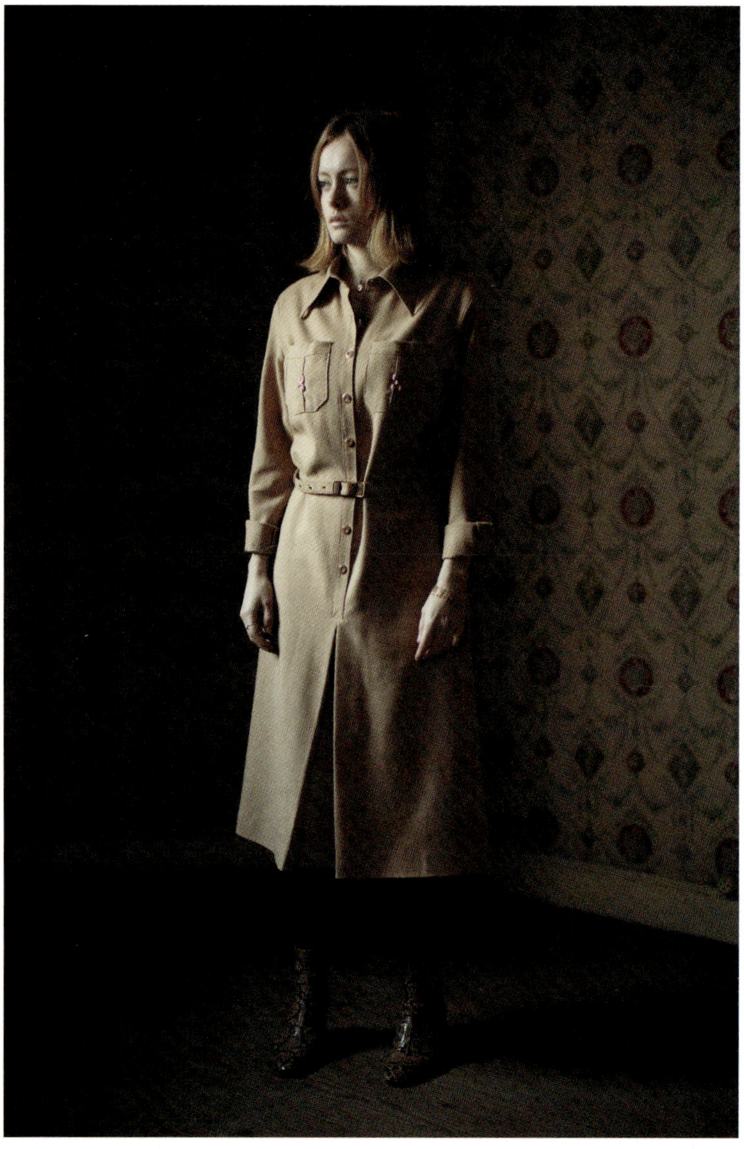

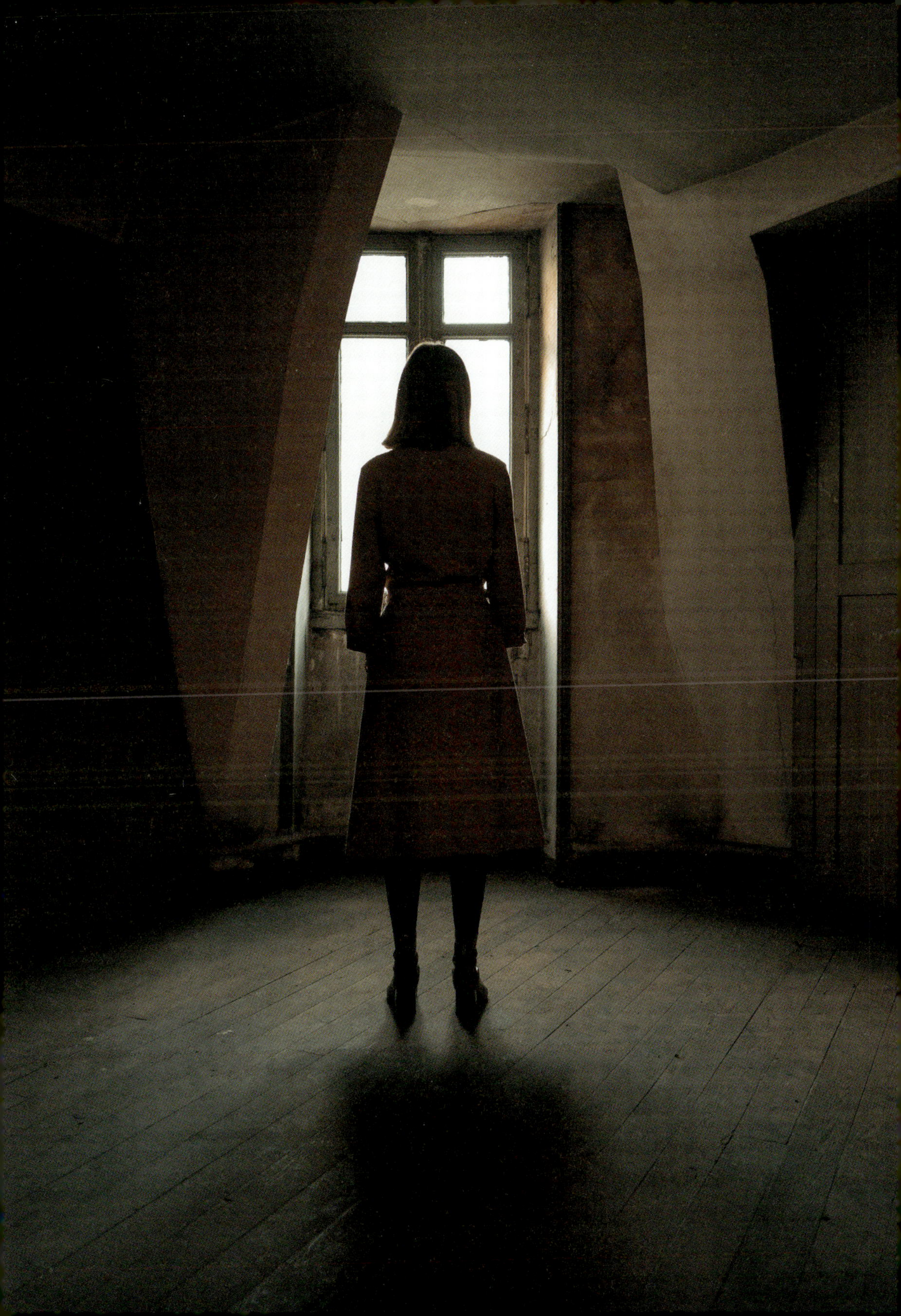

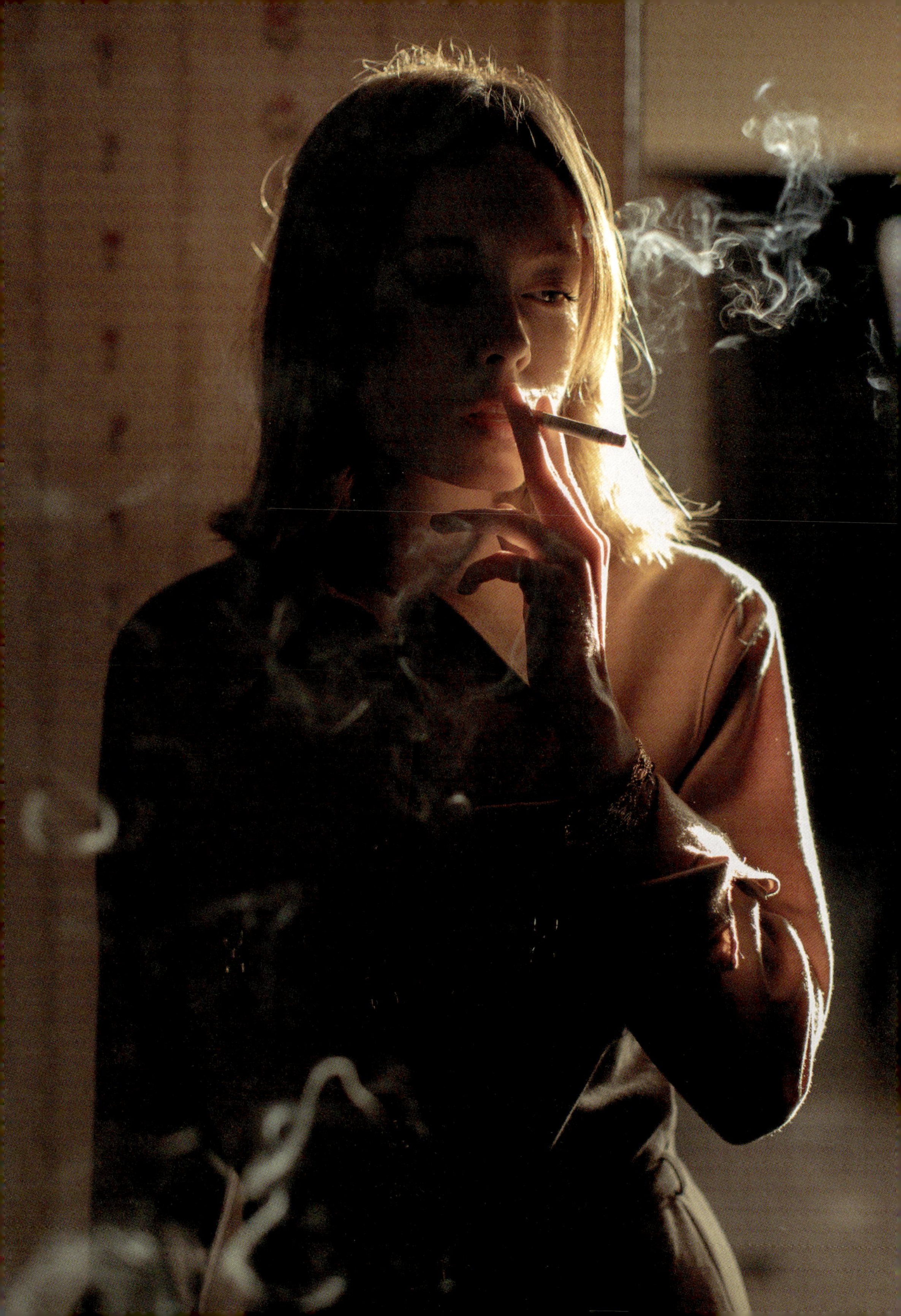

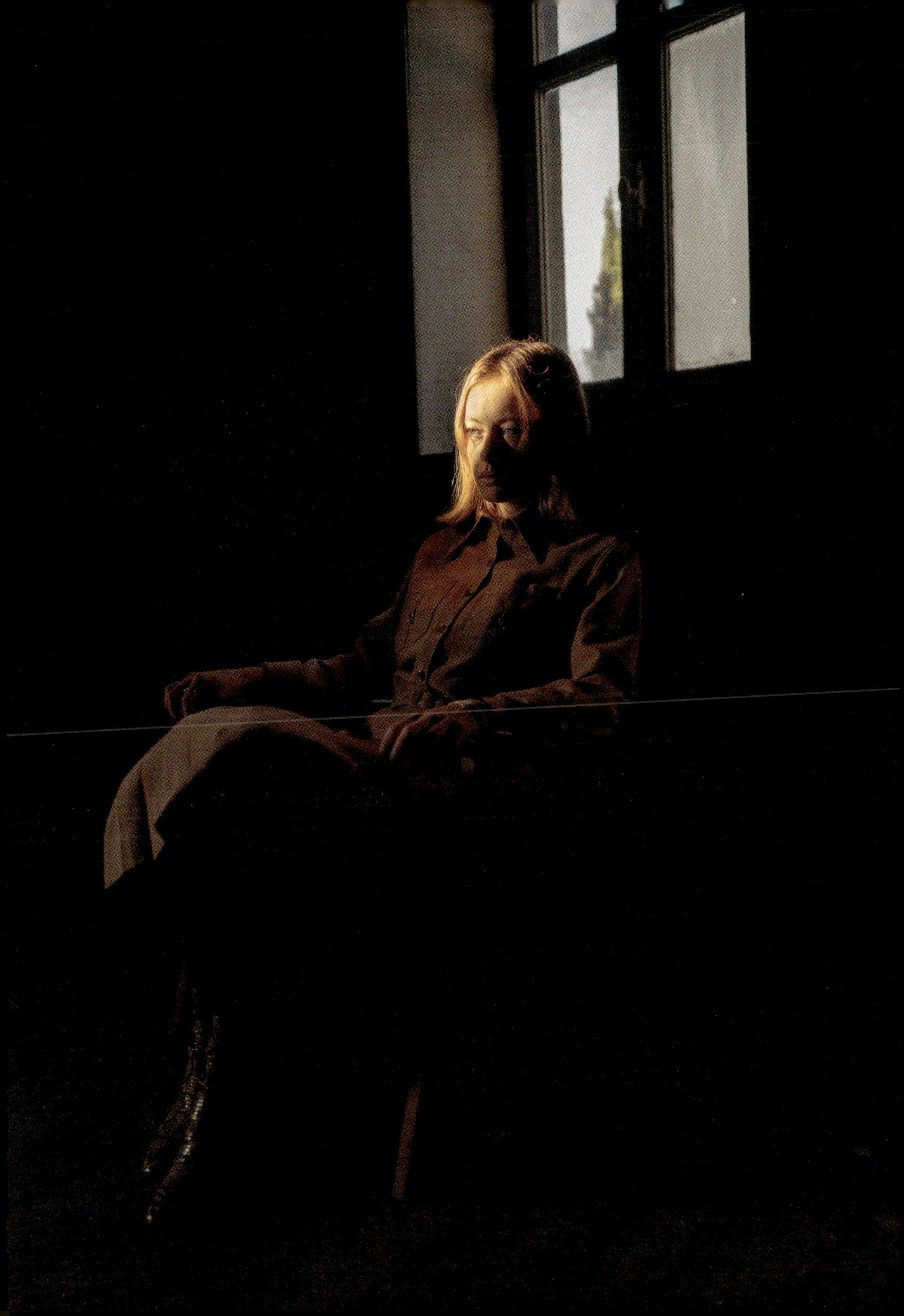

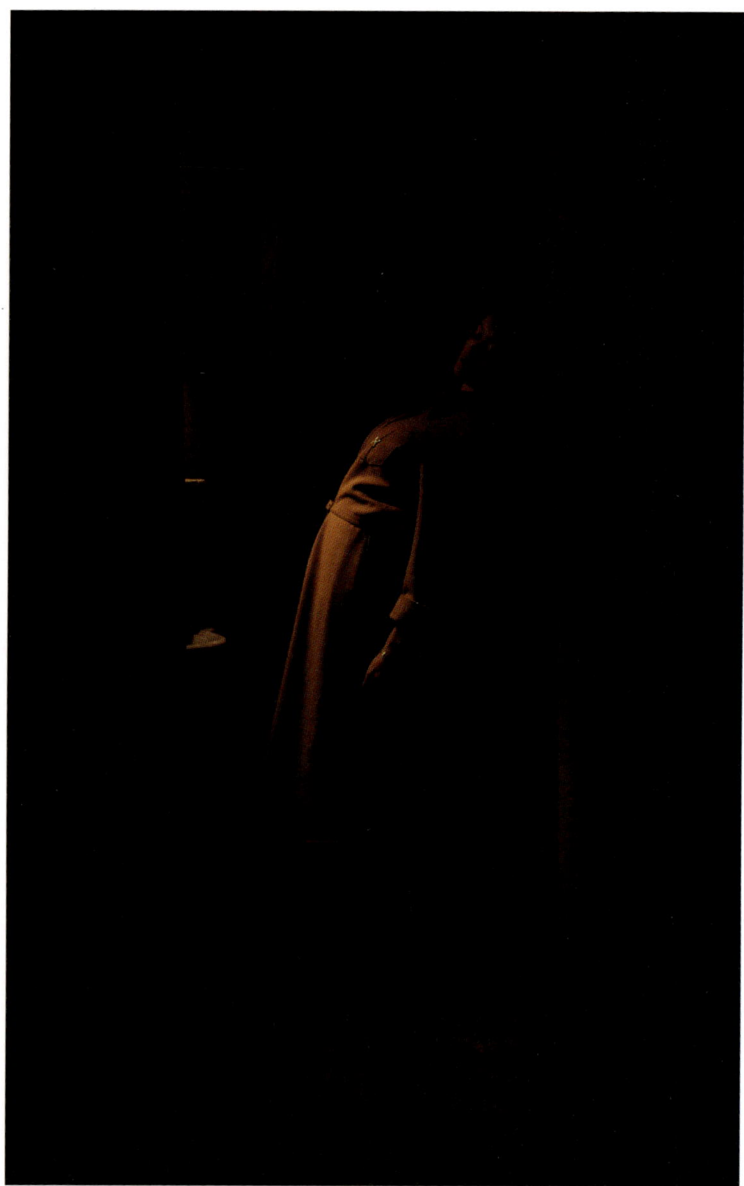

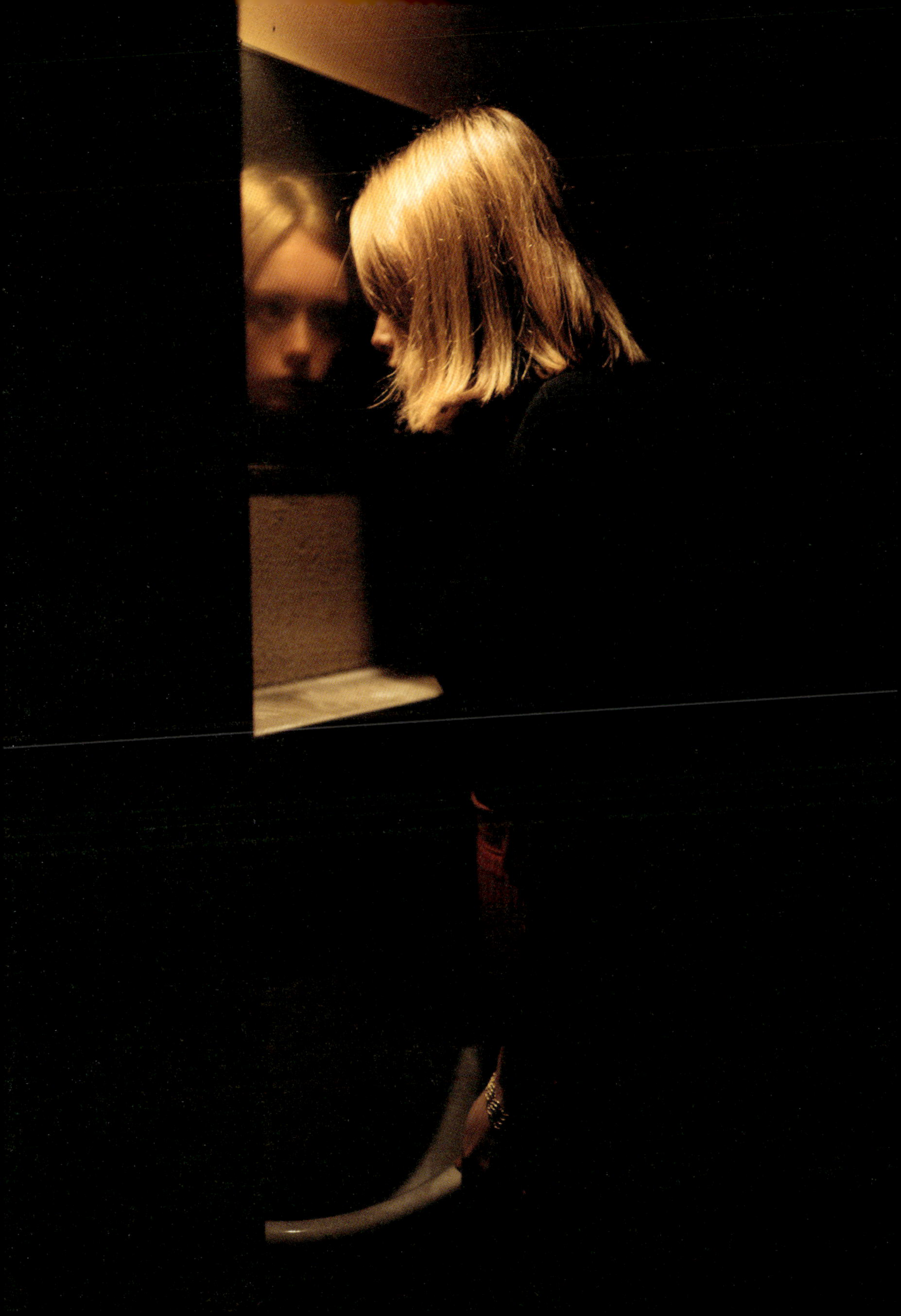

Art is born of constraint, lives in struggle,
and dies in freedom.

– André Gide

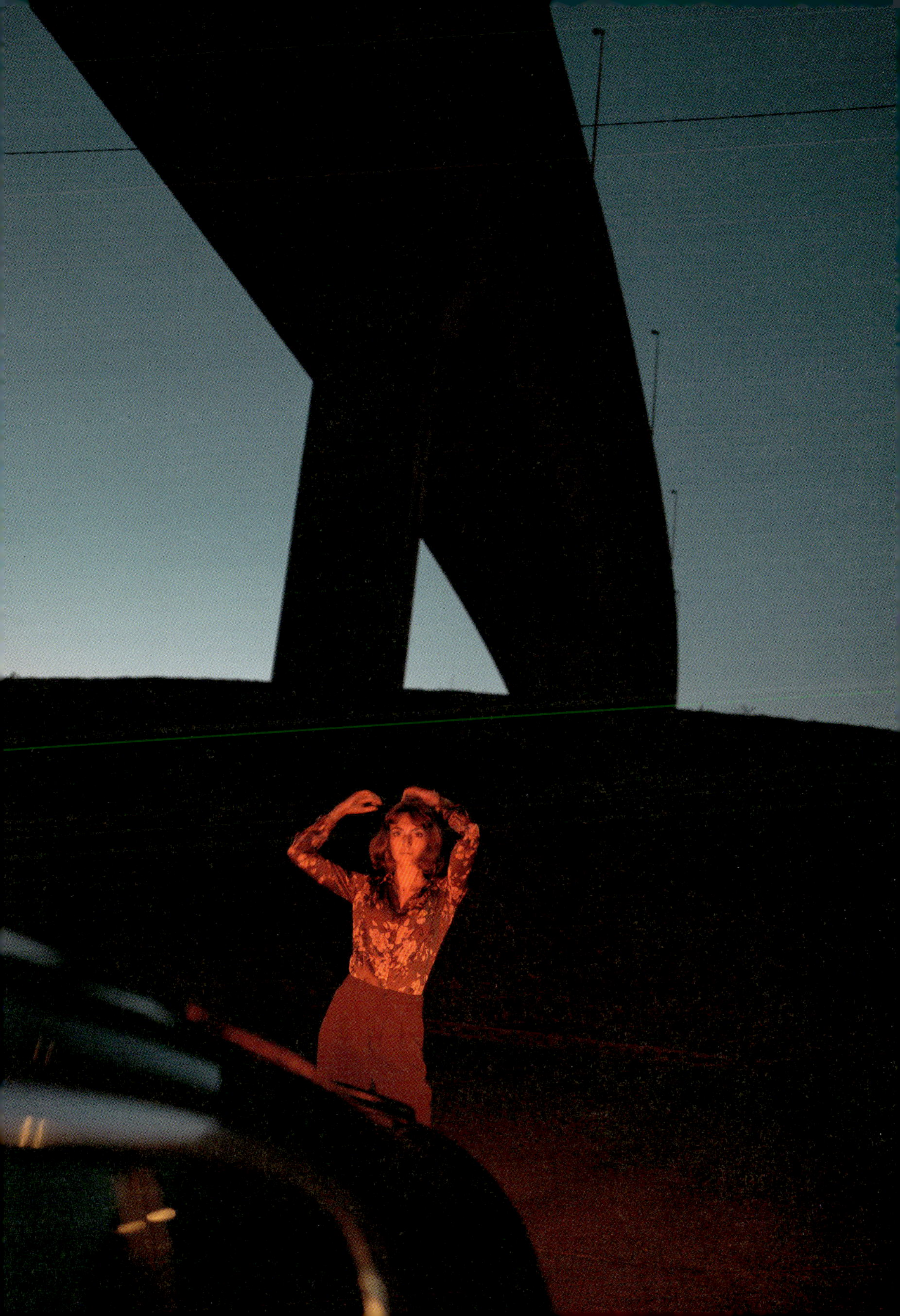

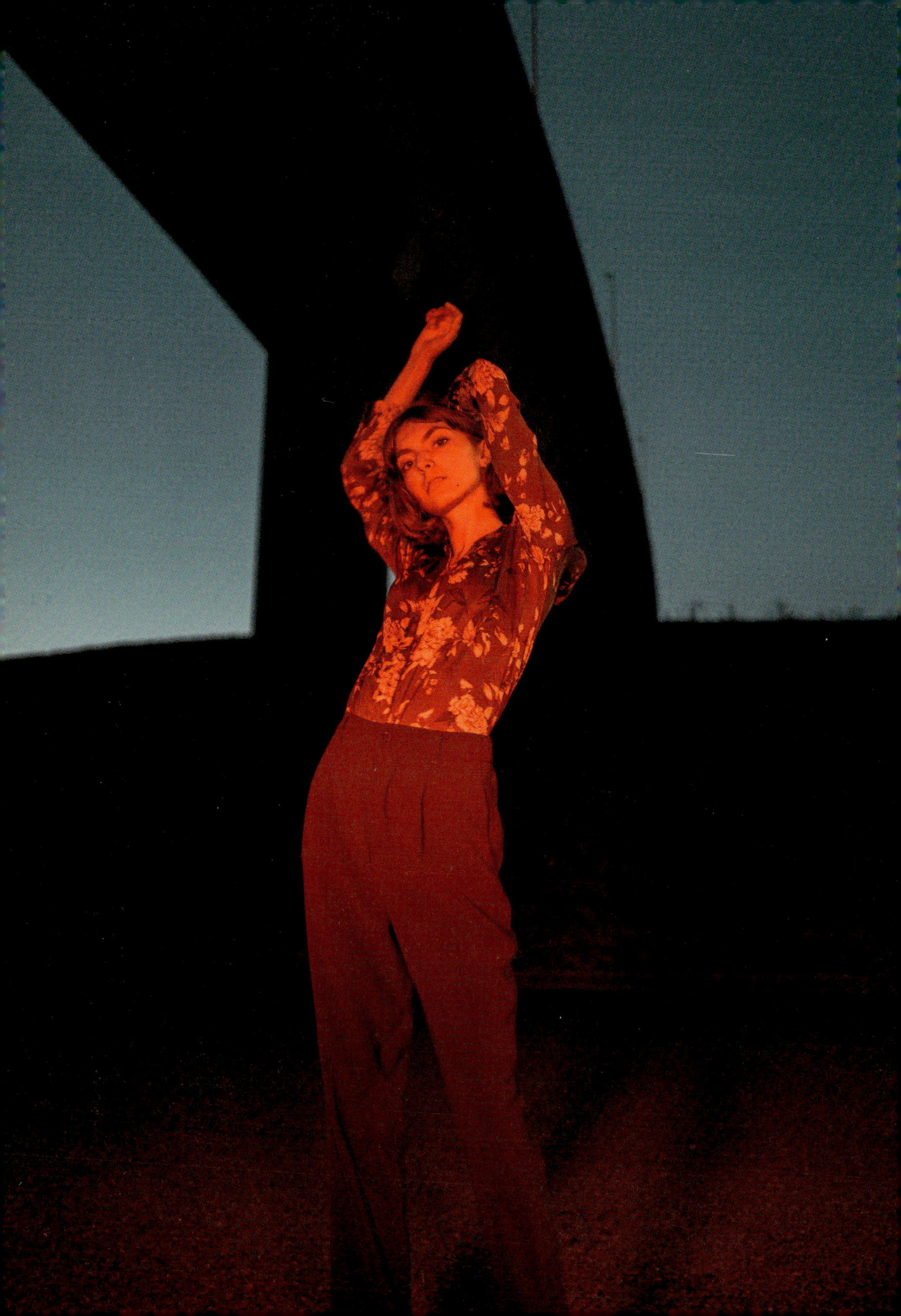

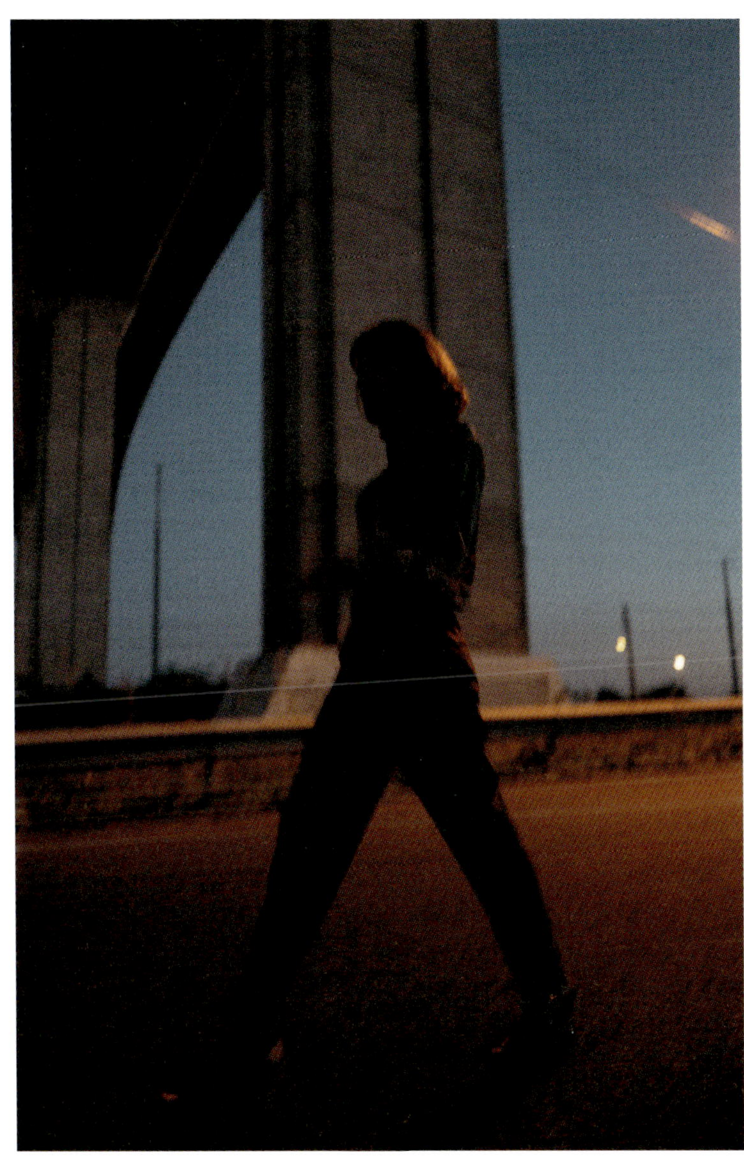

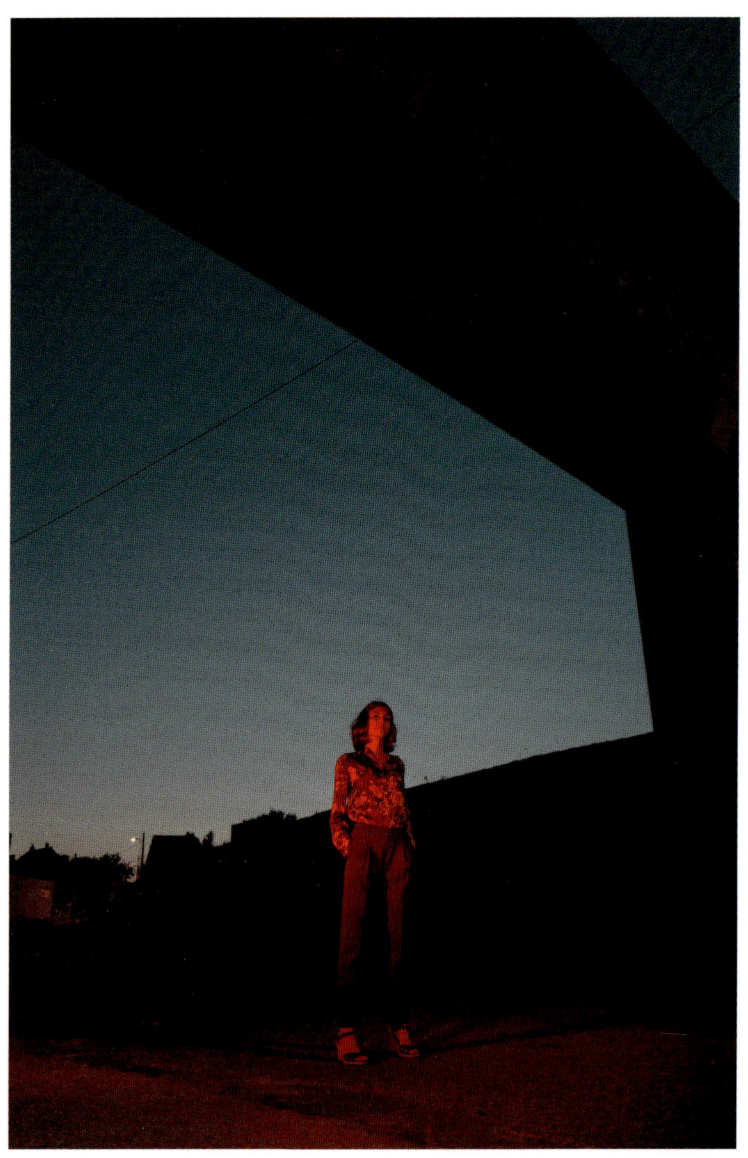

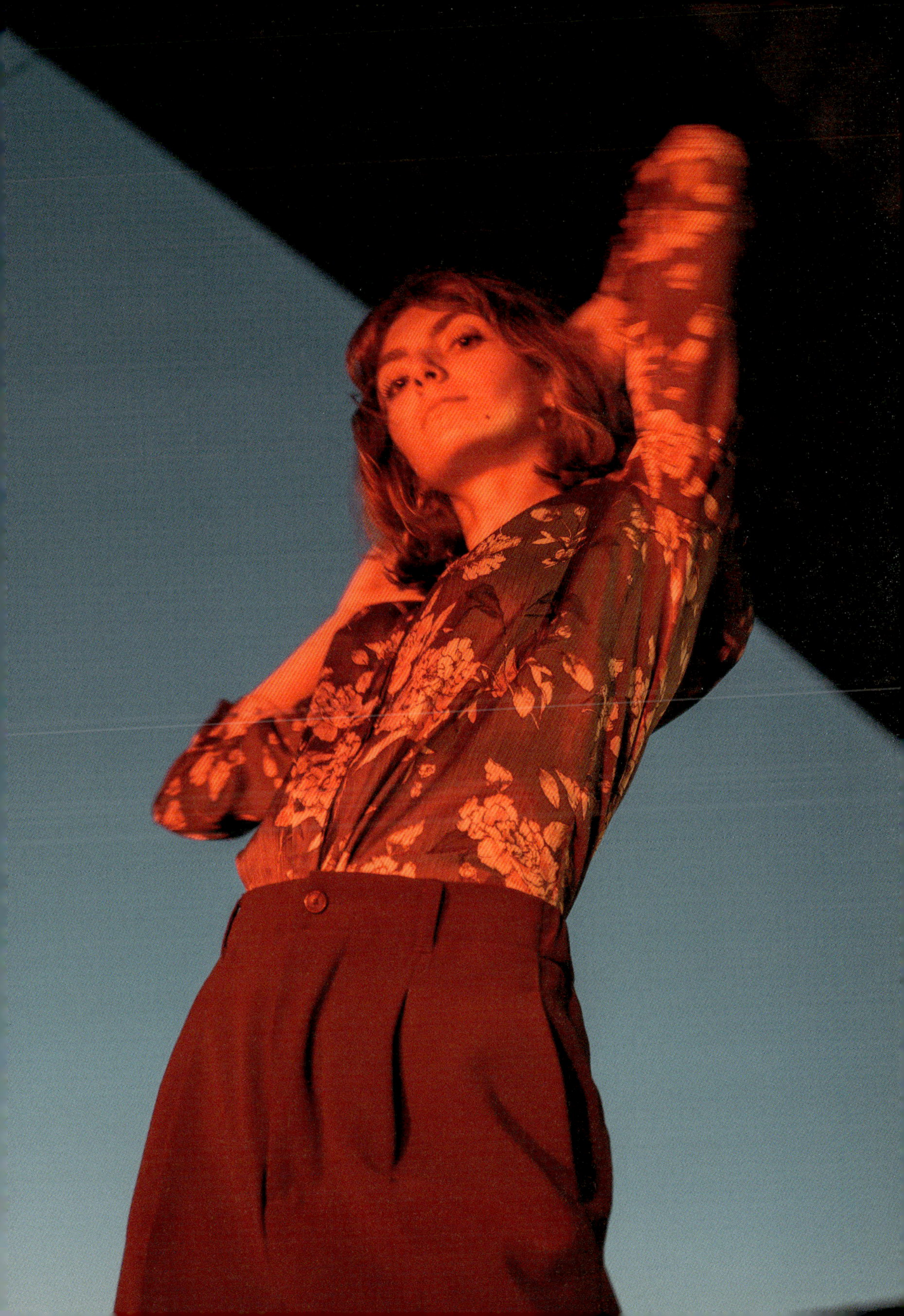

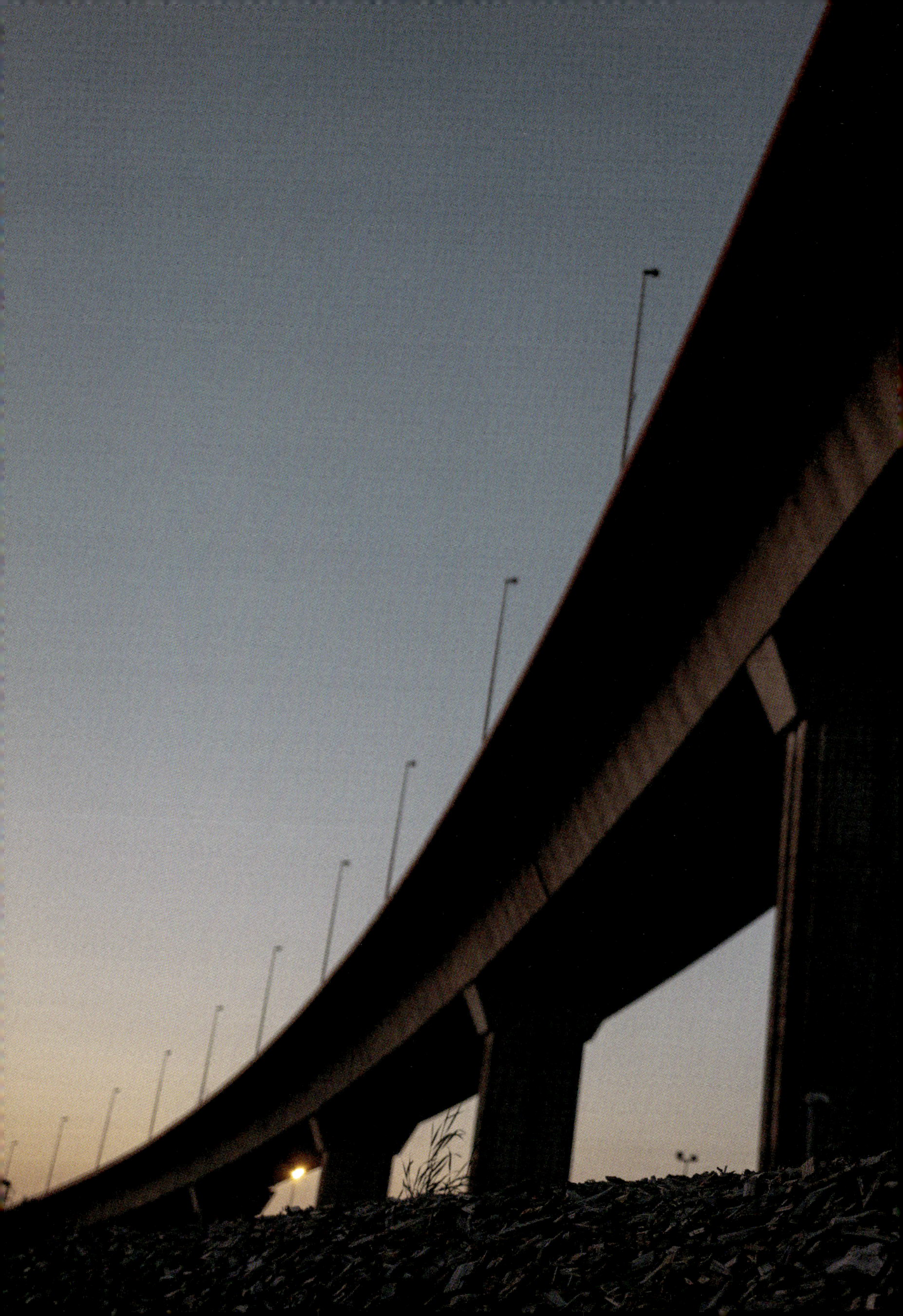

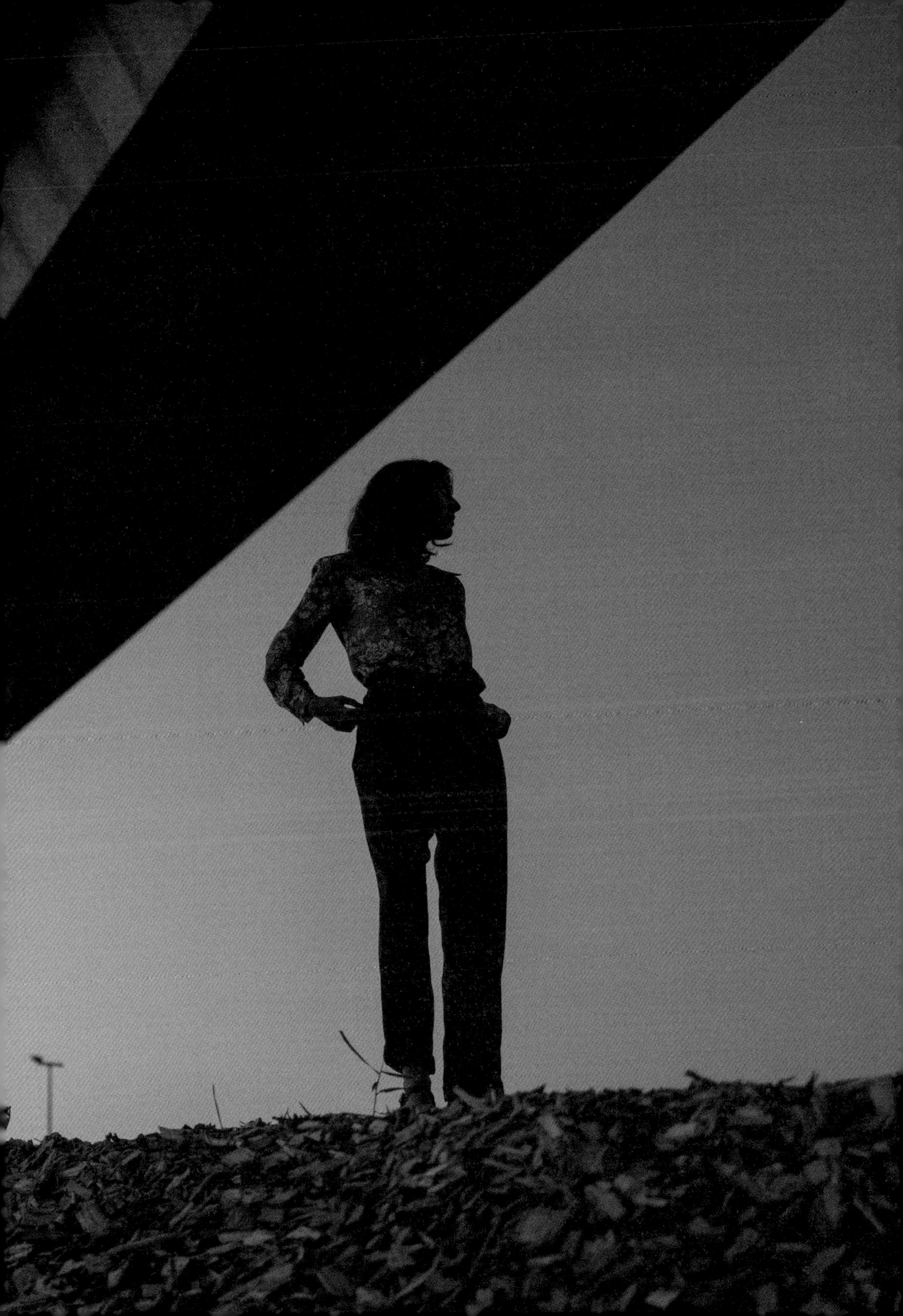

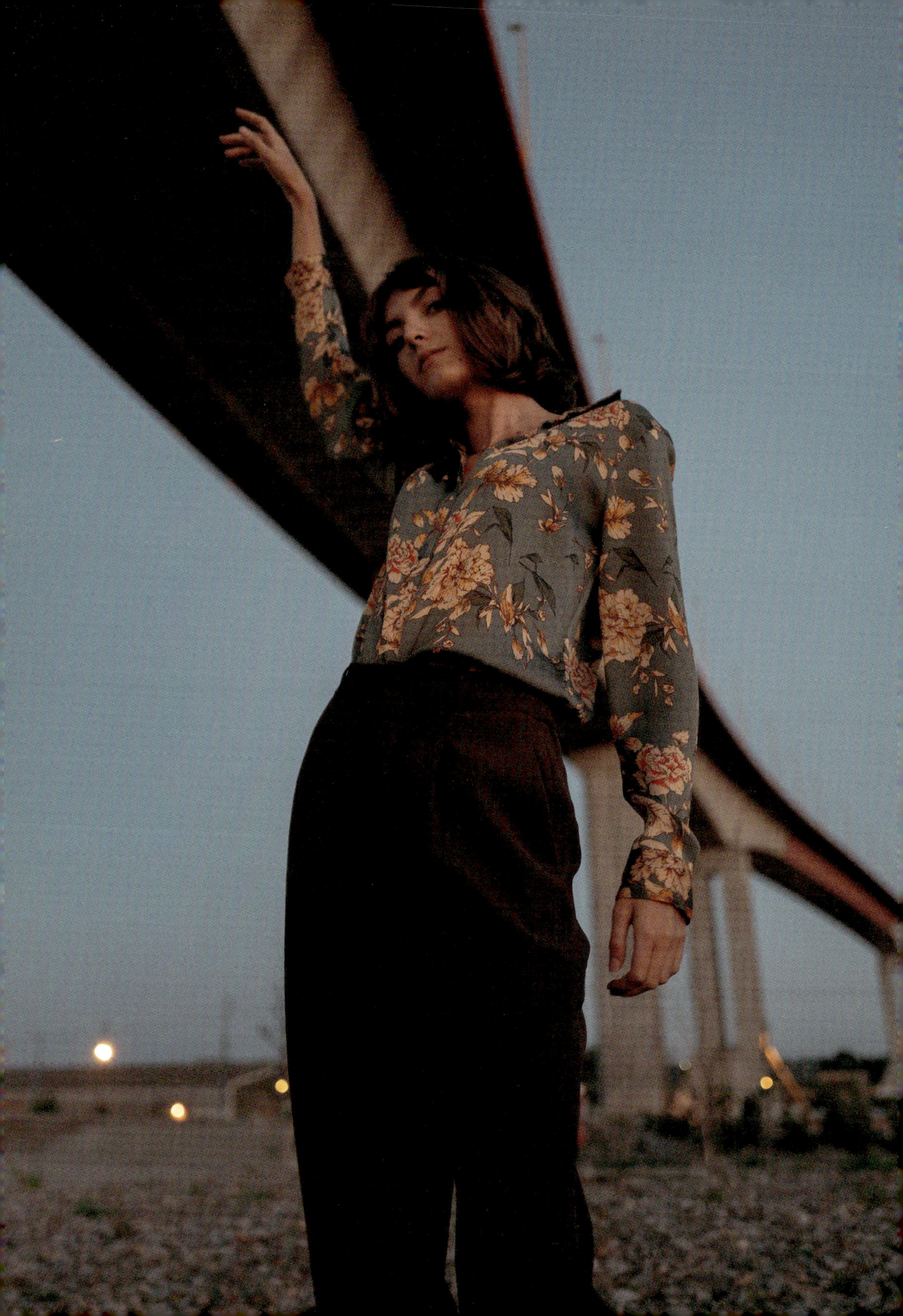

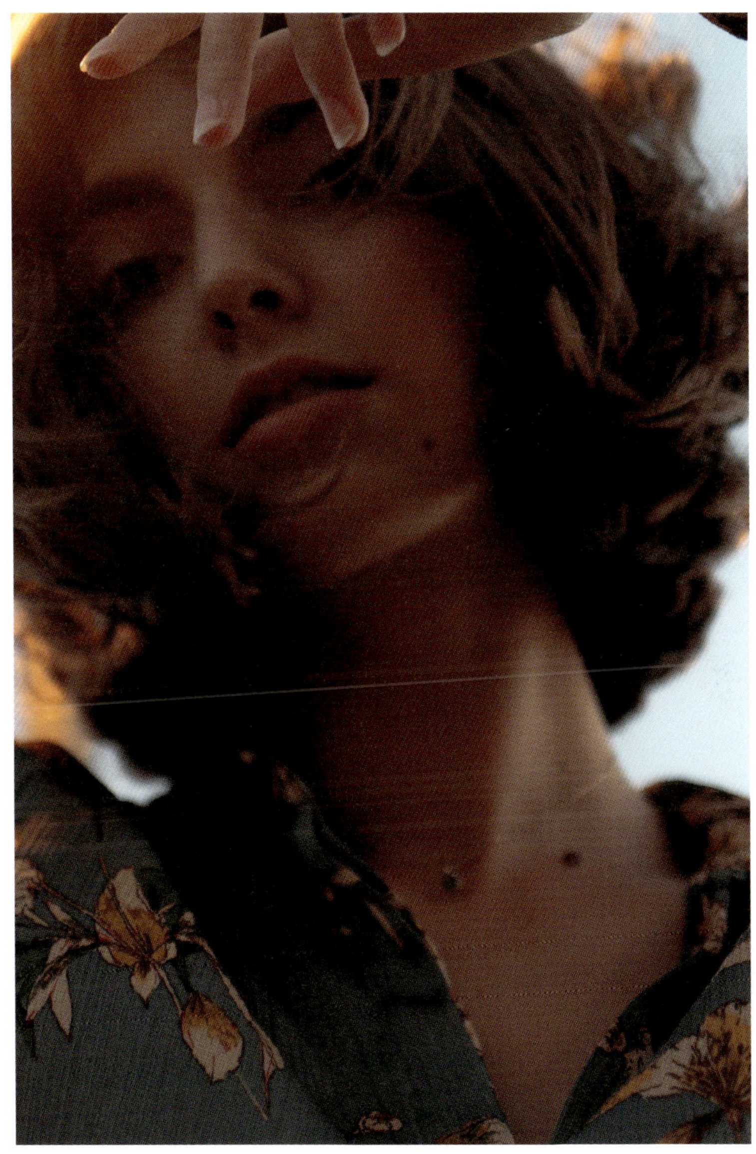

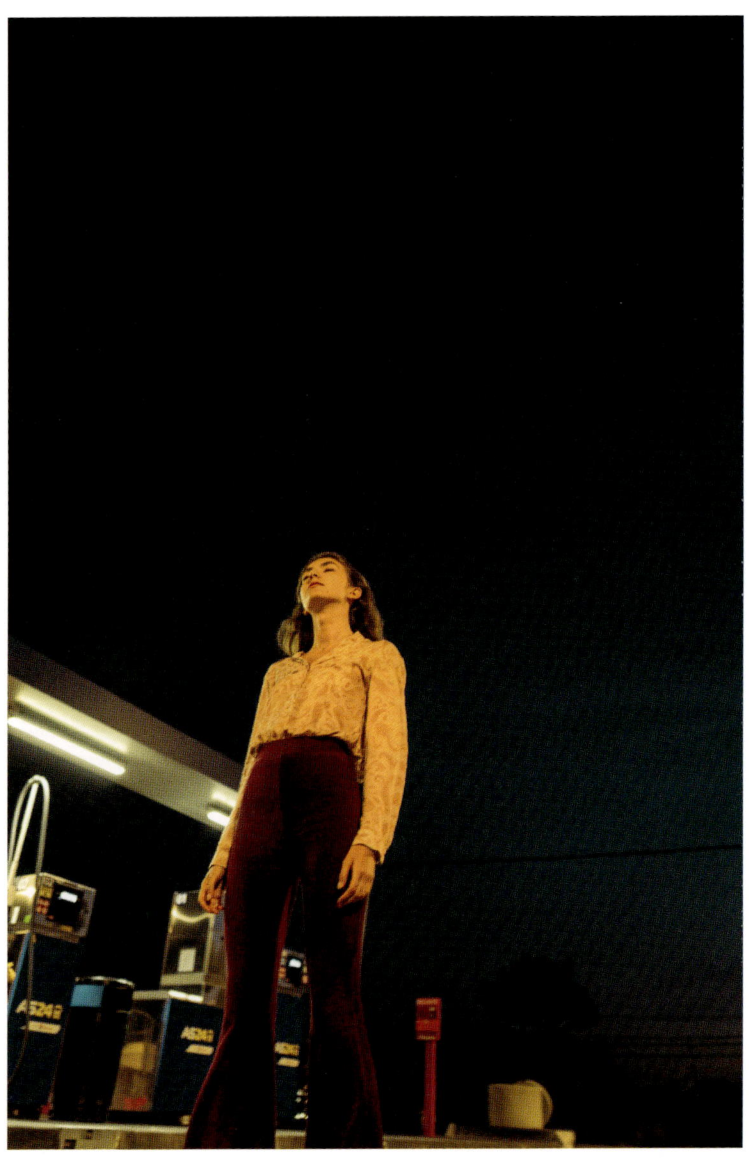

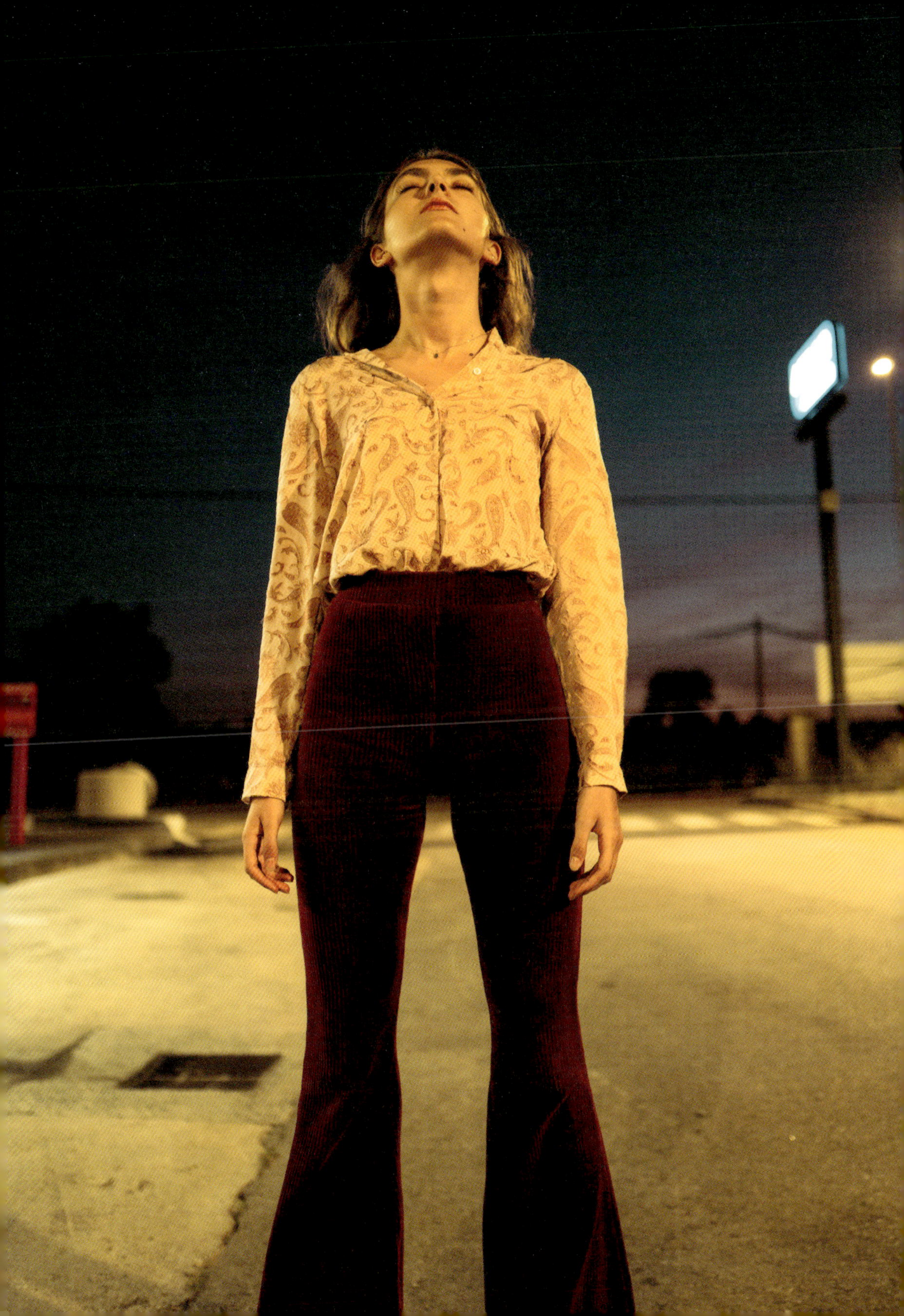

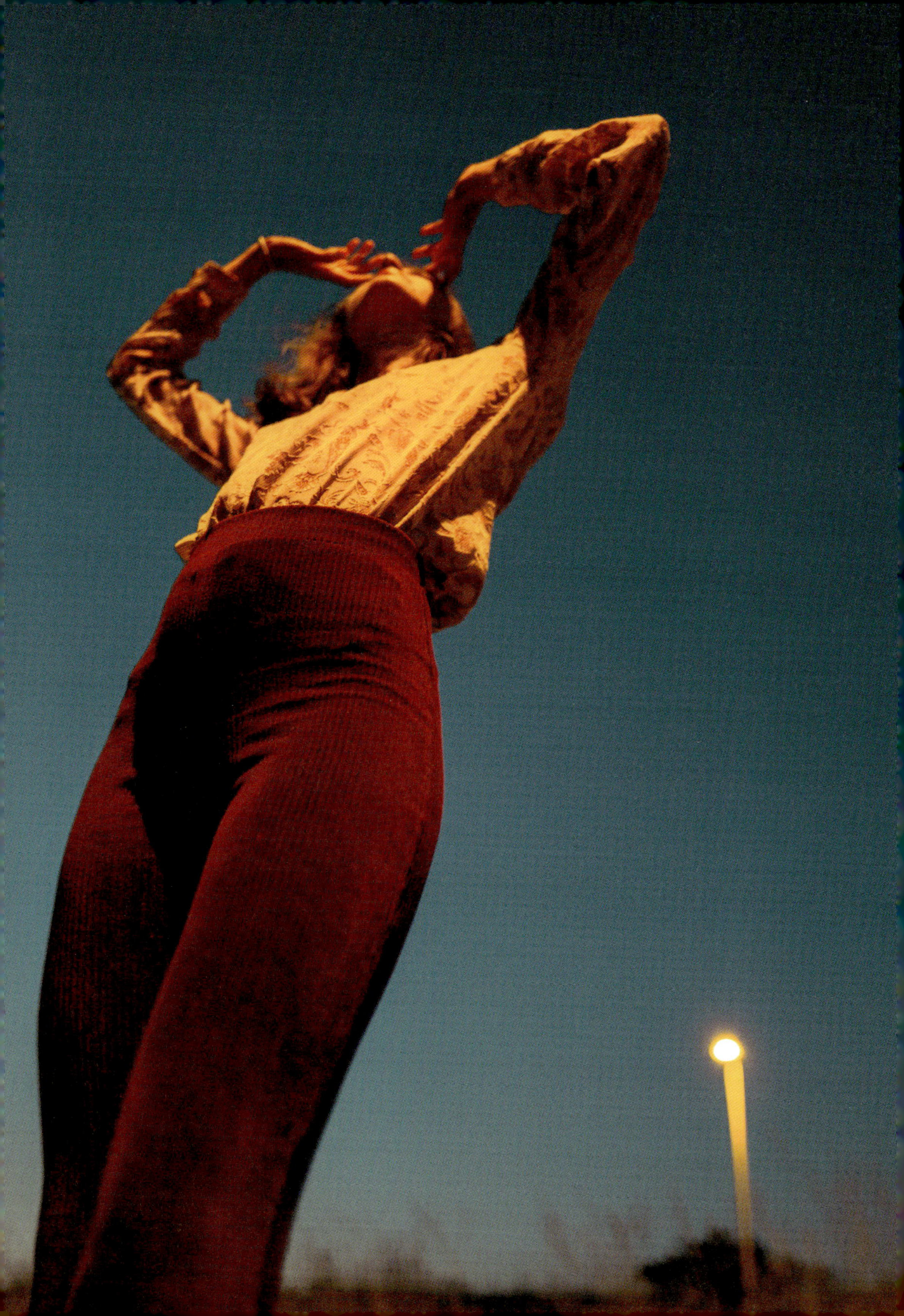

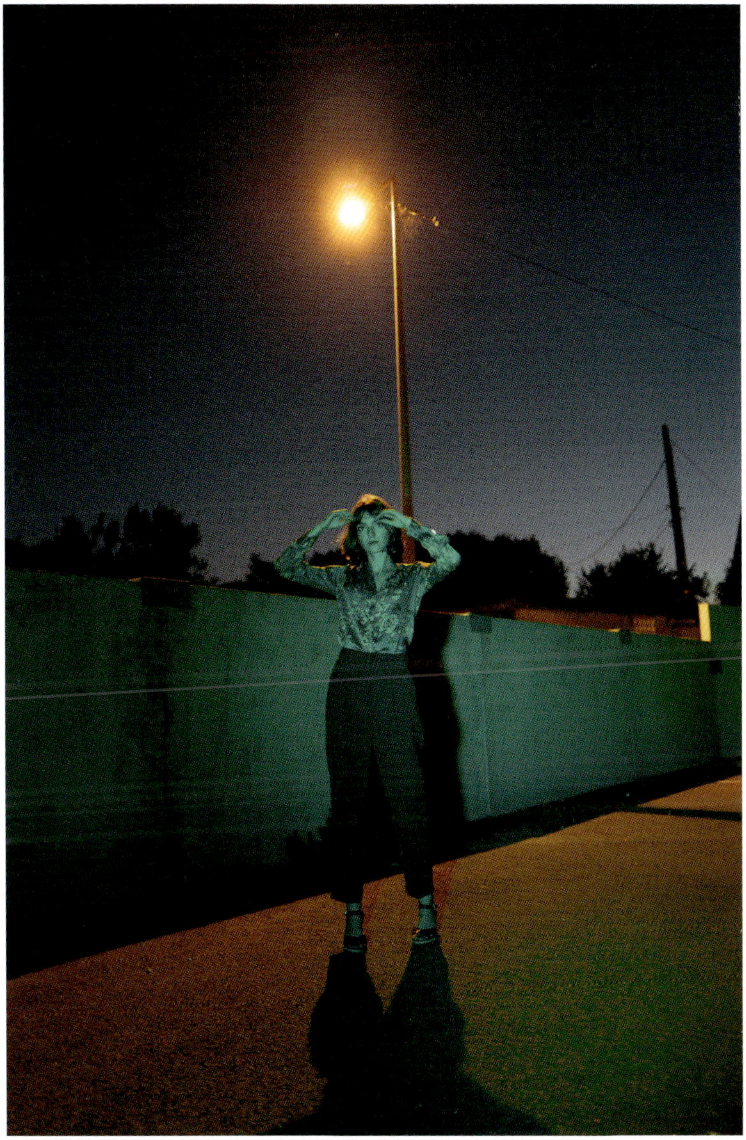

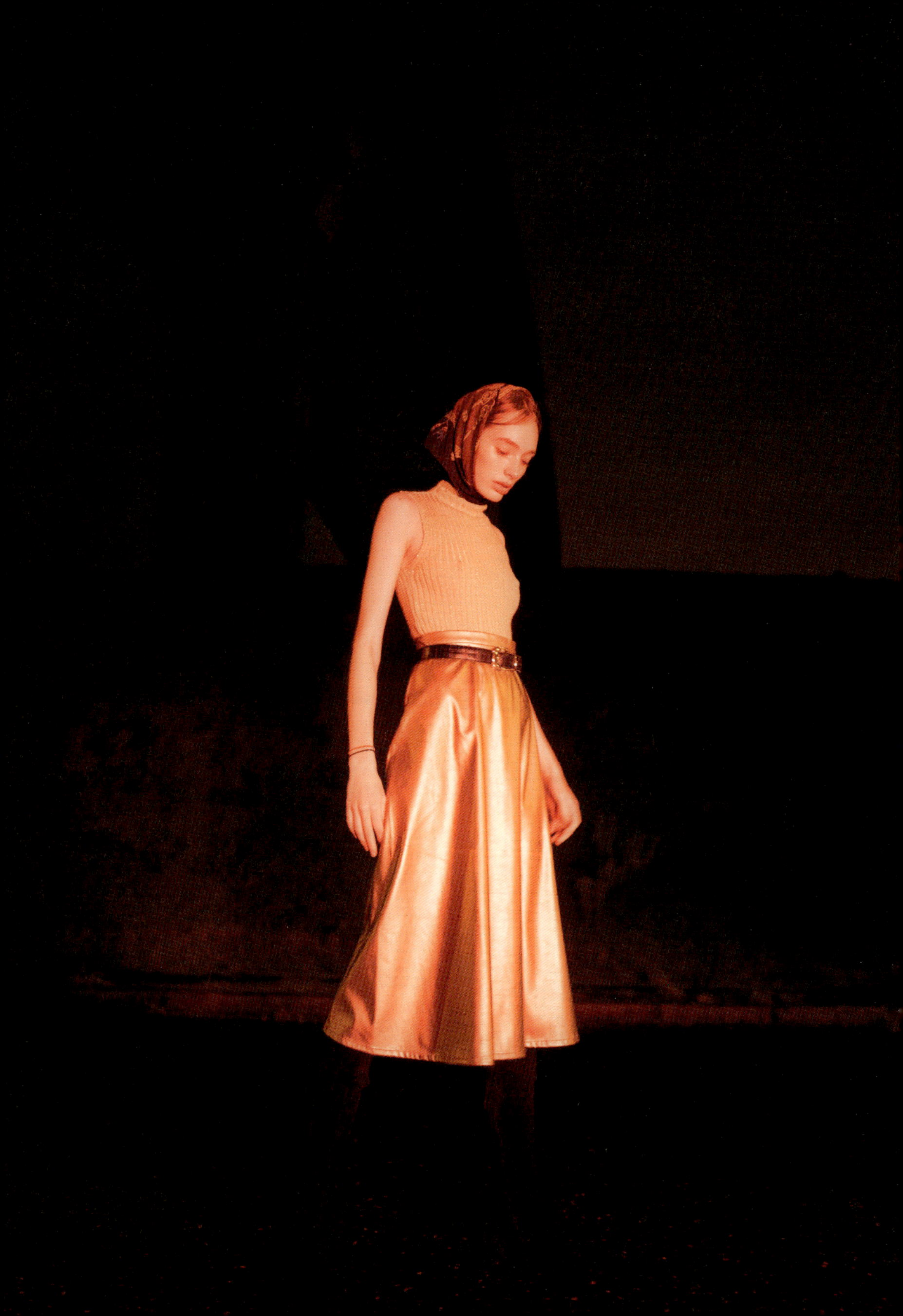

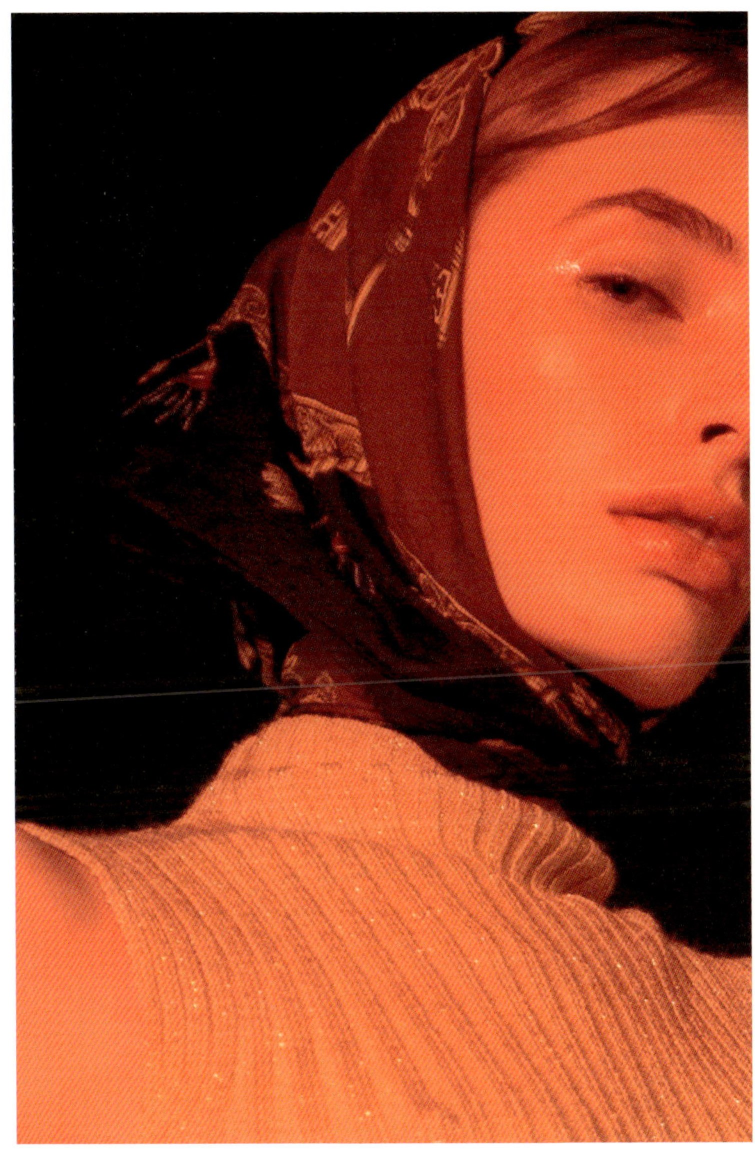

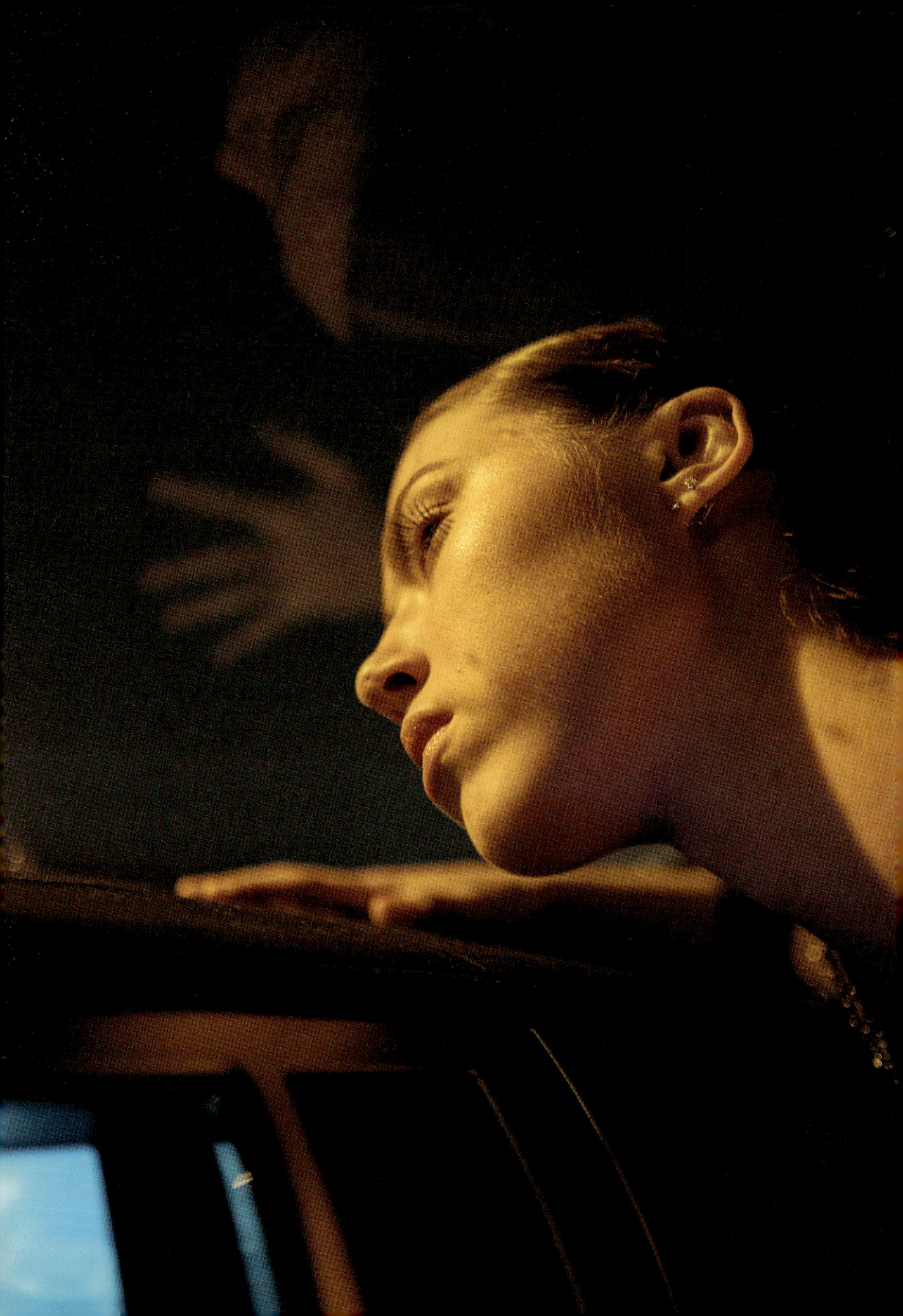

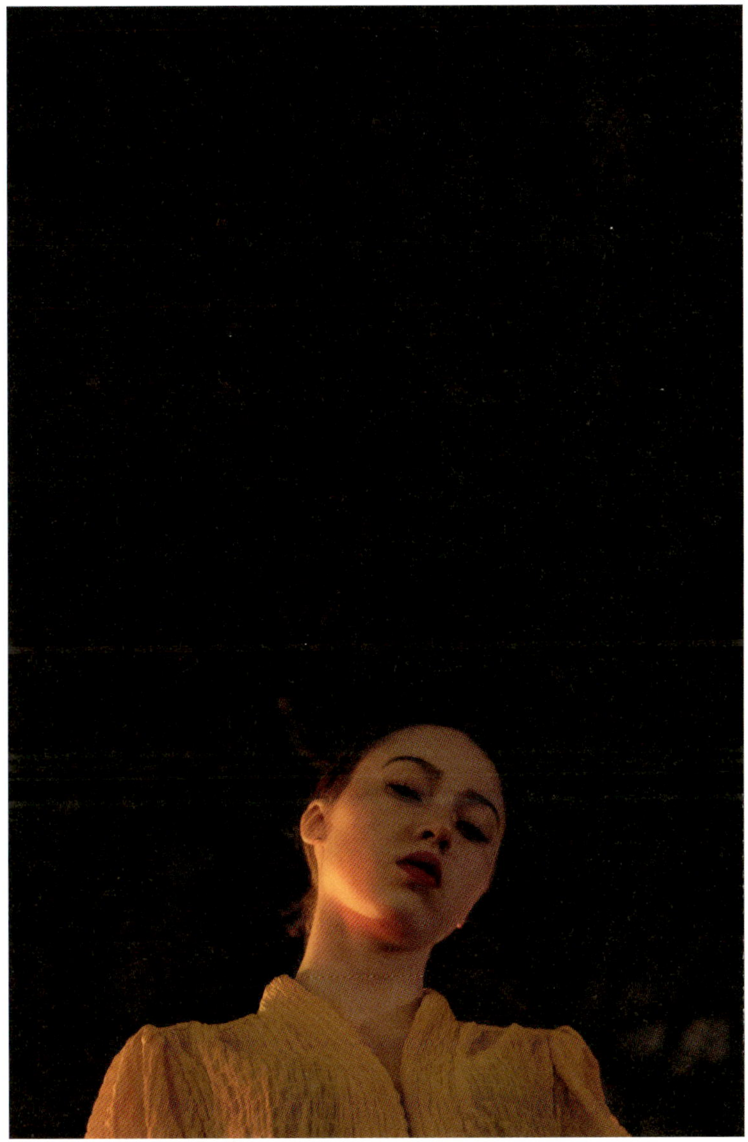

We Are Dreamers

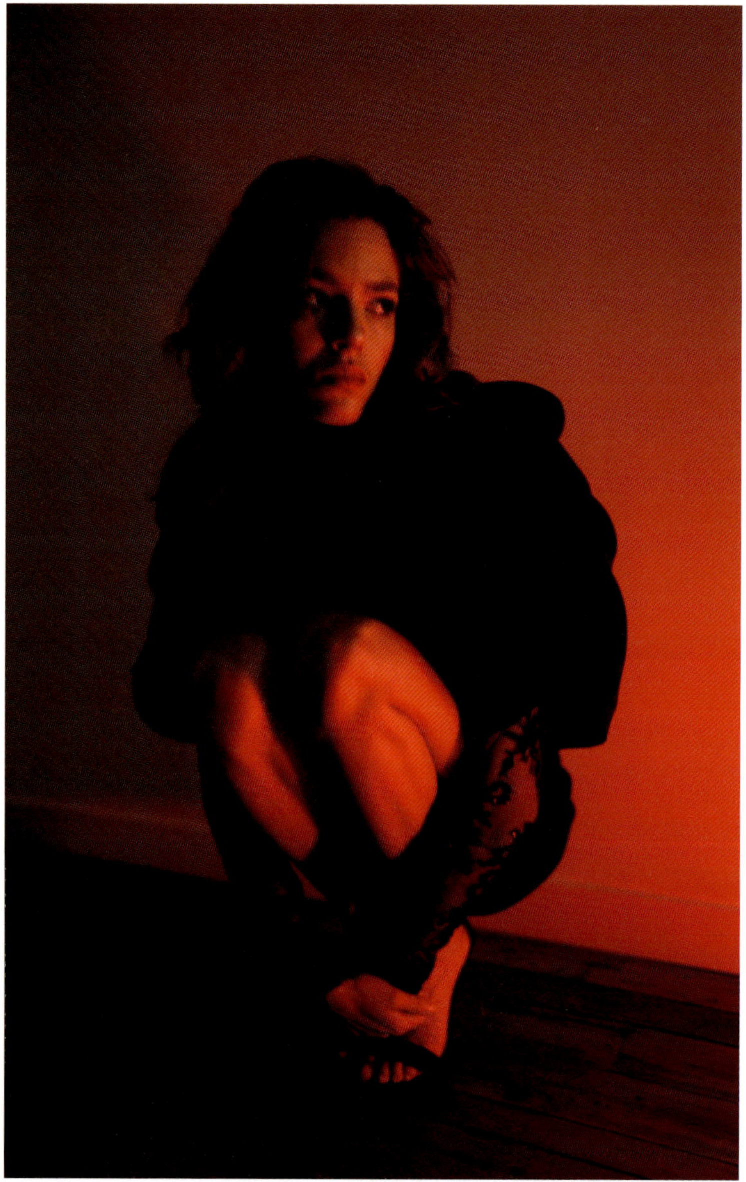

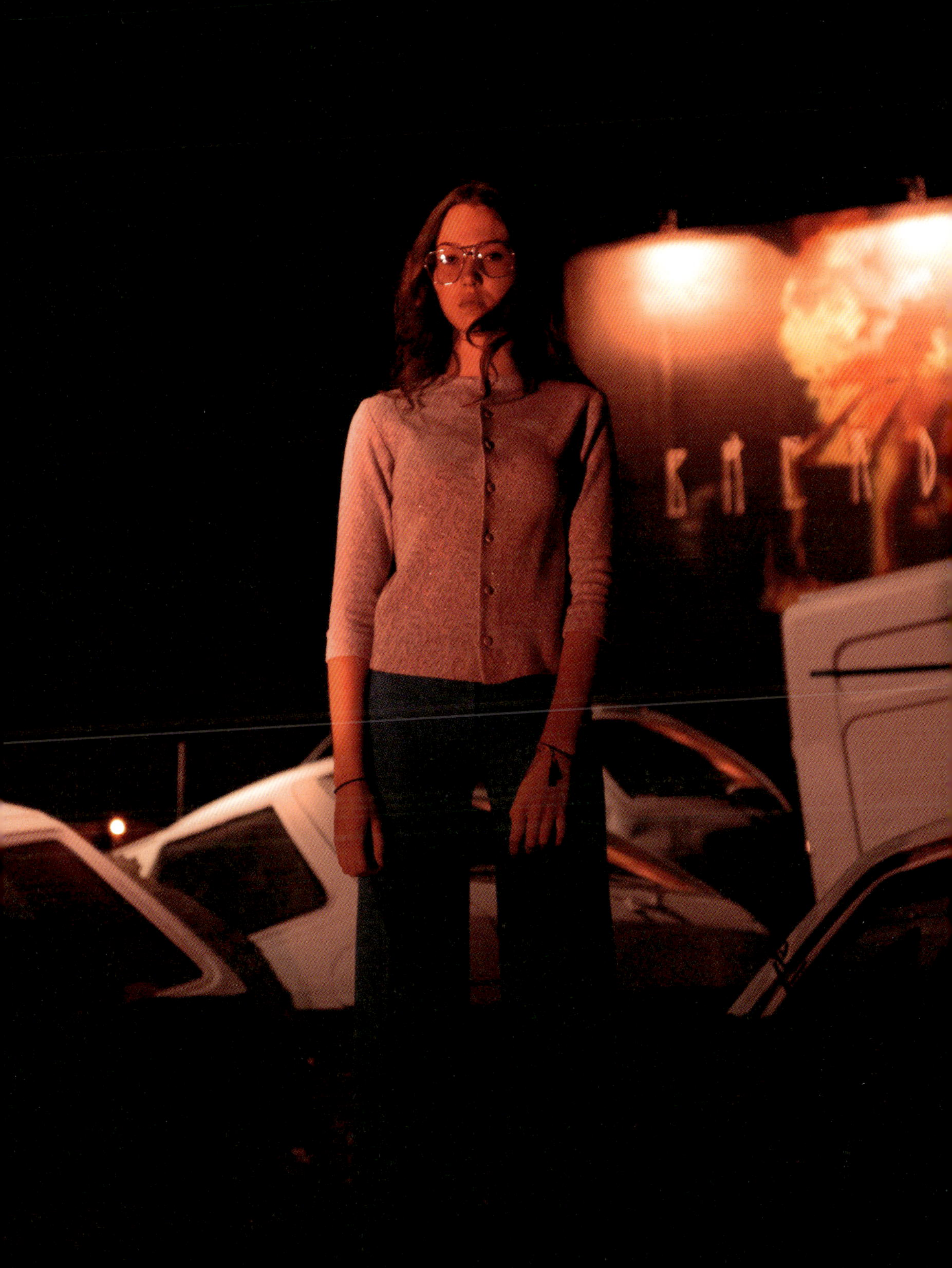

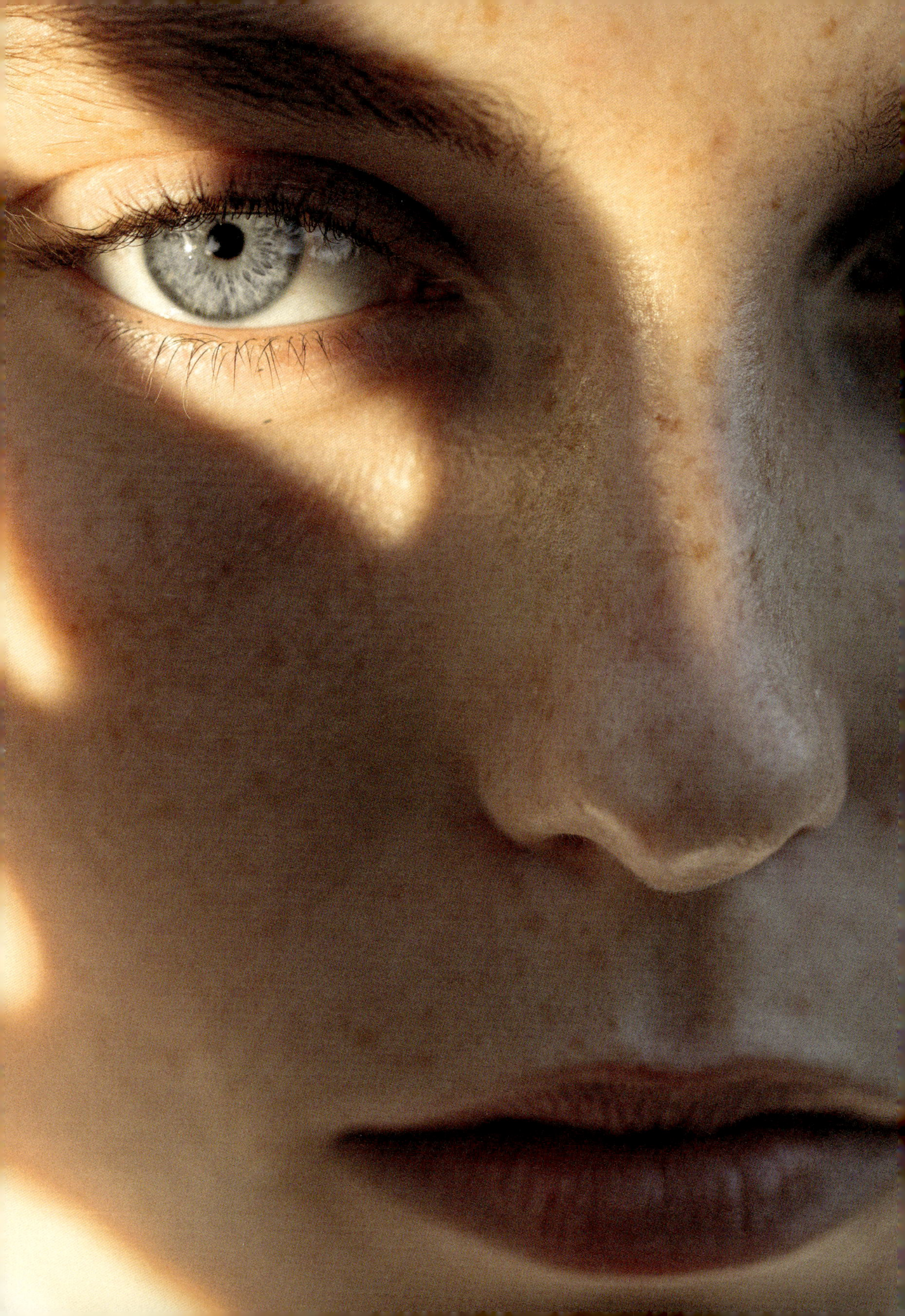

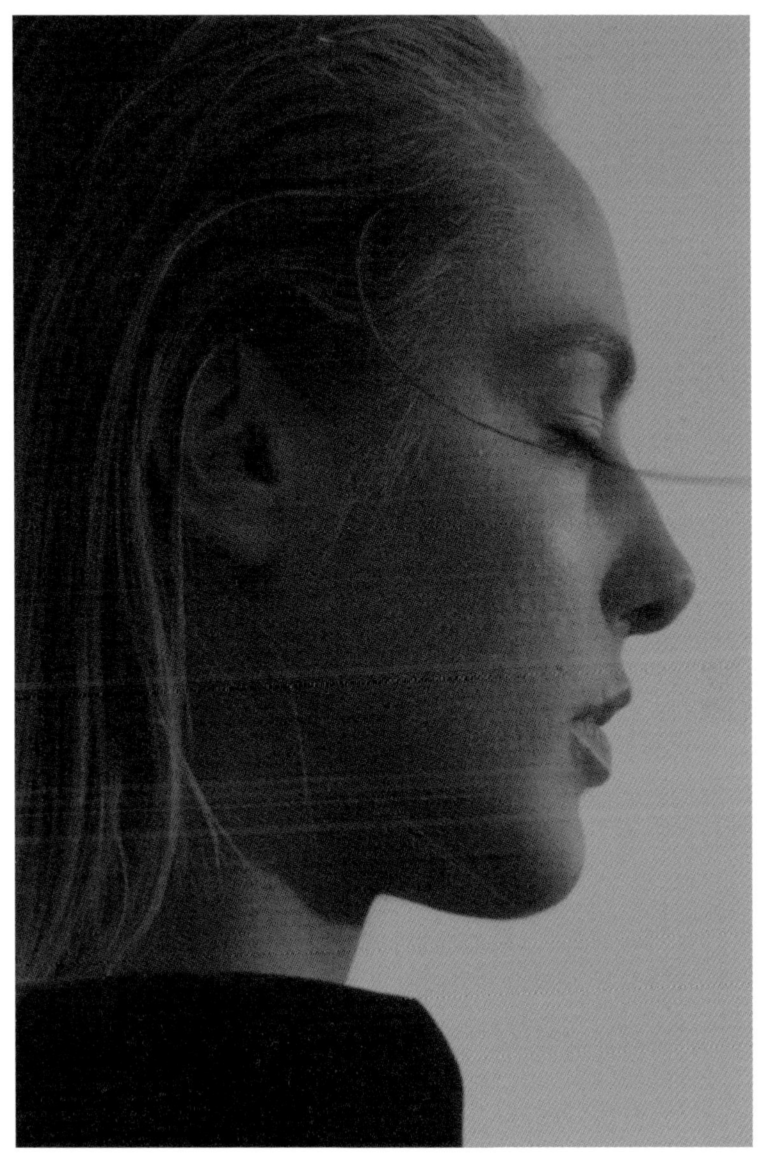

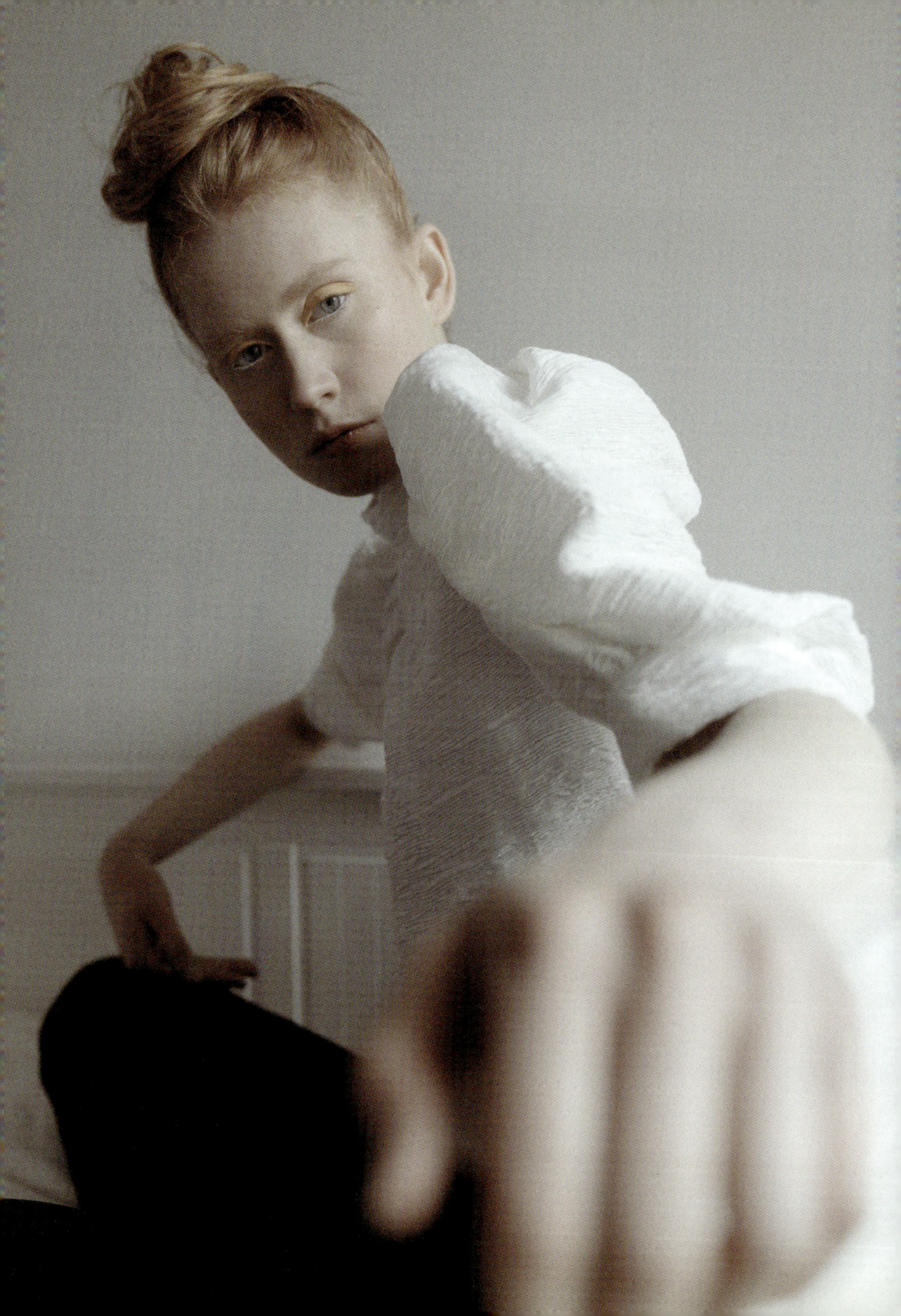

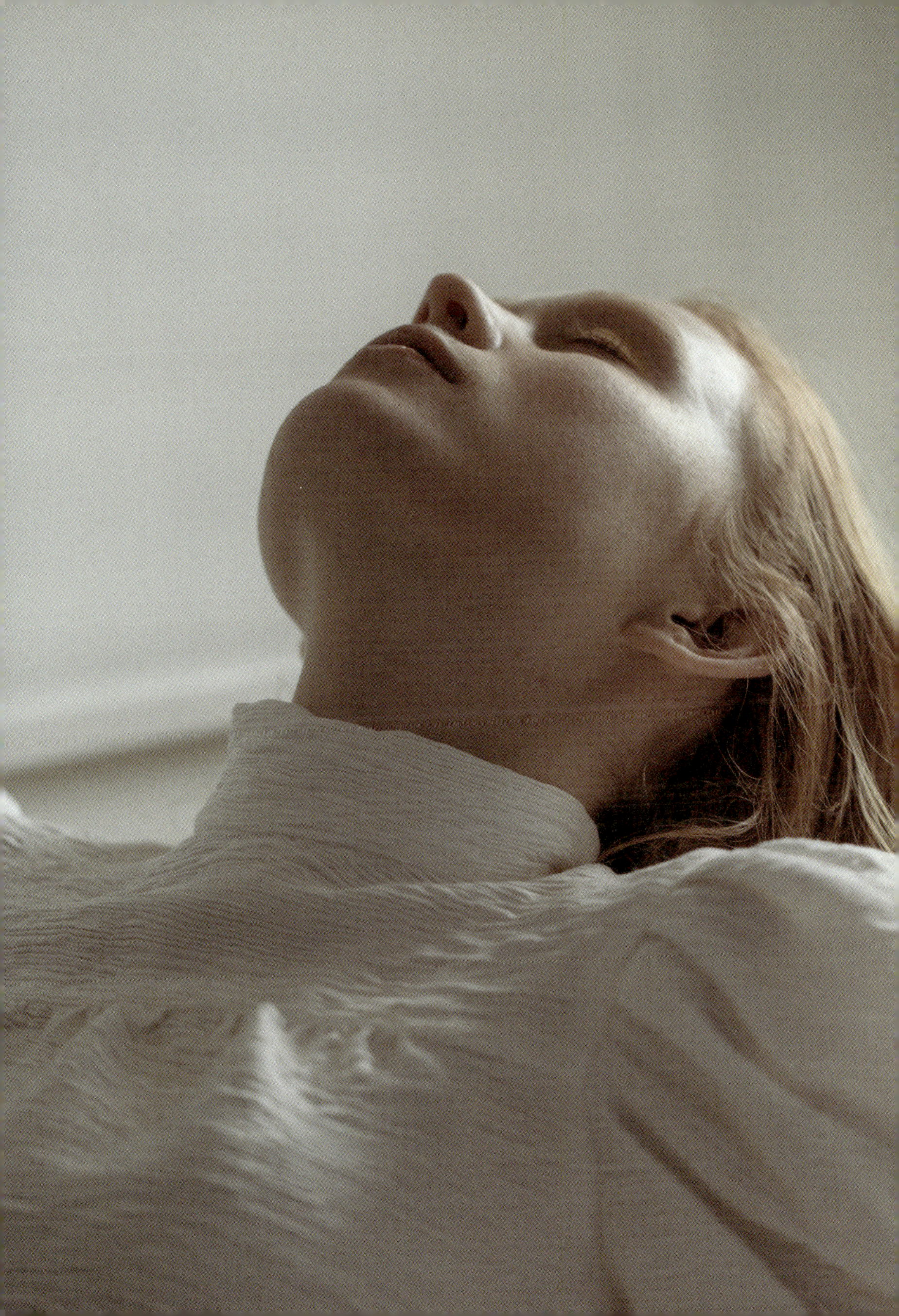

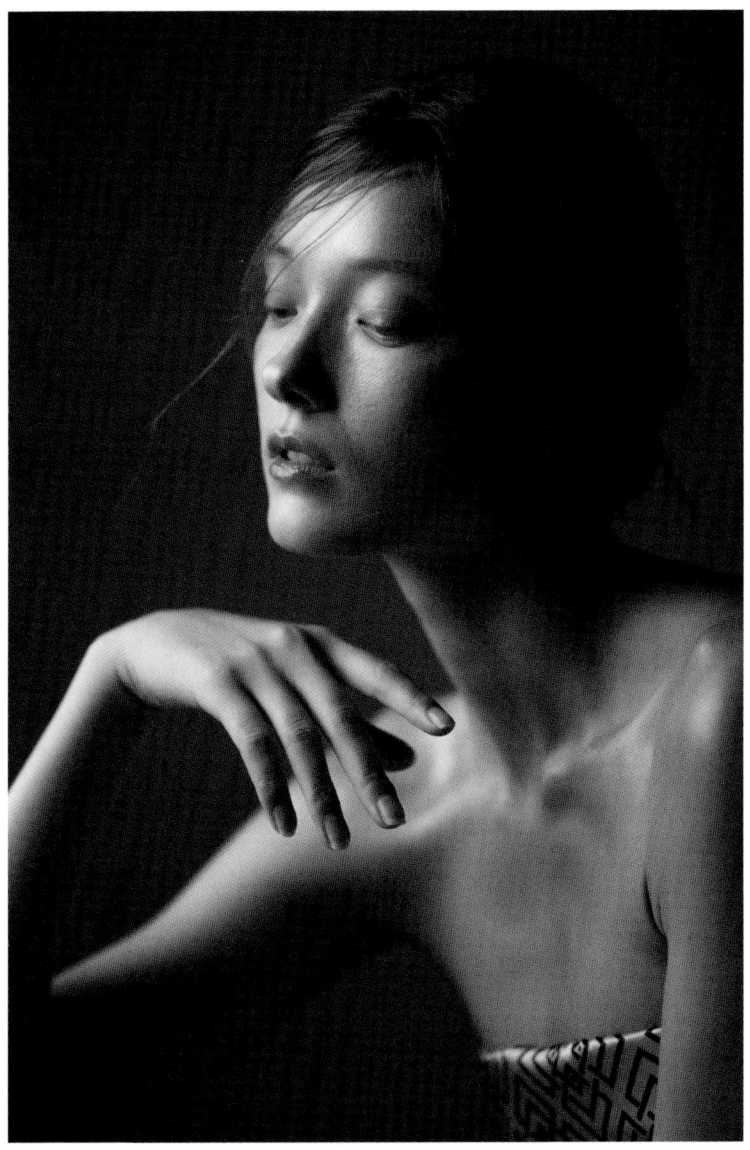

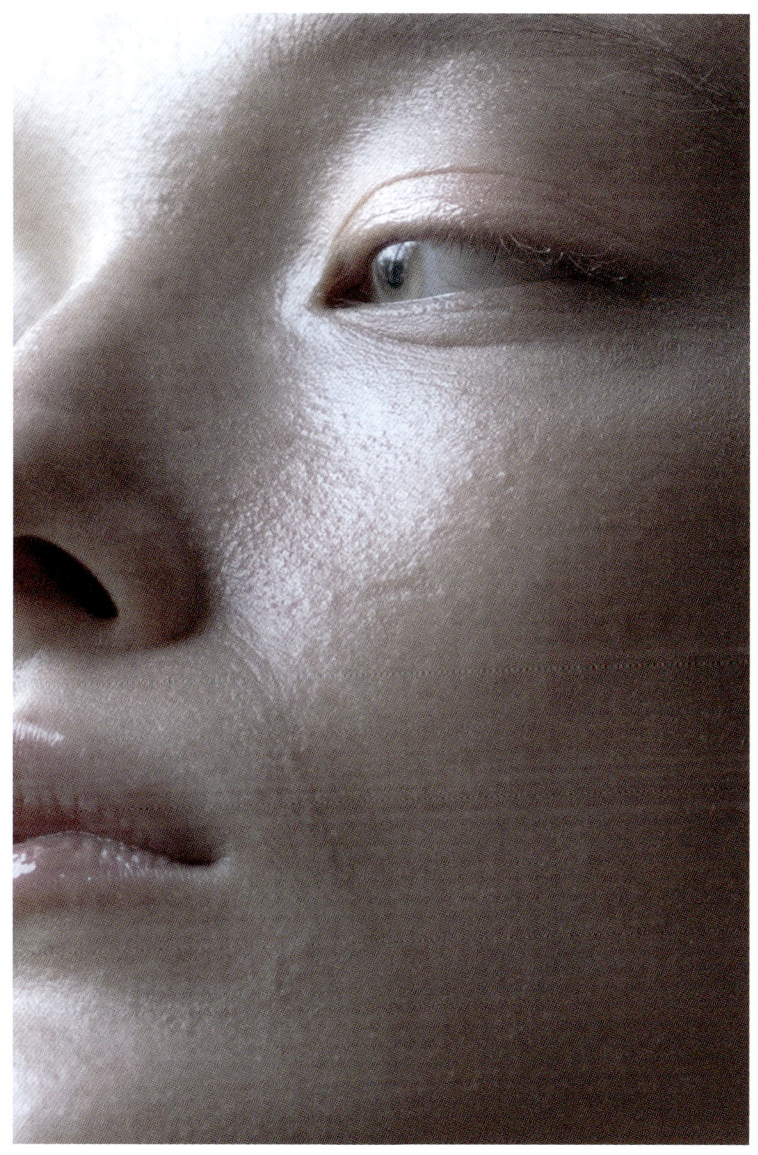

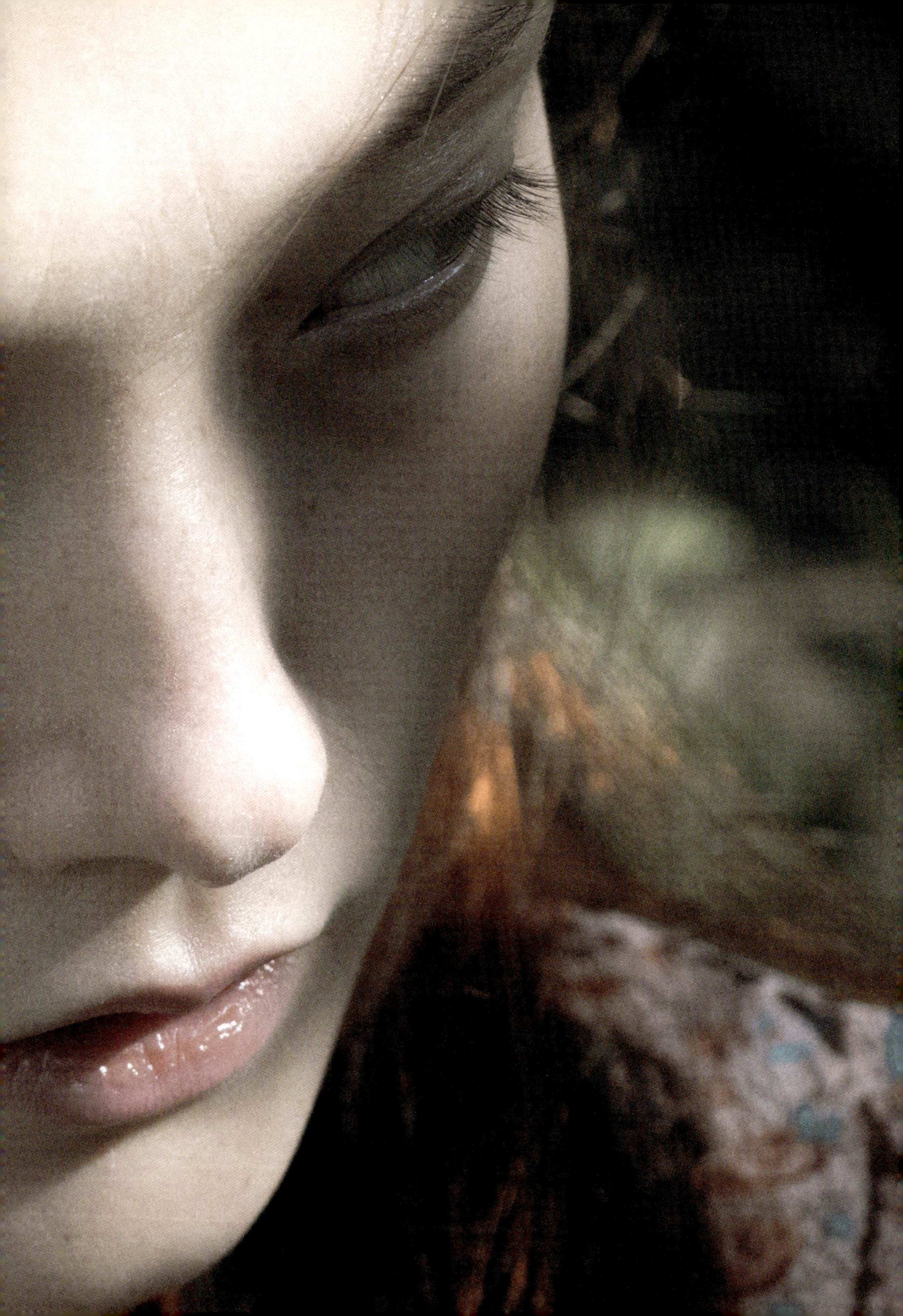

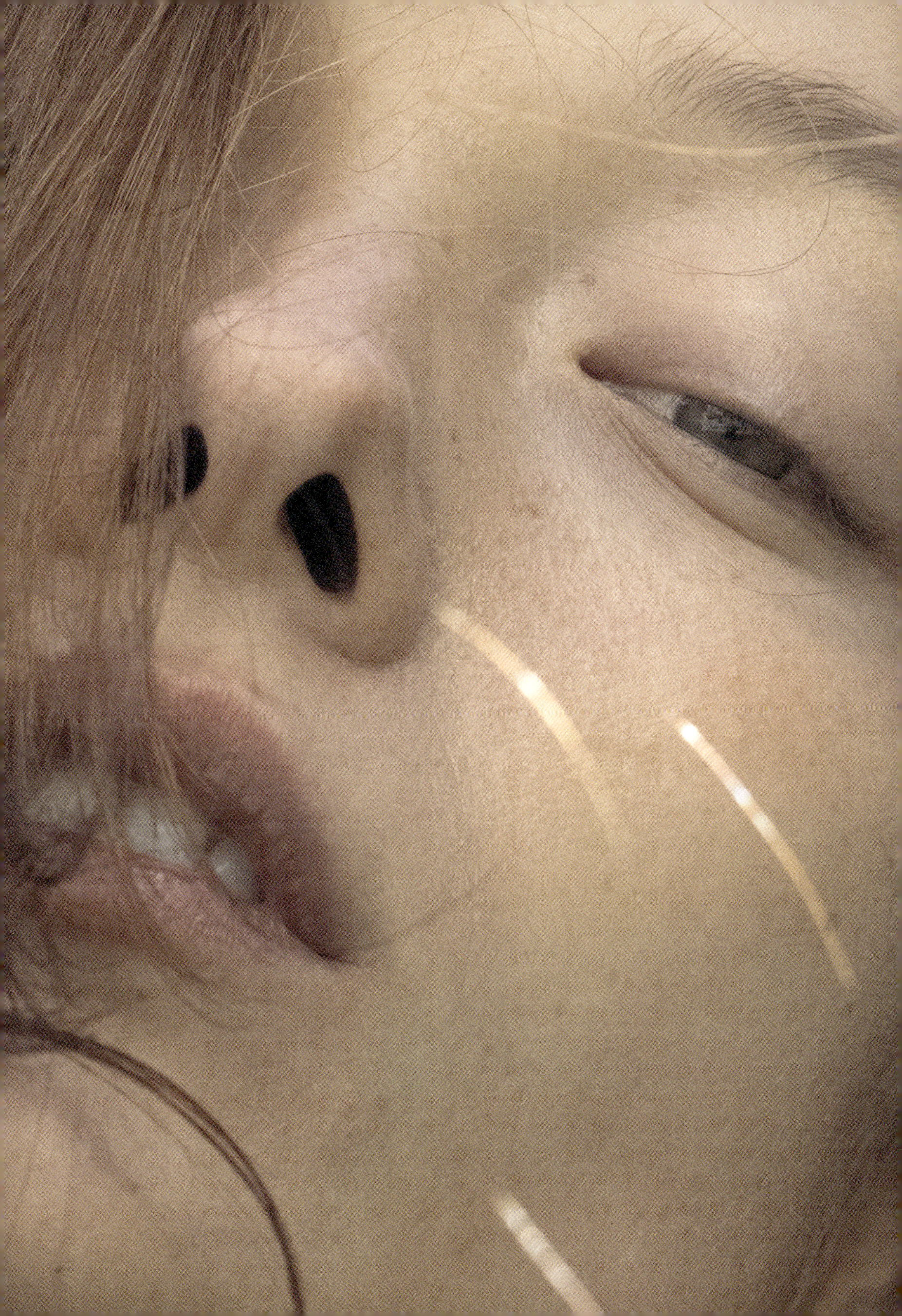

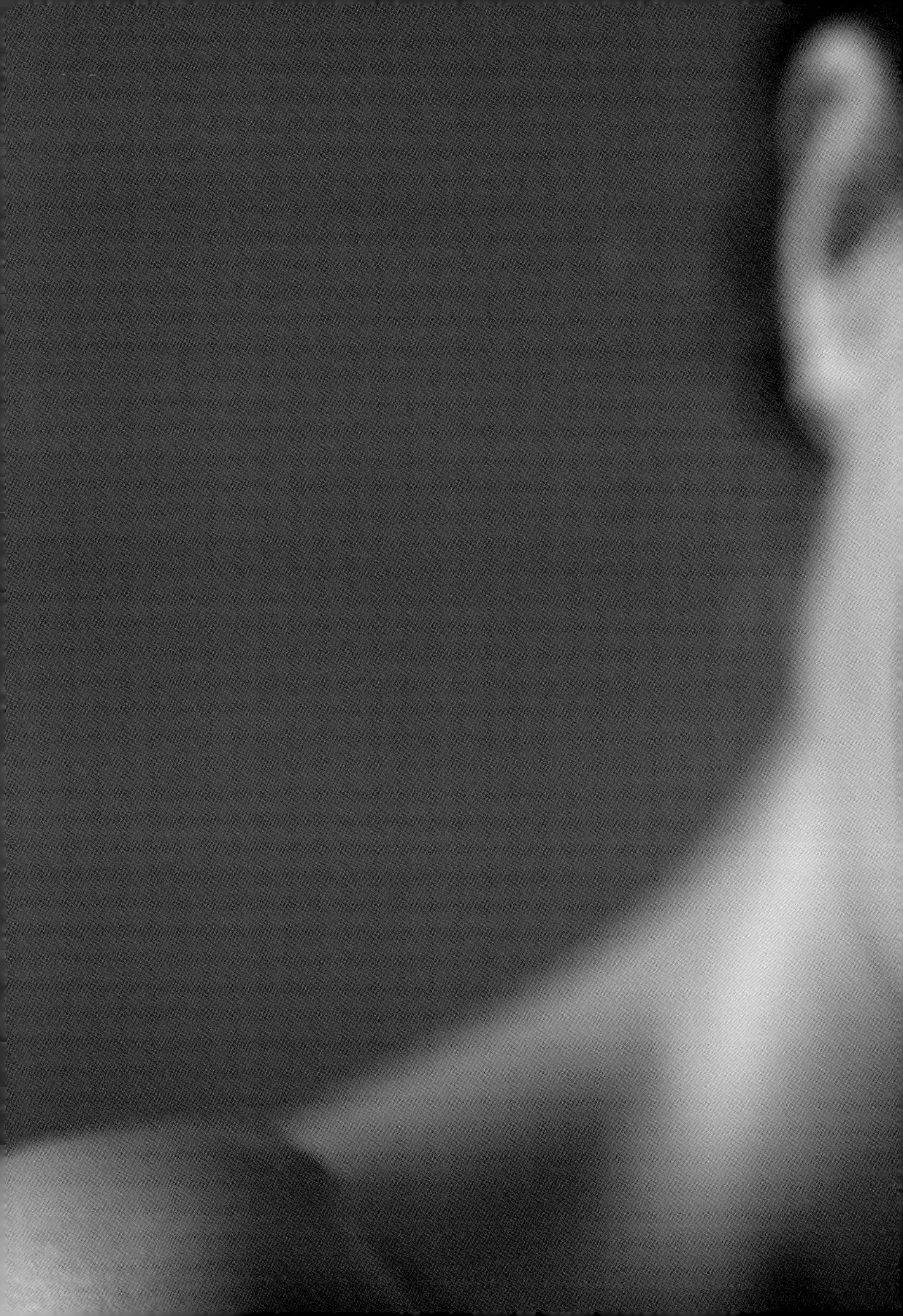

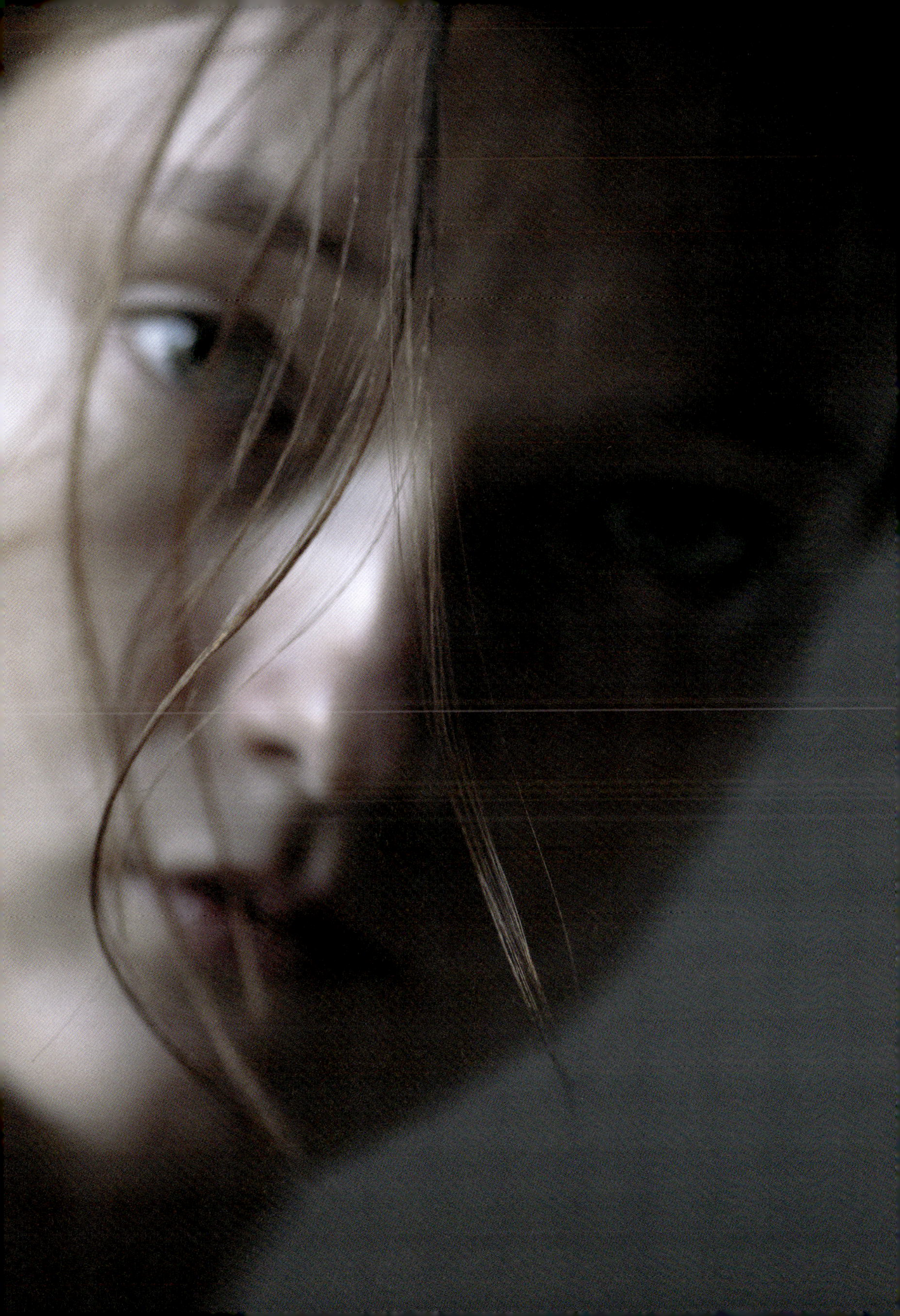

Beauté Brute

Men's weaknesses are women's strength.

– Voltaire

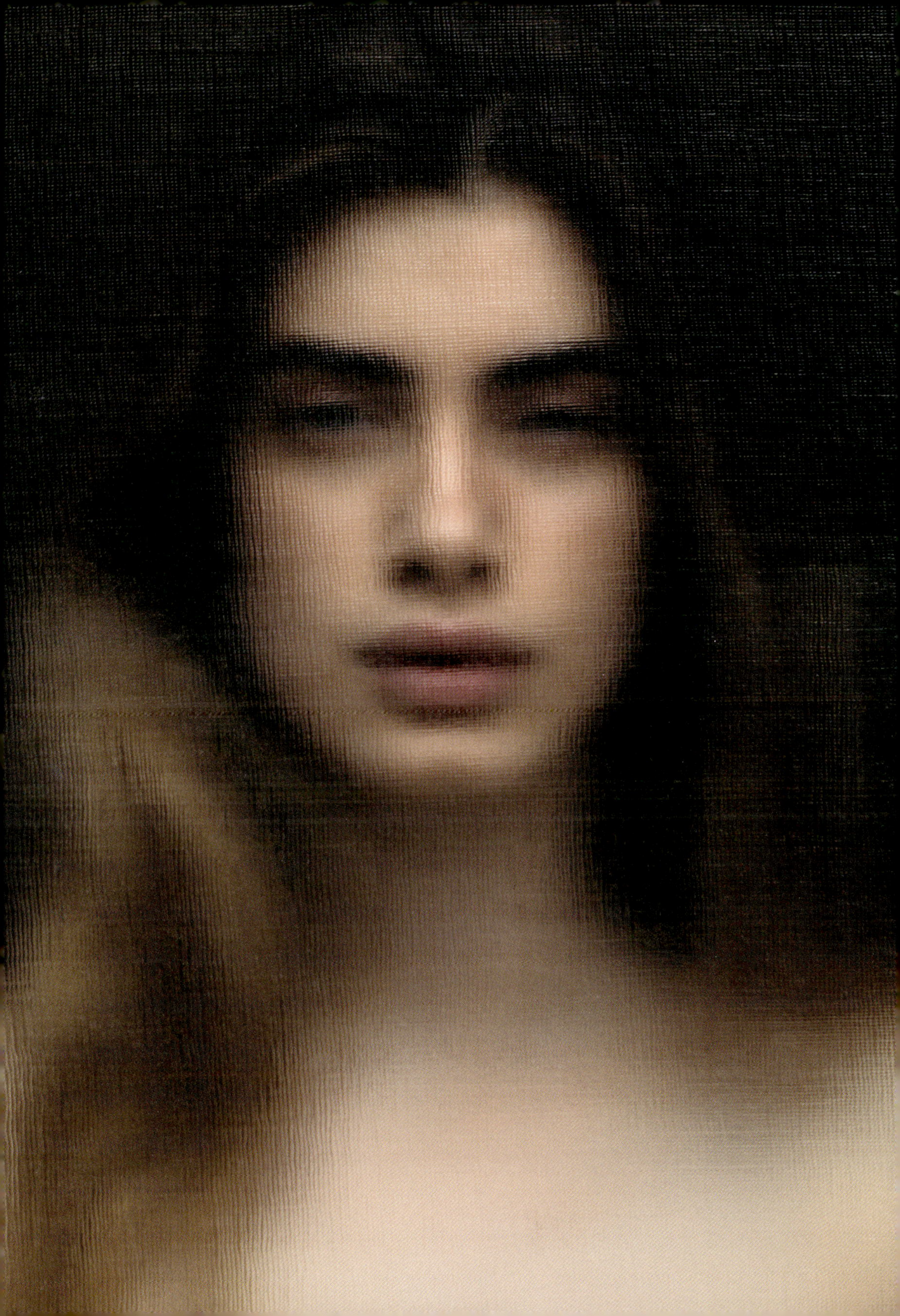

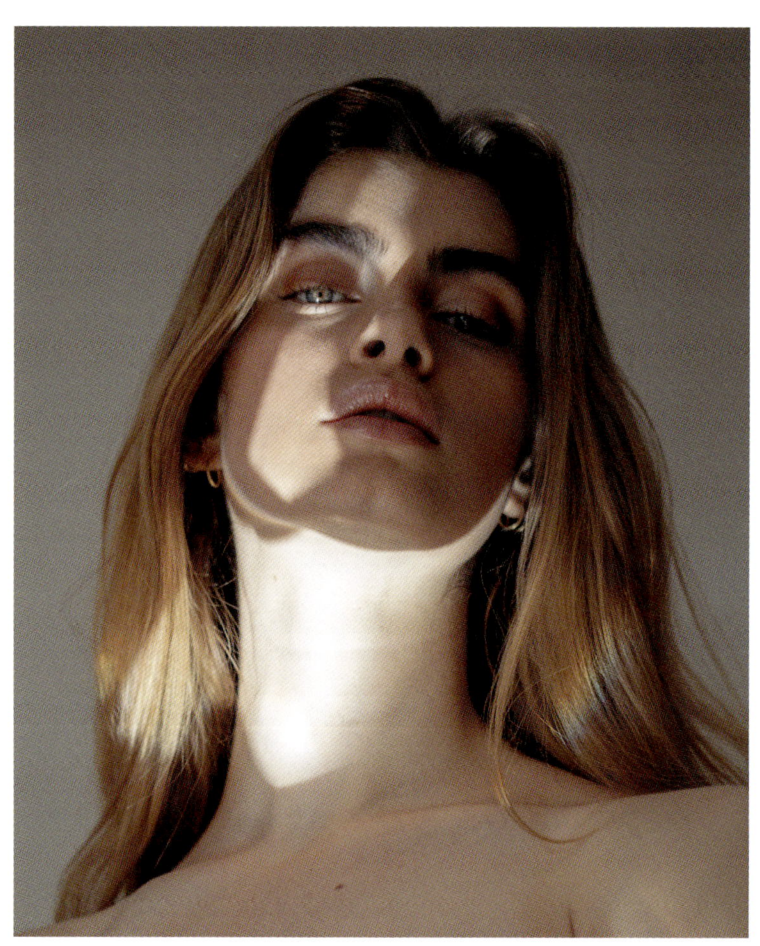

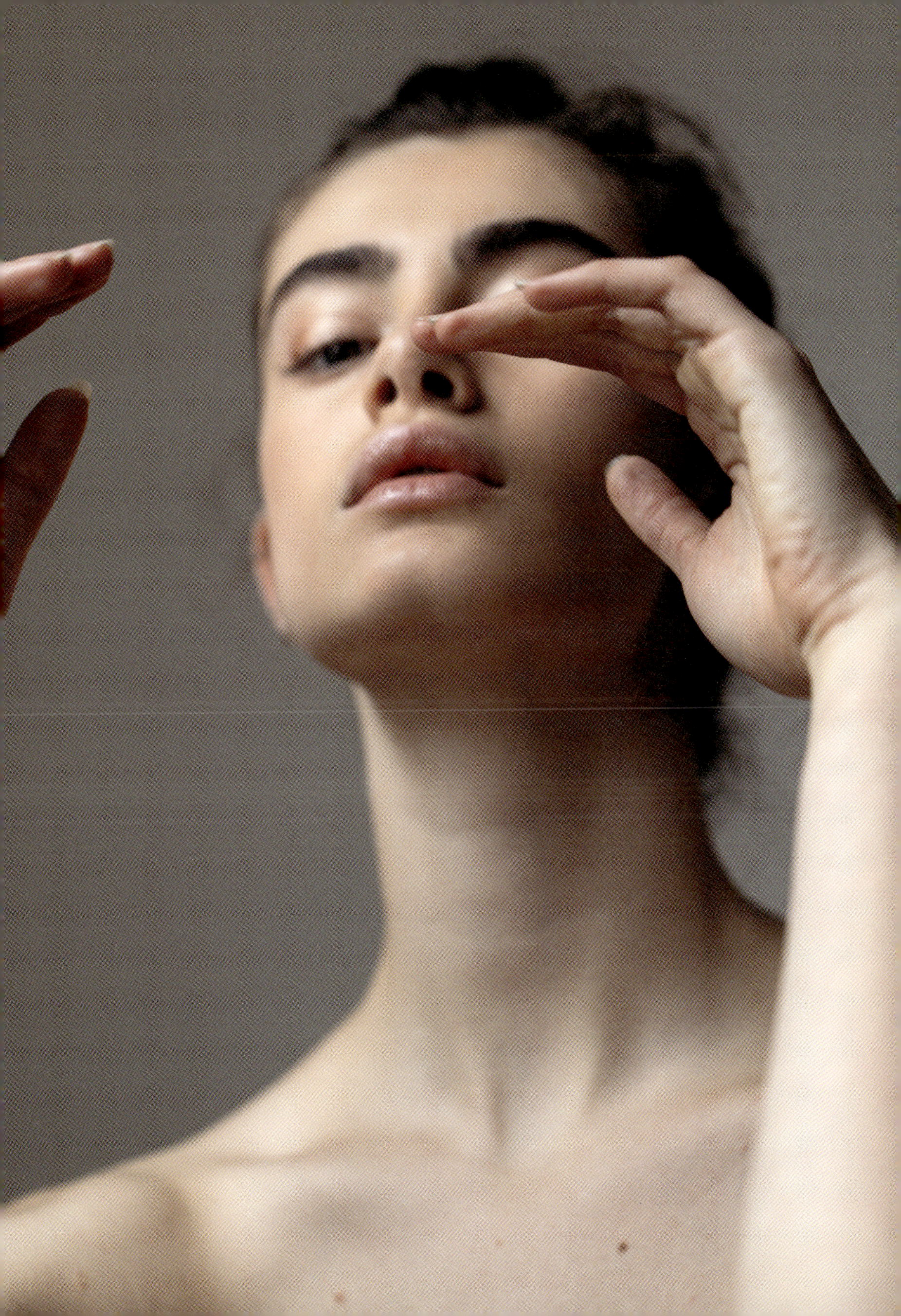

Body Expression

Art wasn't supposed to look nice; it was supposed to make you feel something.

– Rainbow Rowell

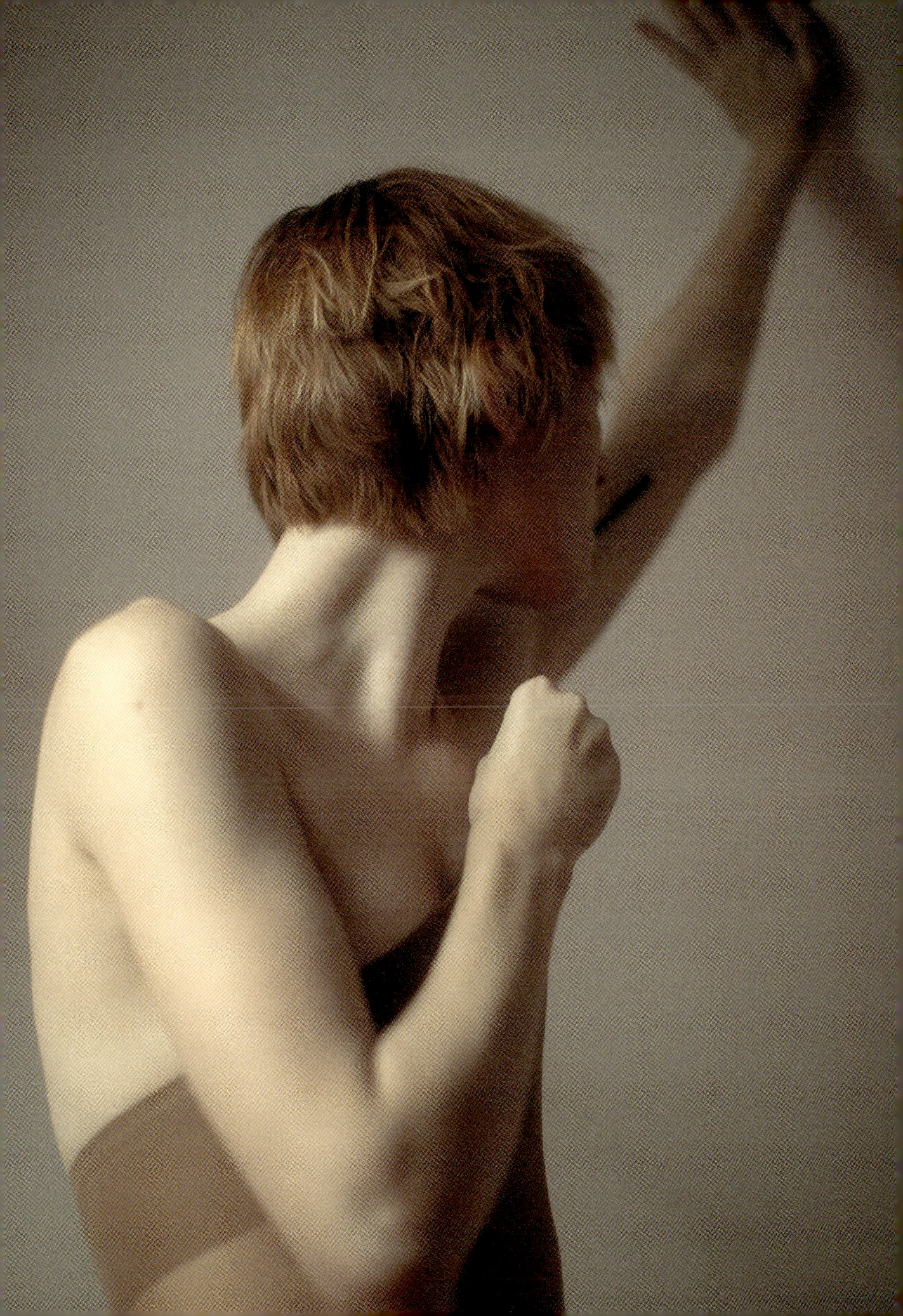

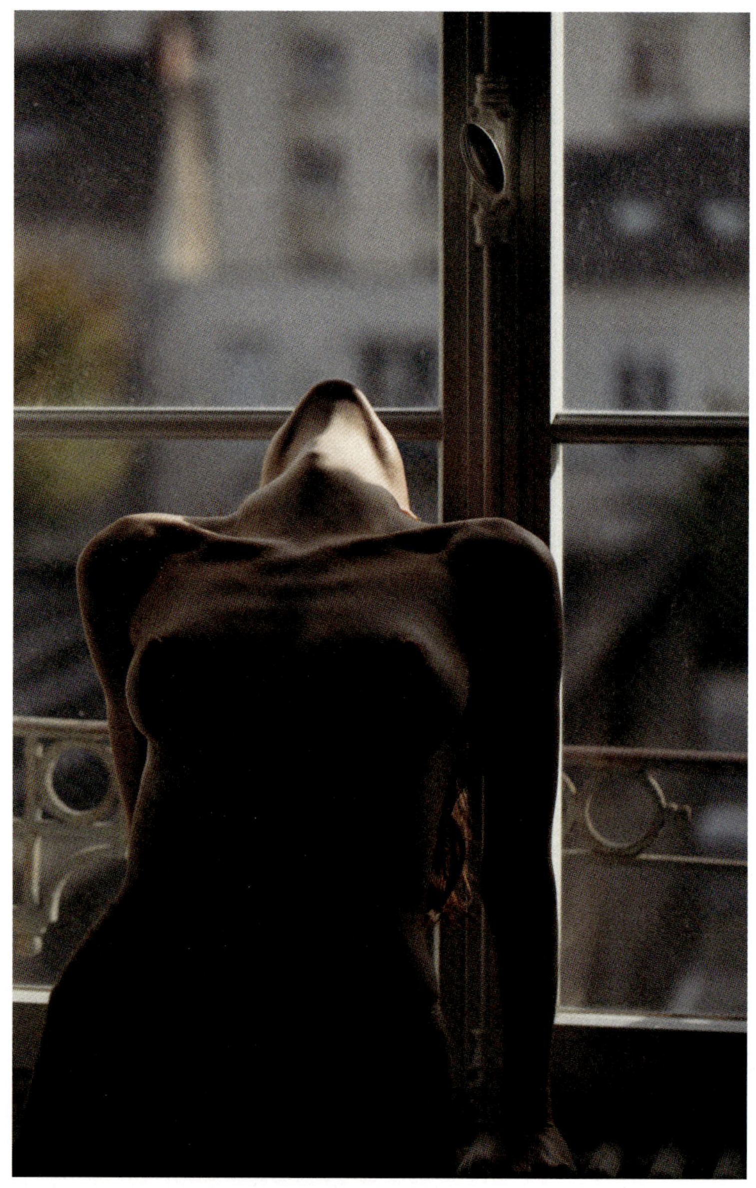

46

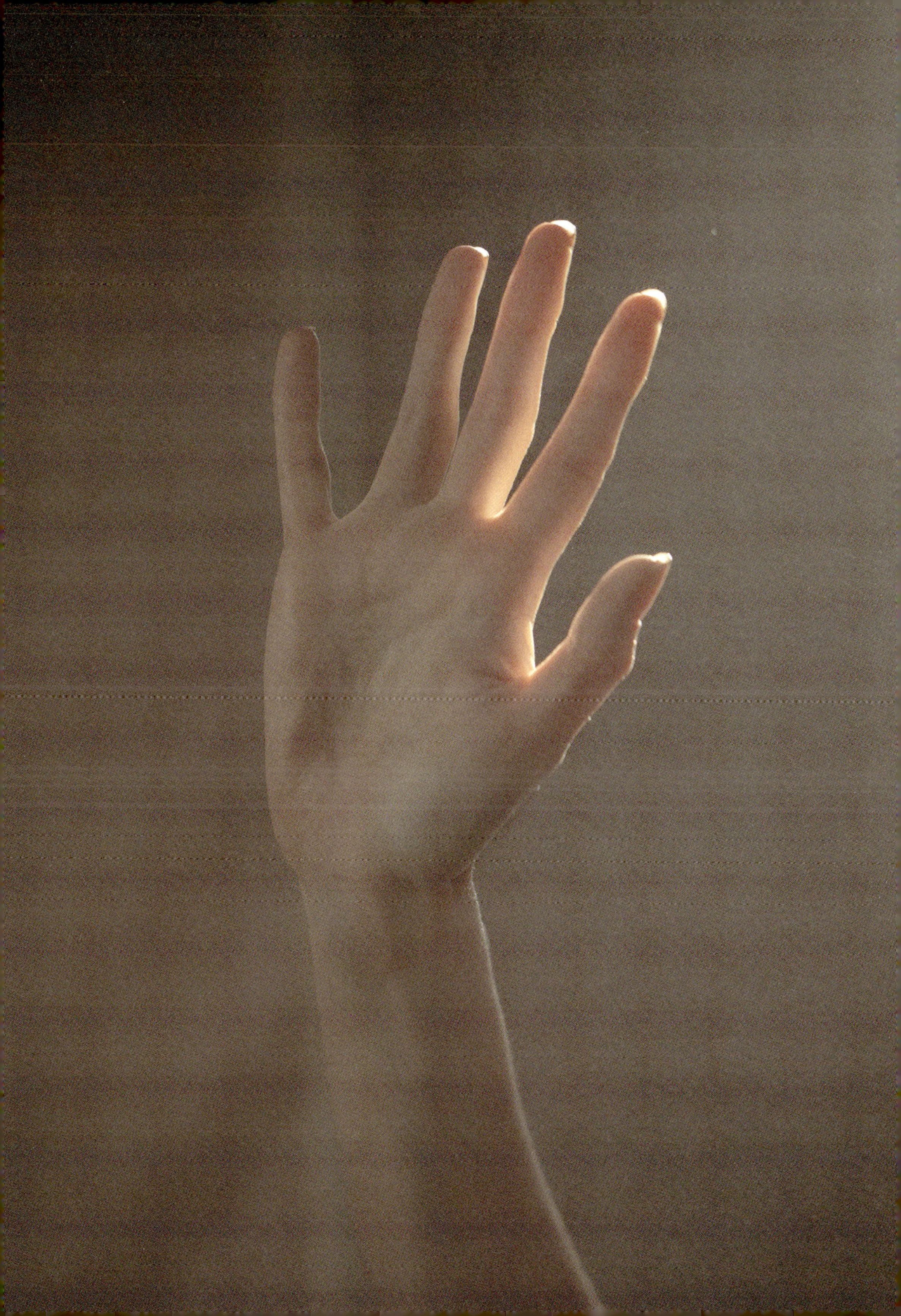

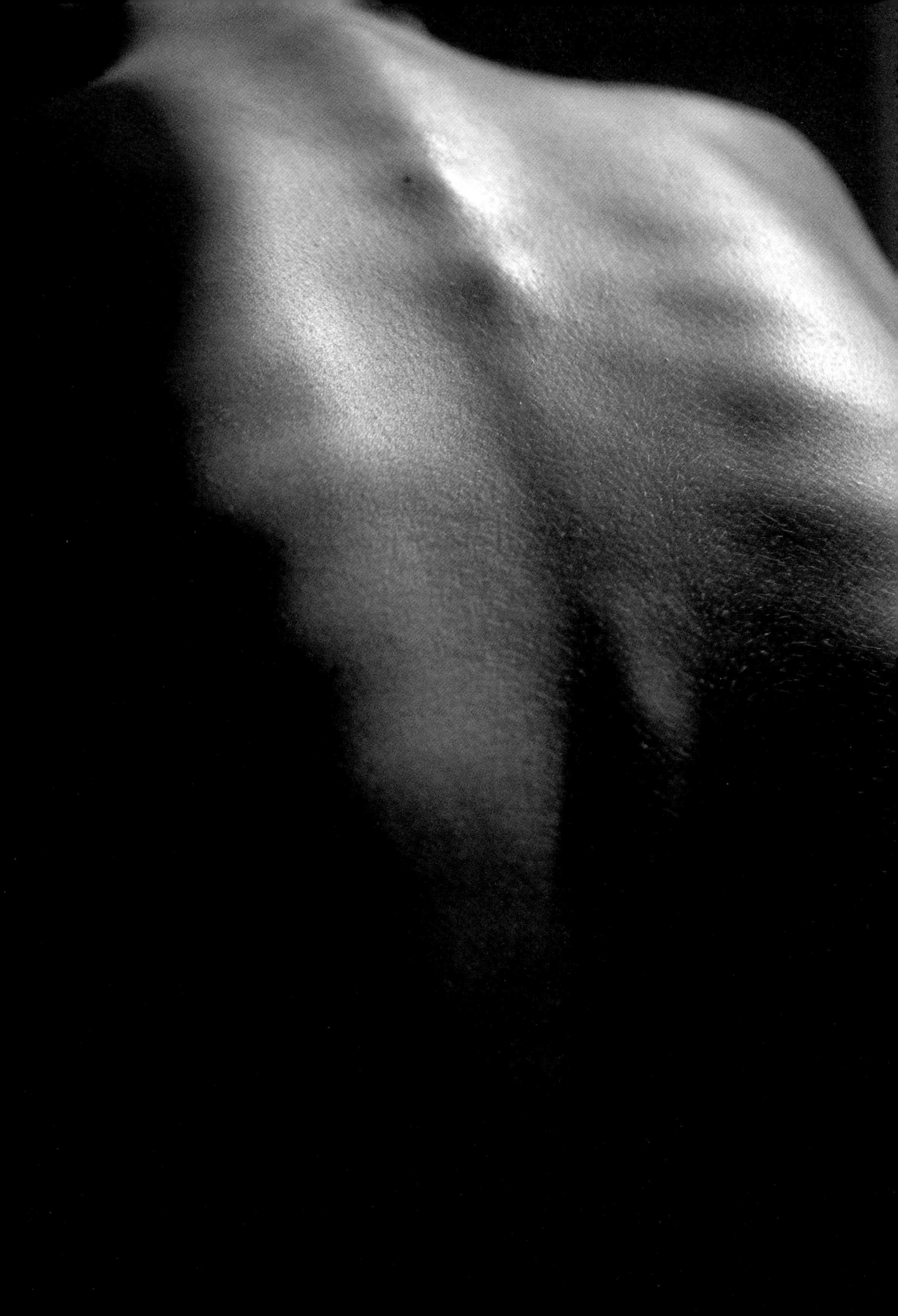

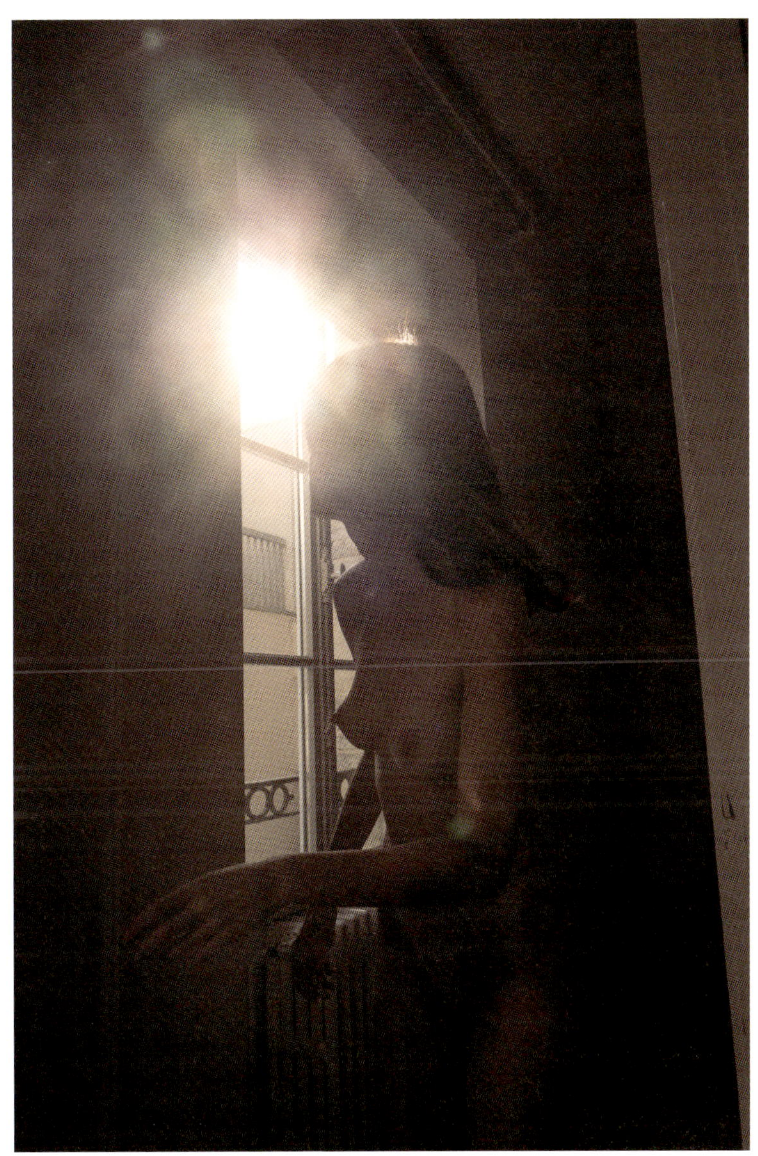

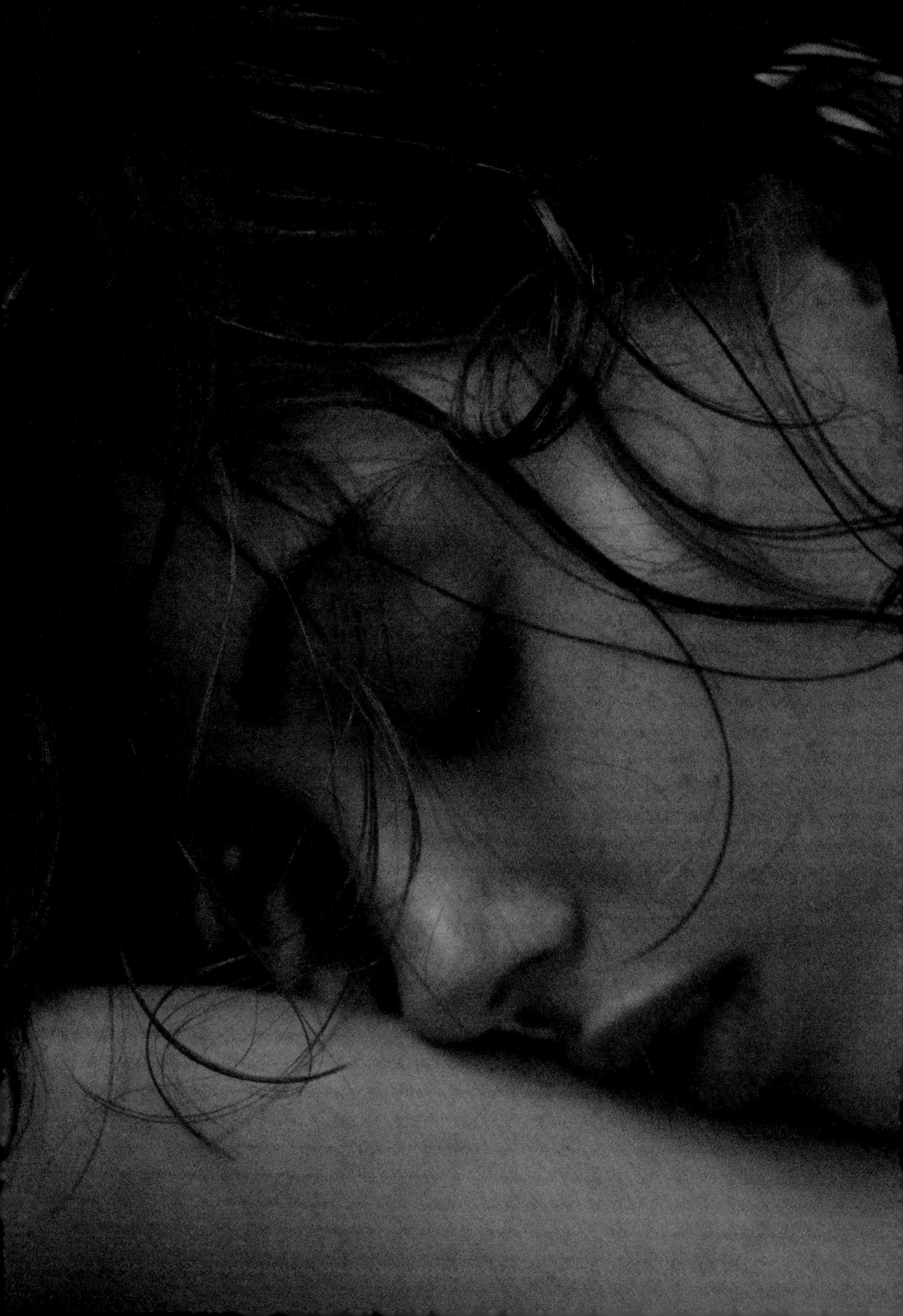

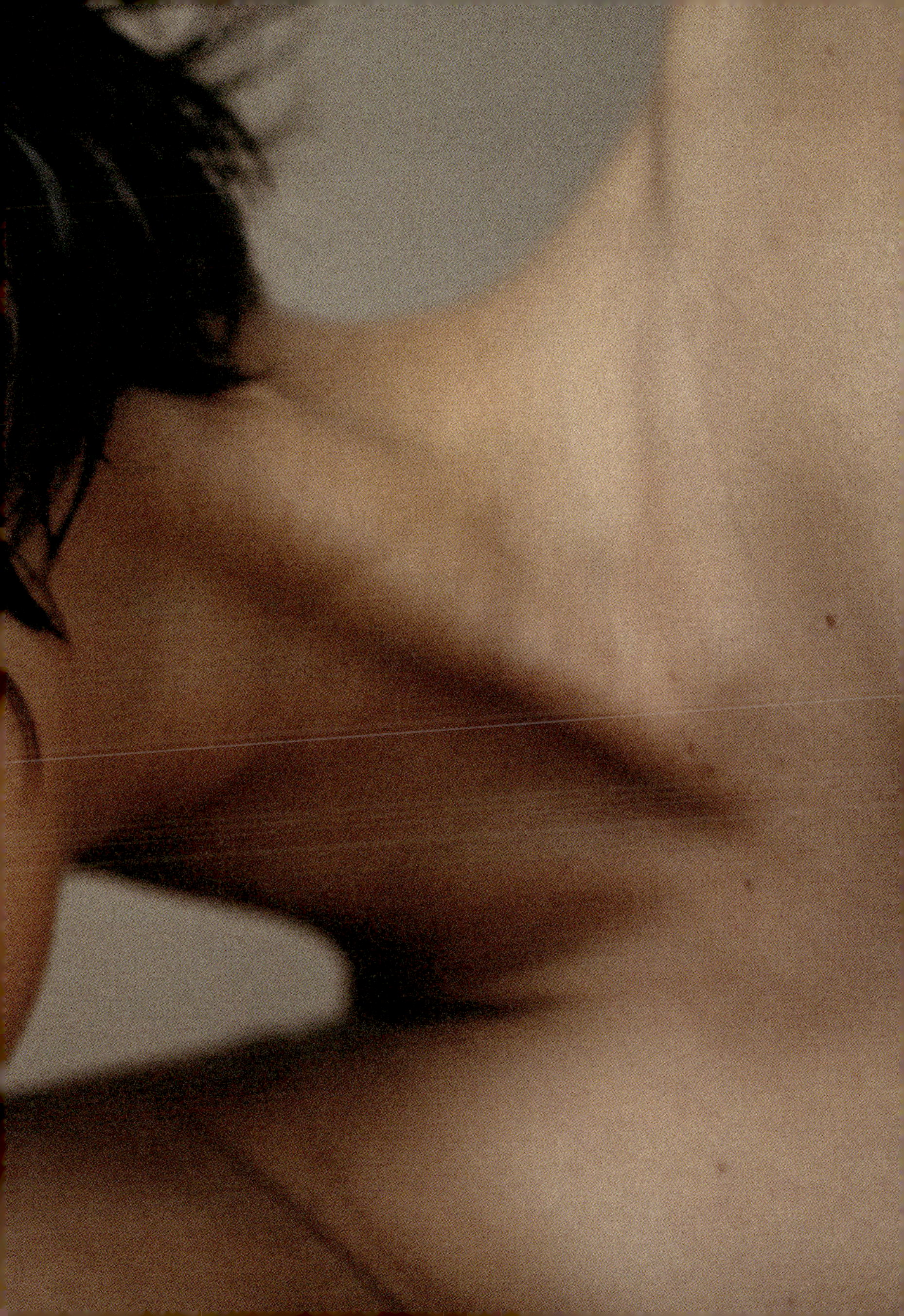

Danse Solaire

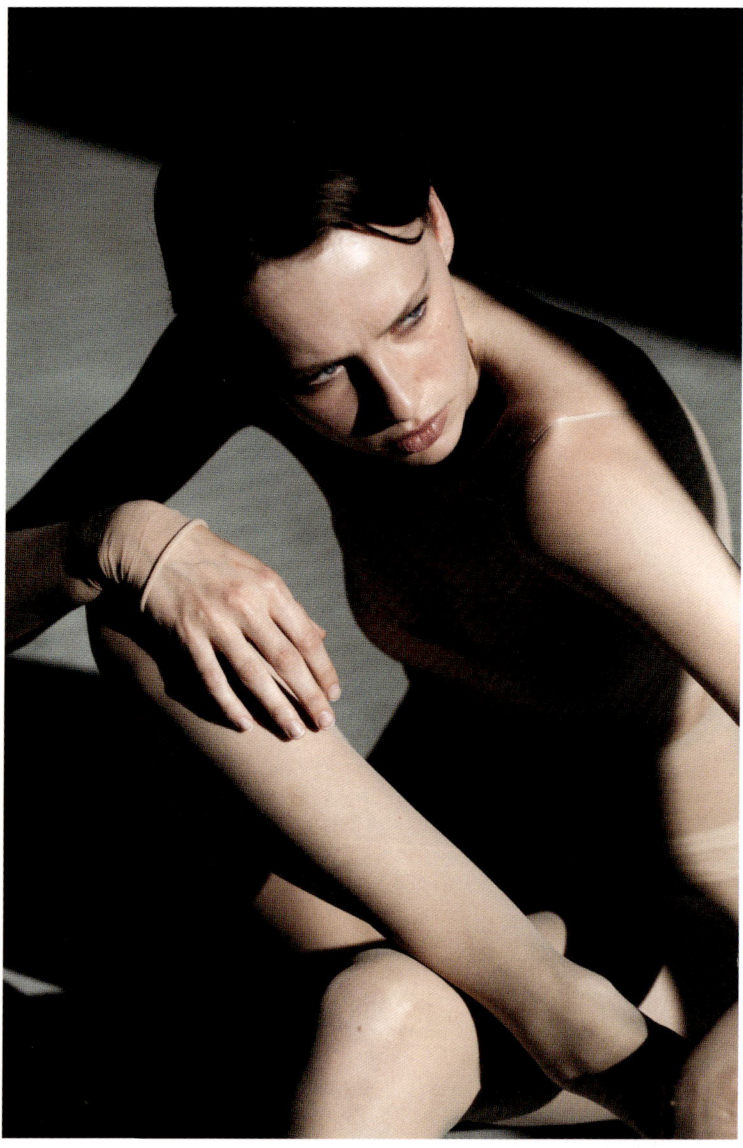

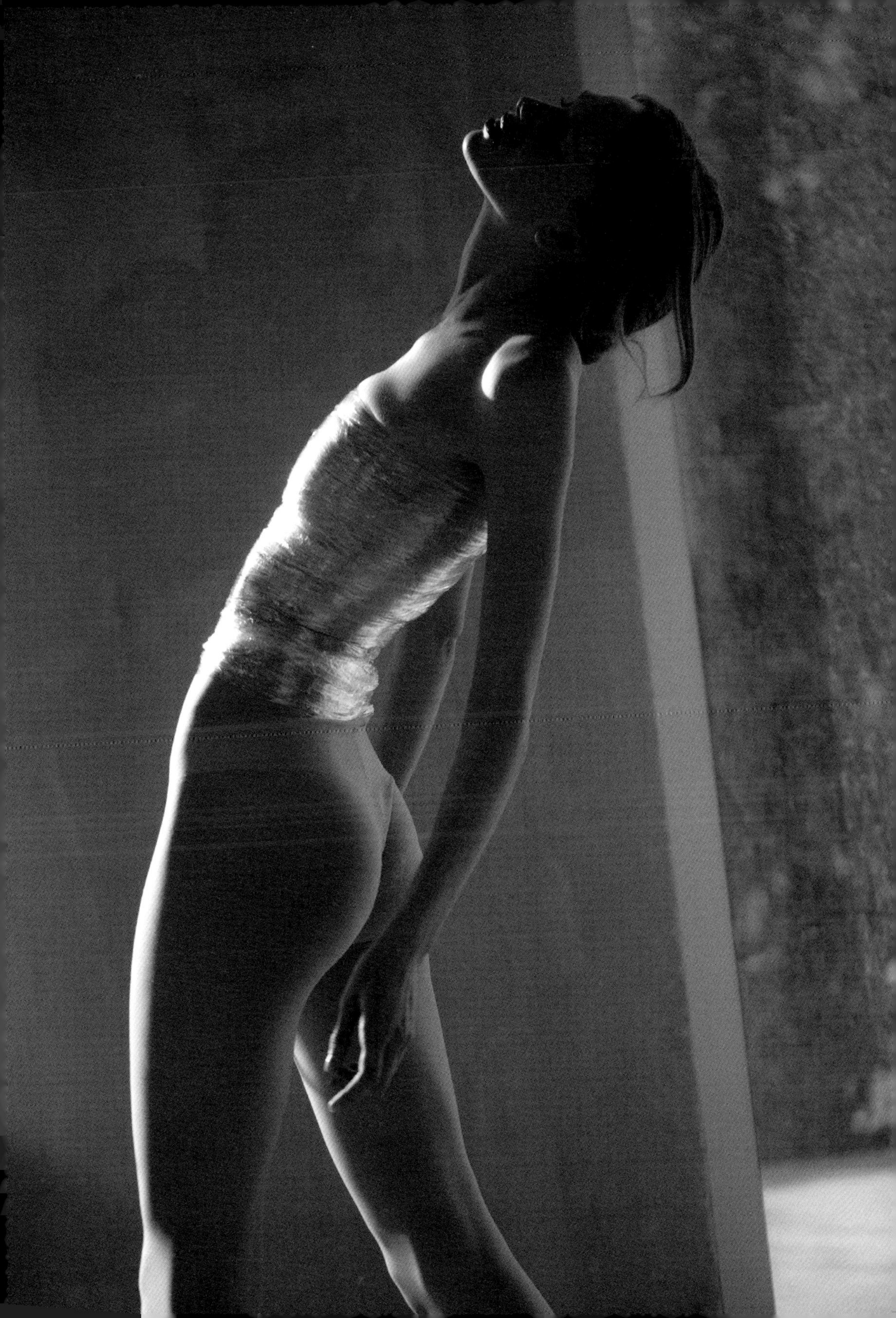

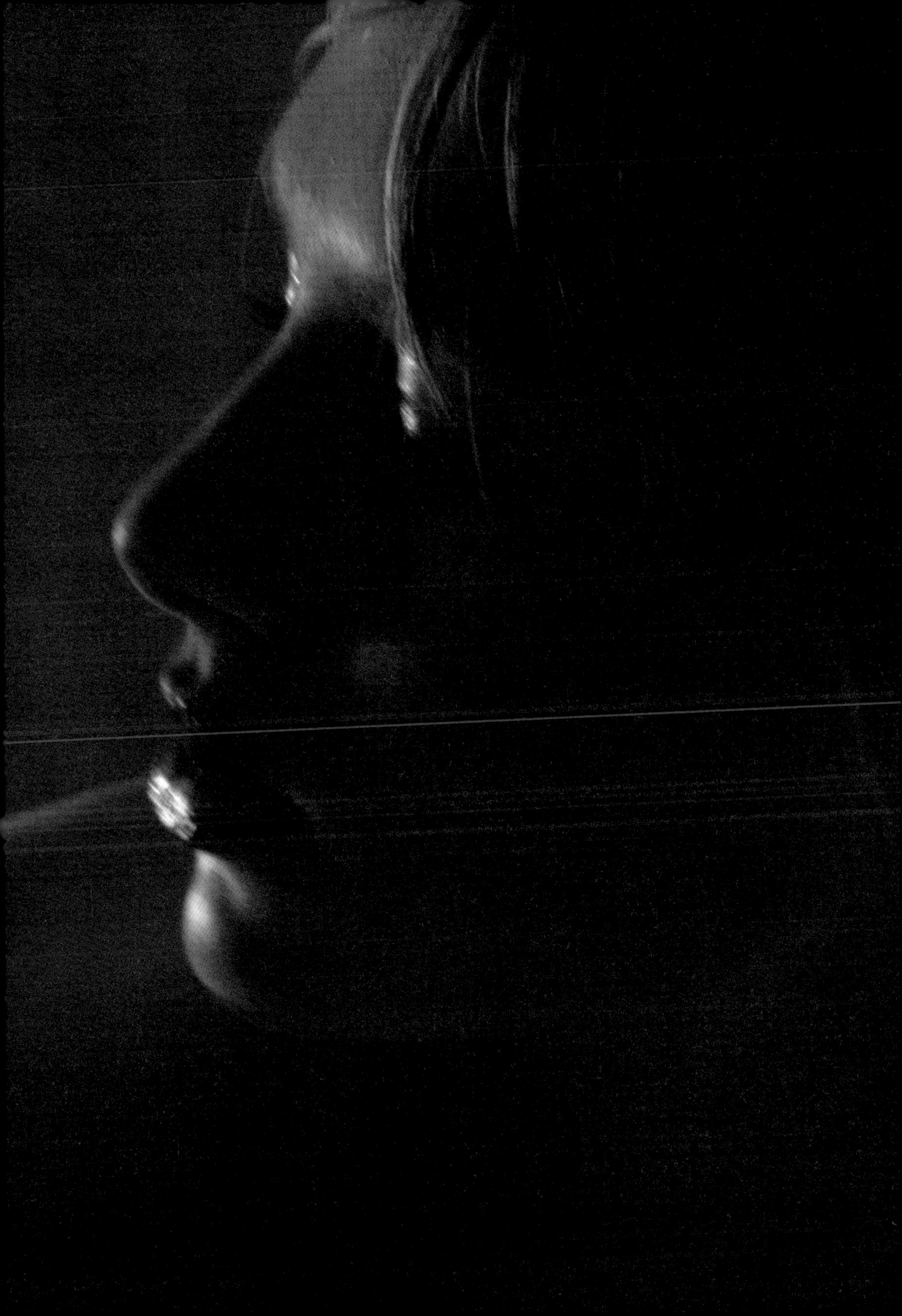

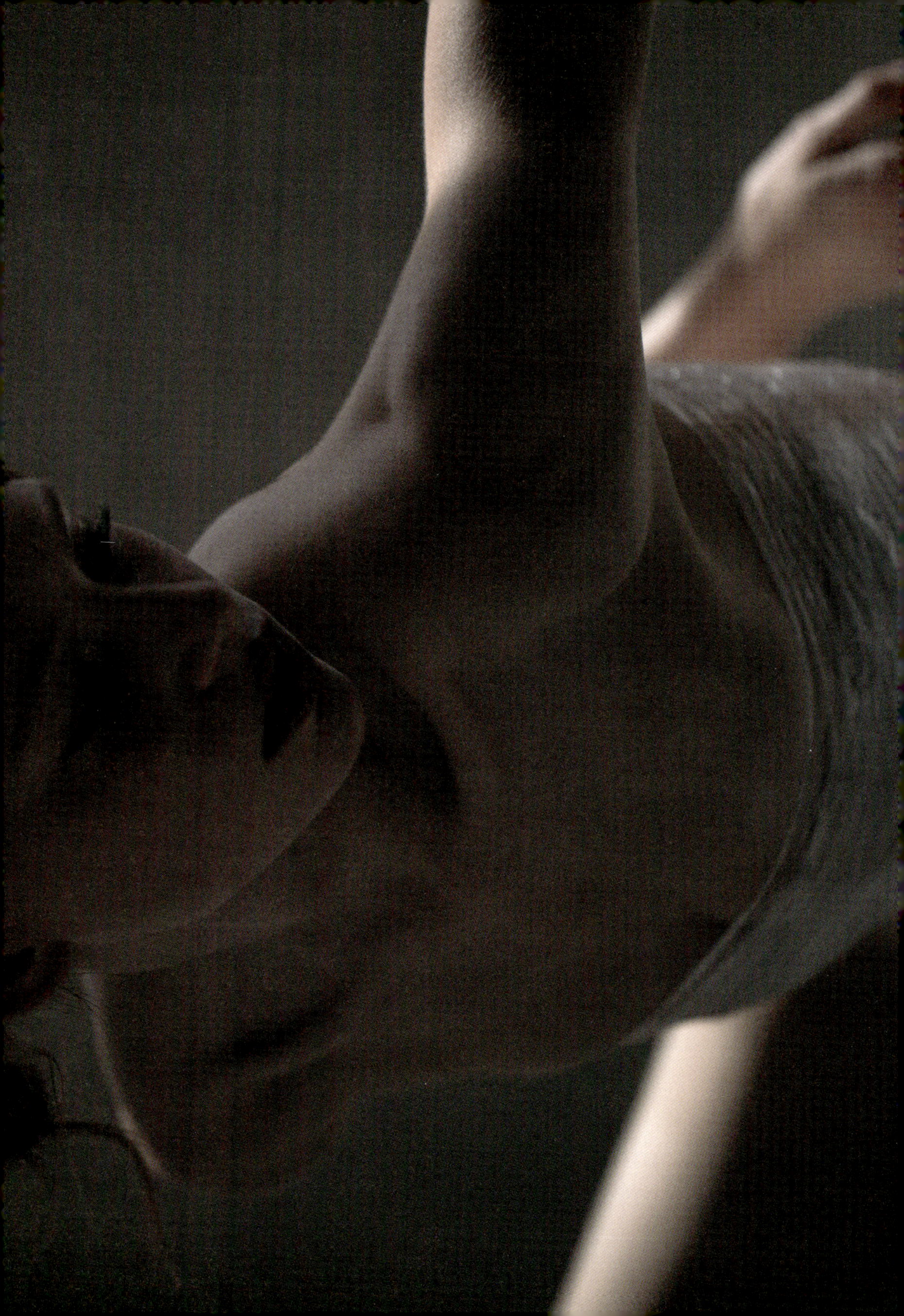

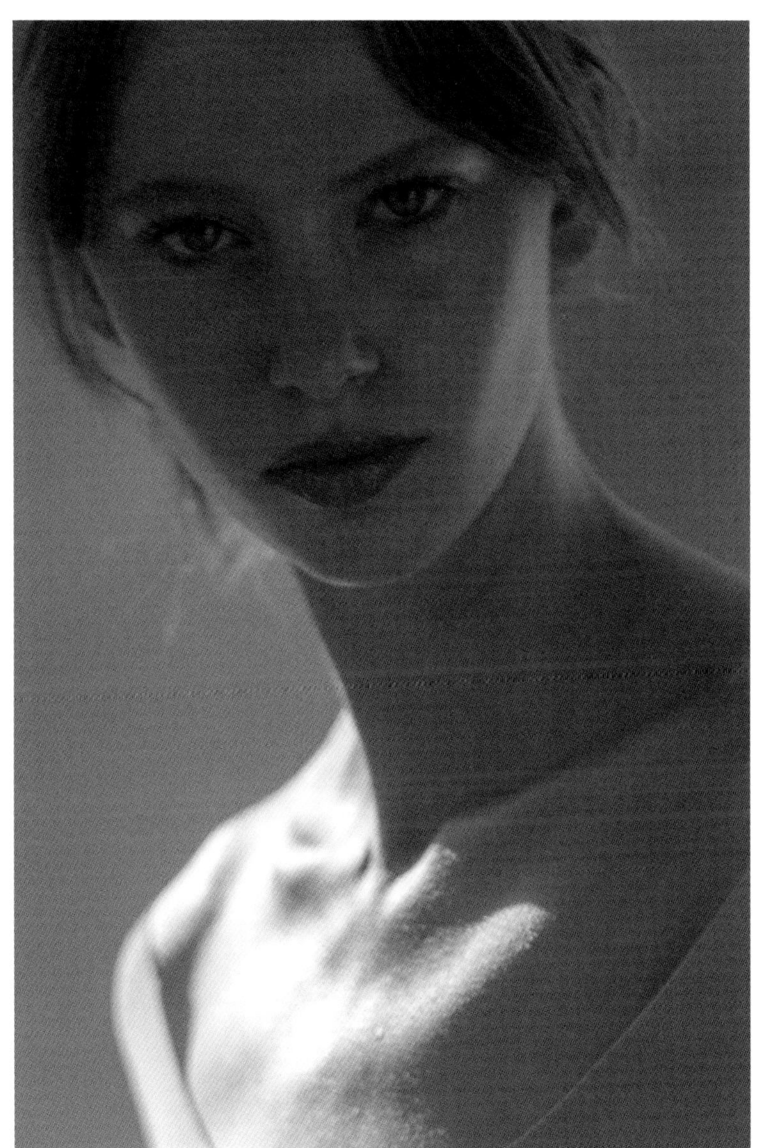

Un Soir d'Eté

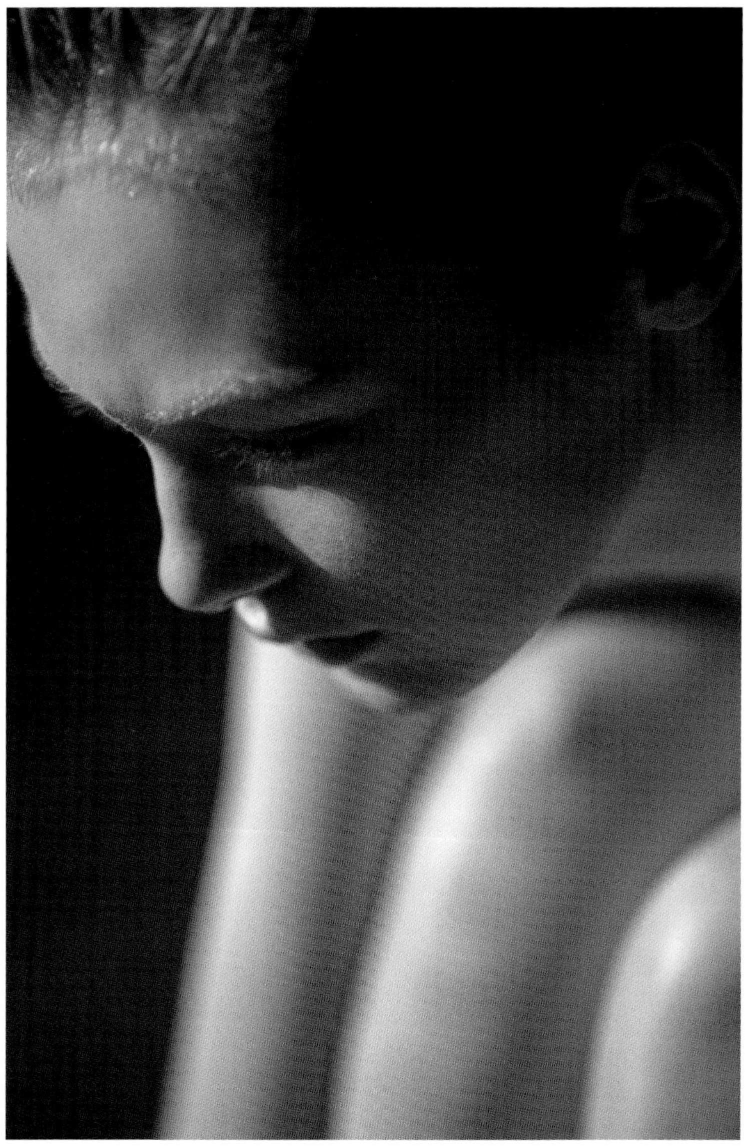

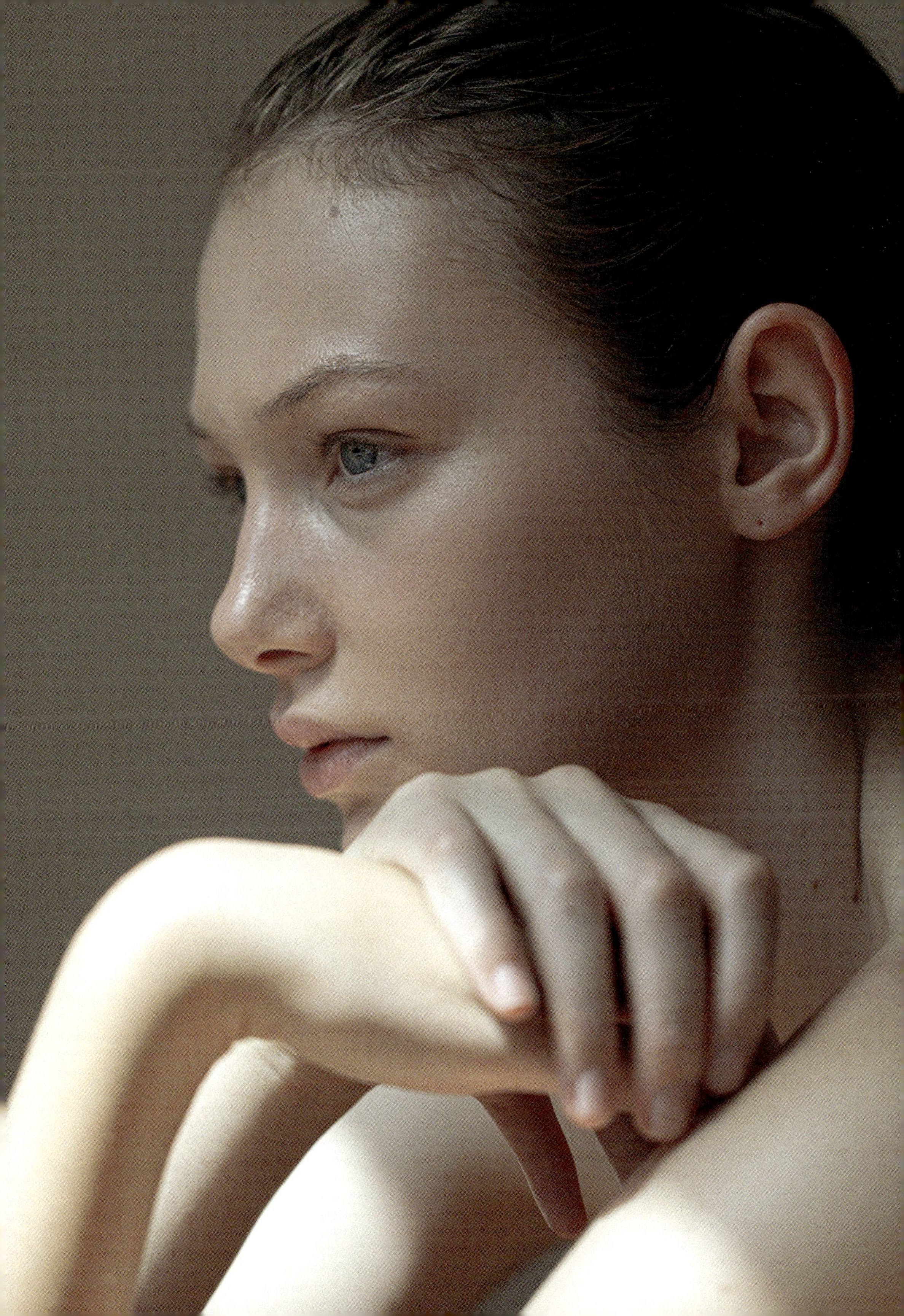

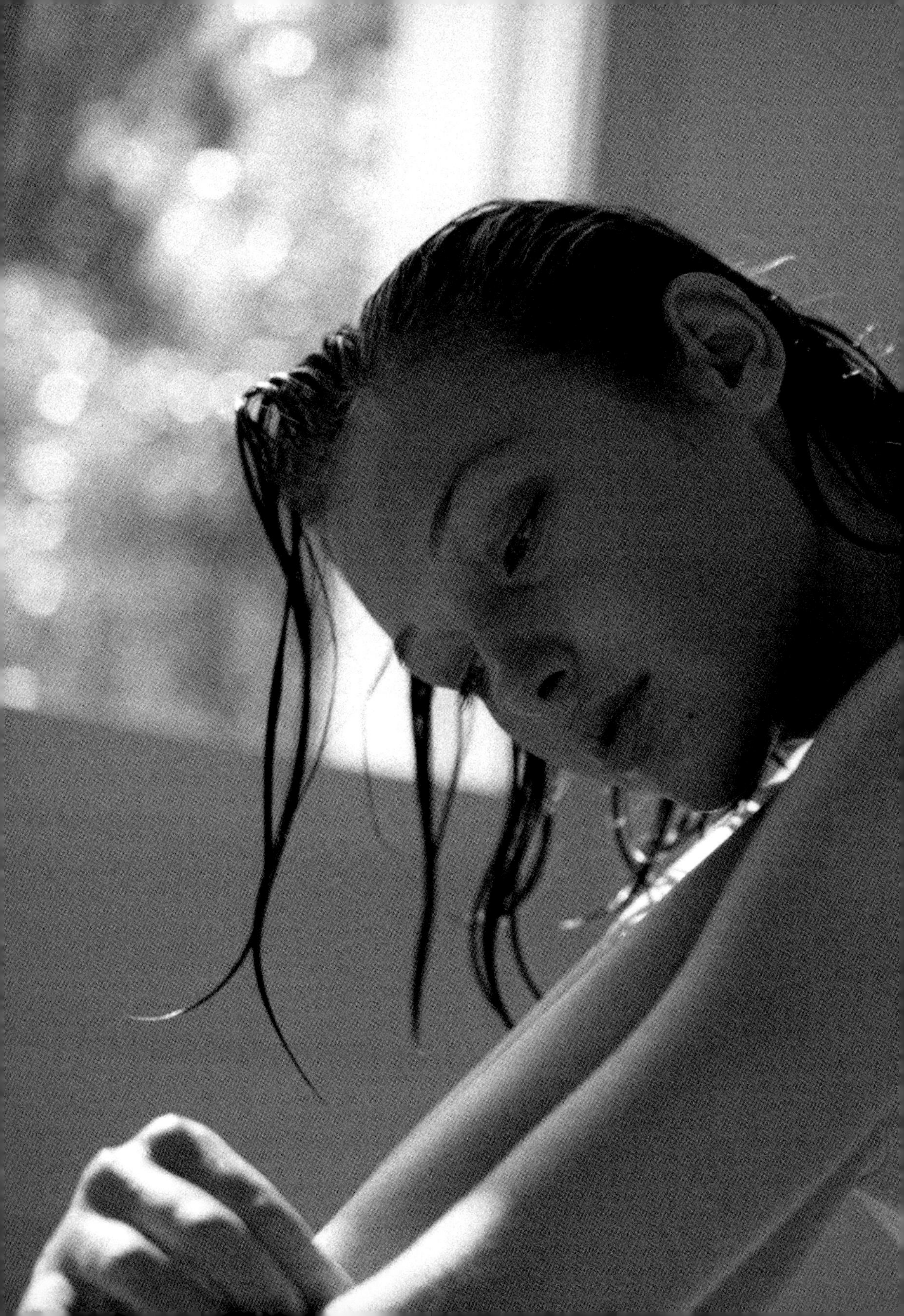

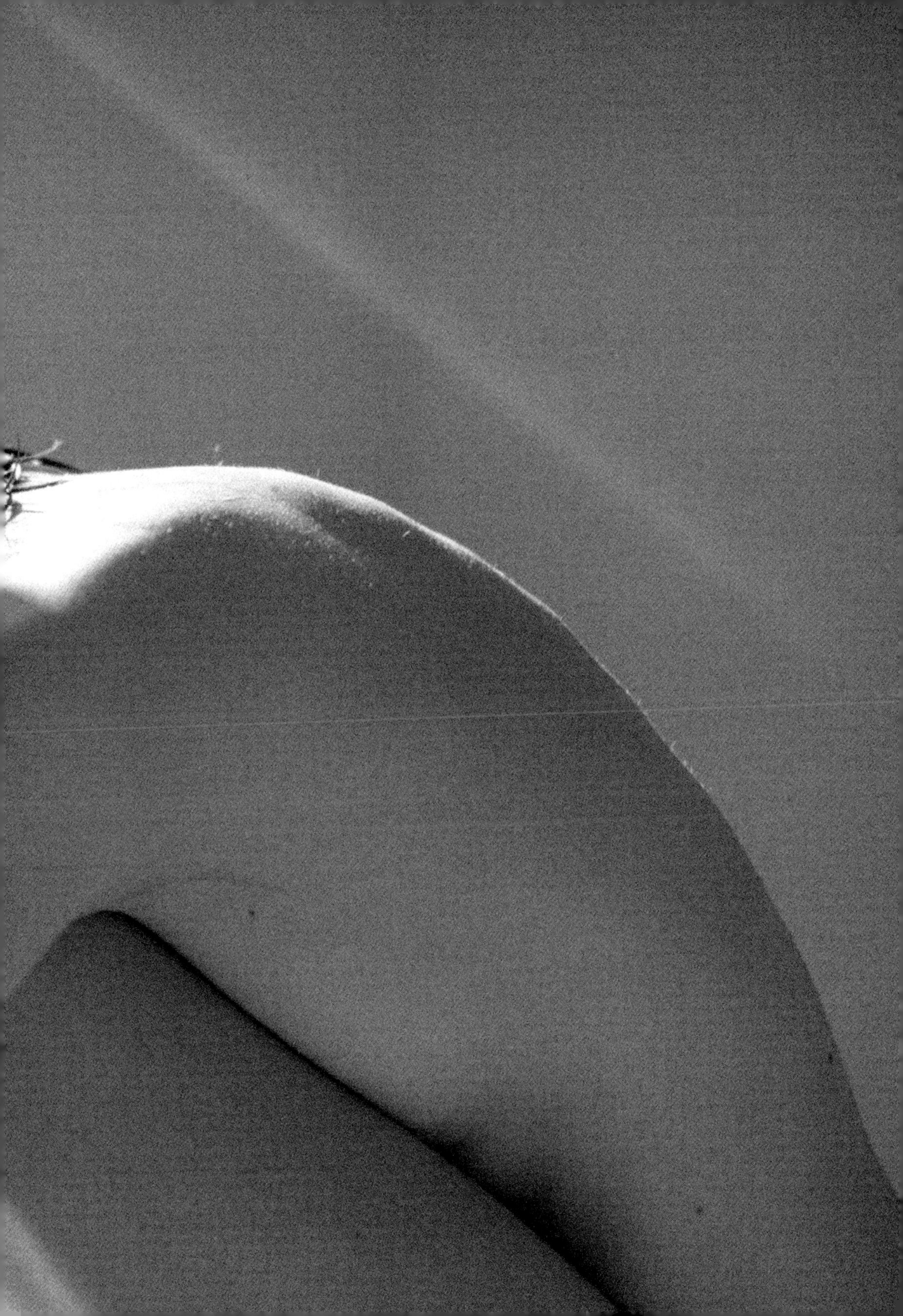

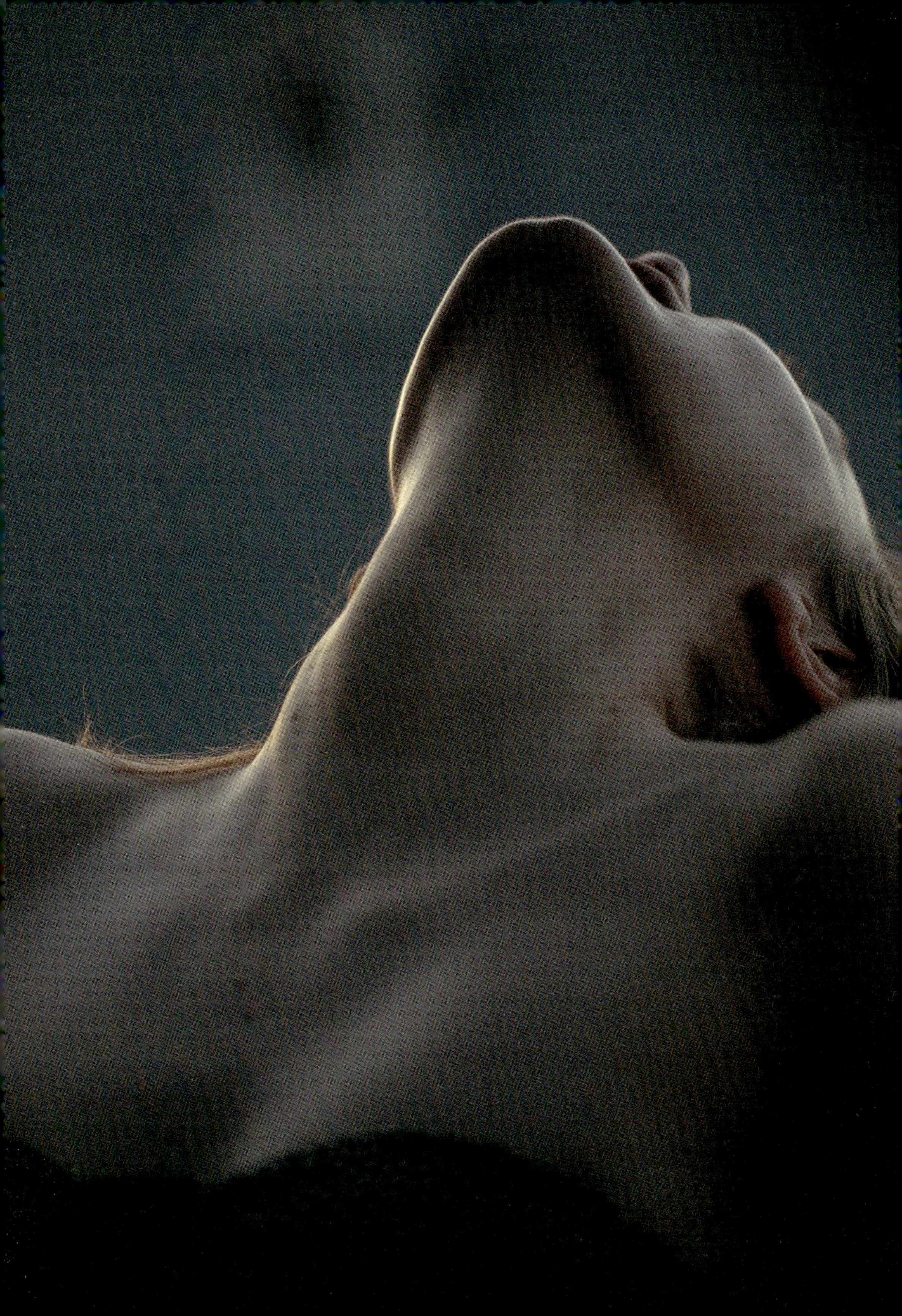

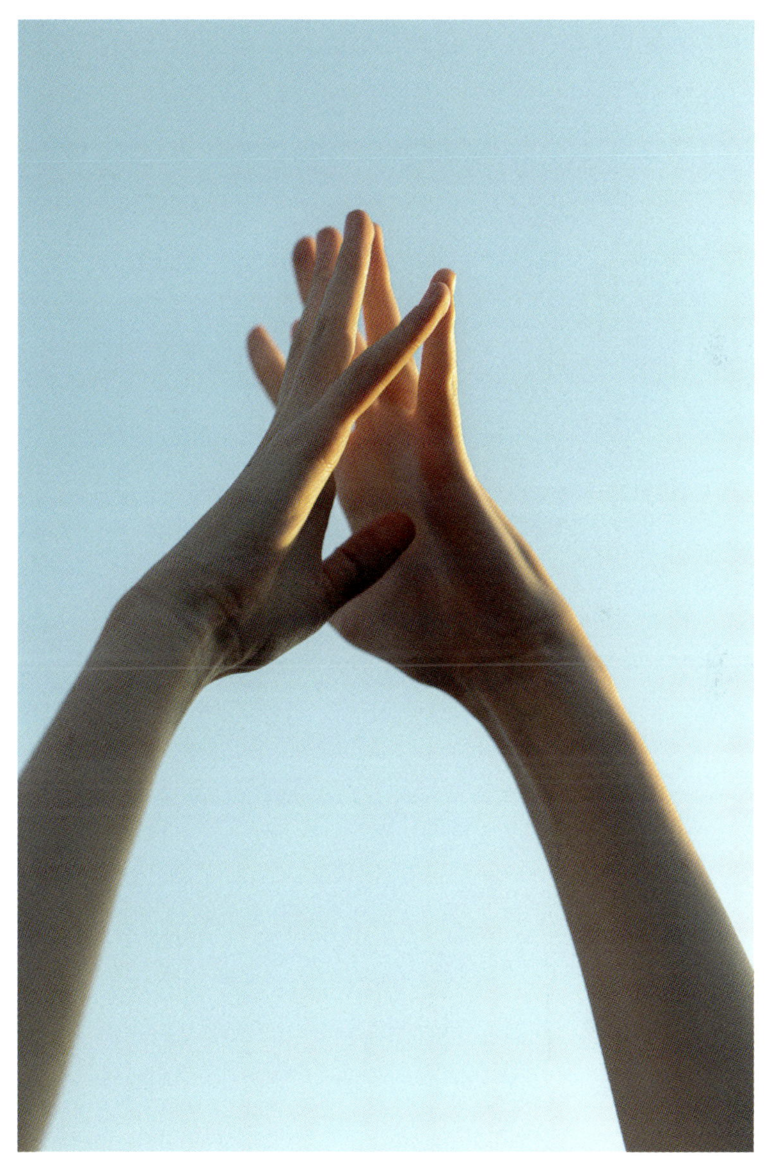

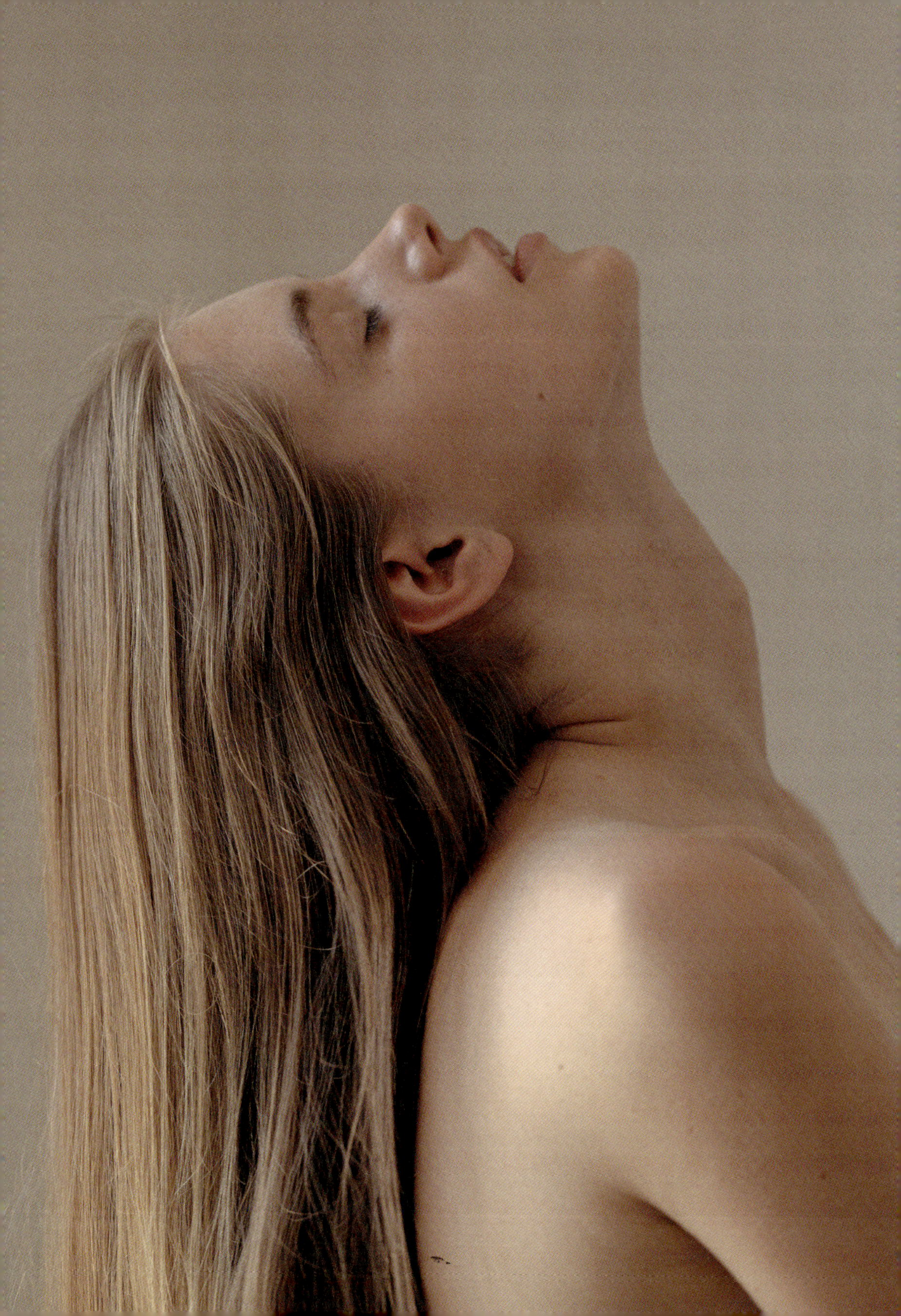

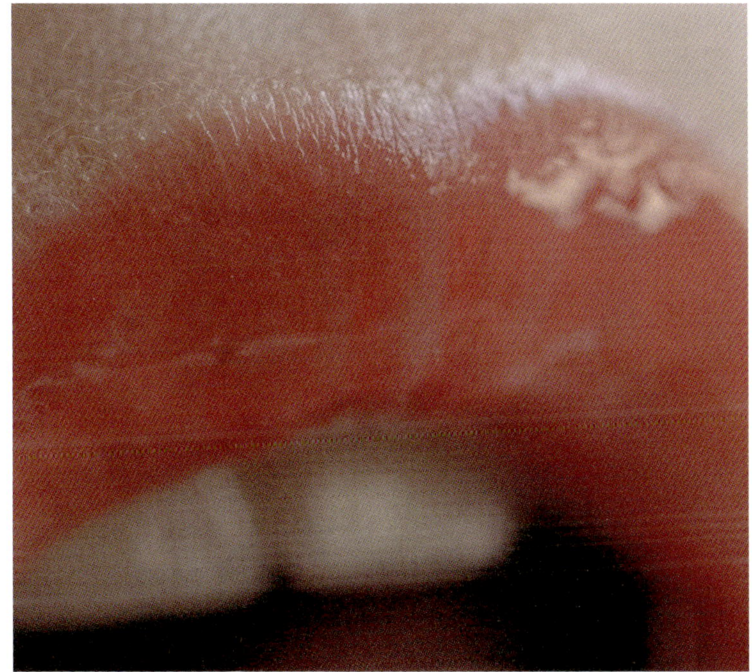

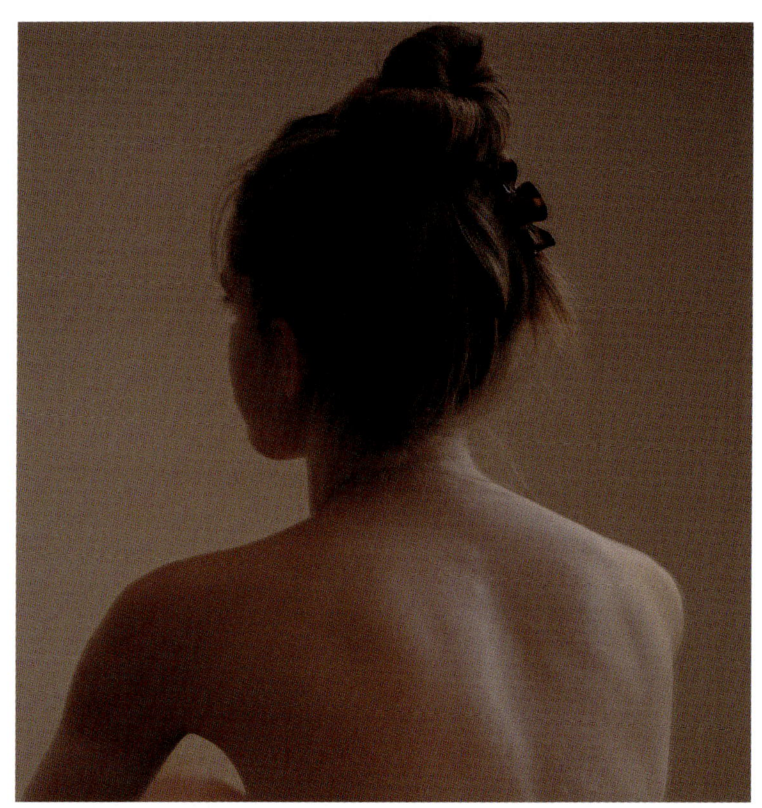

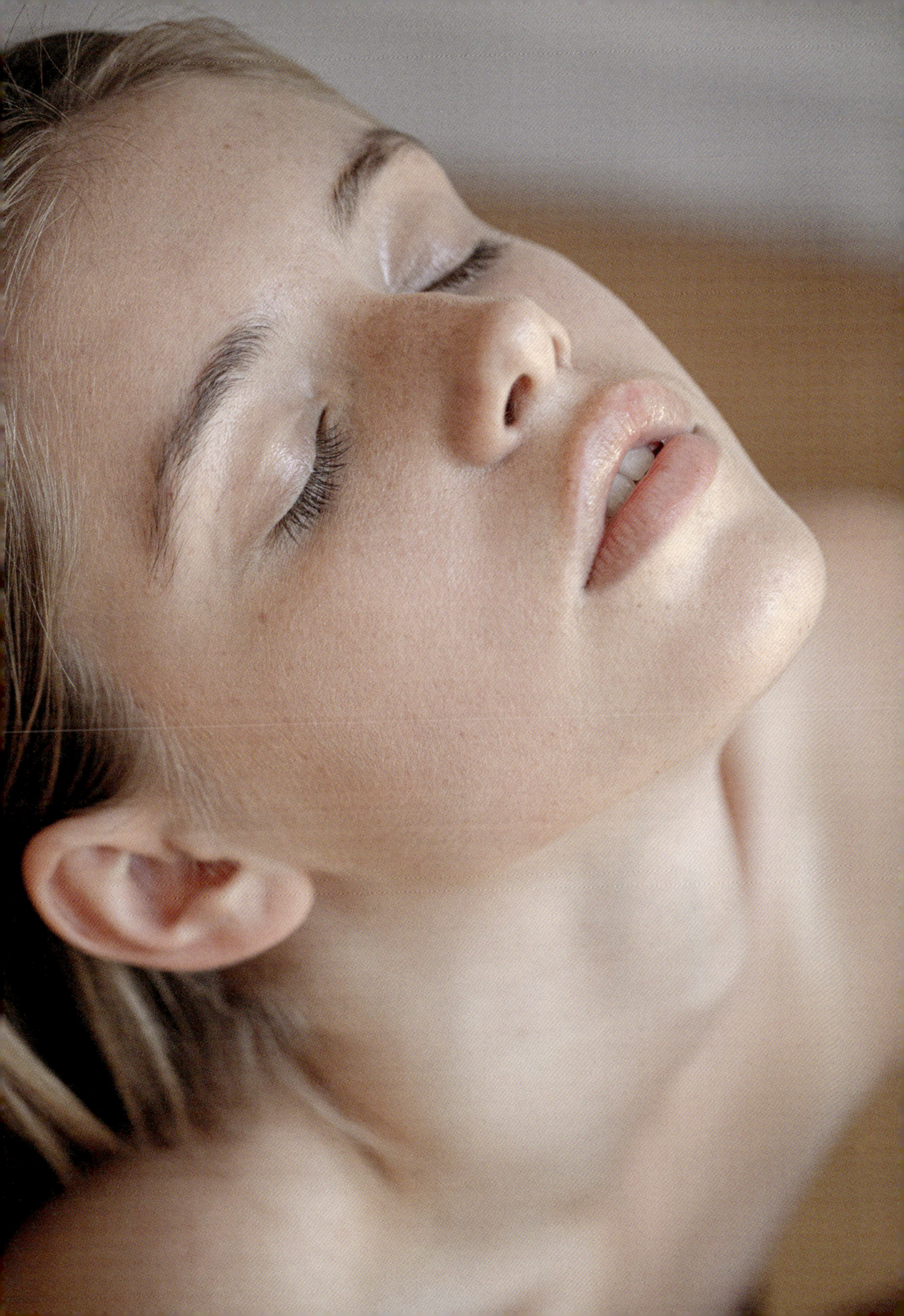

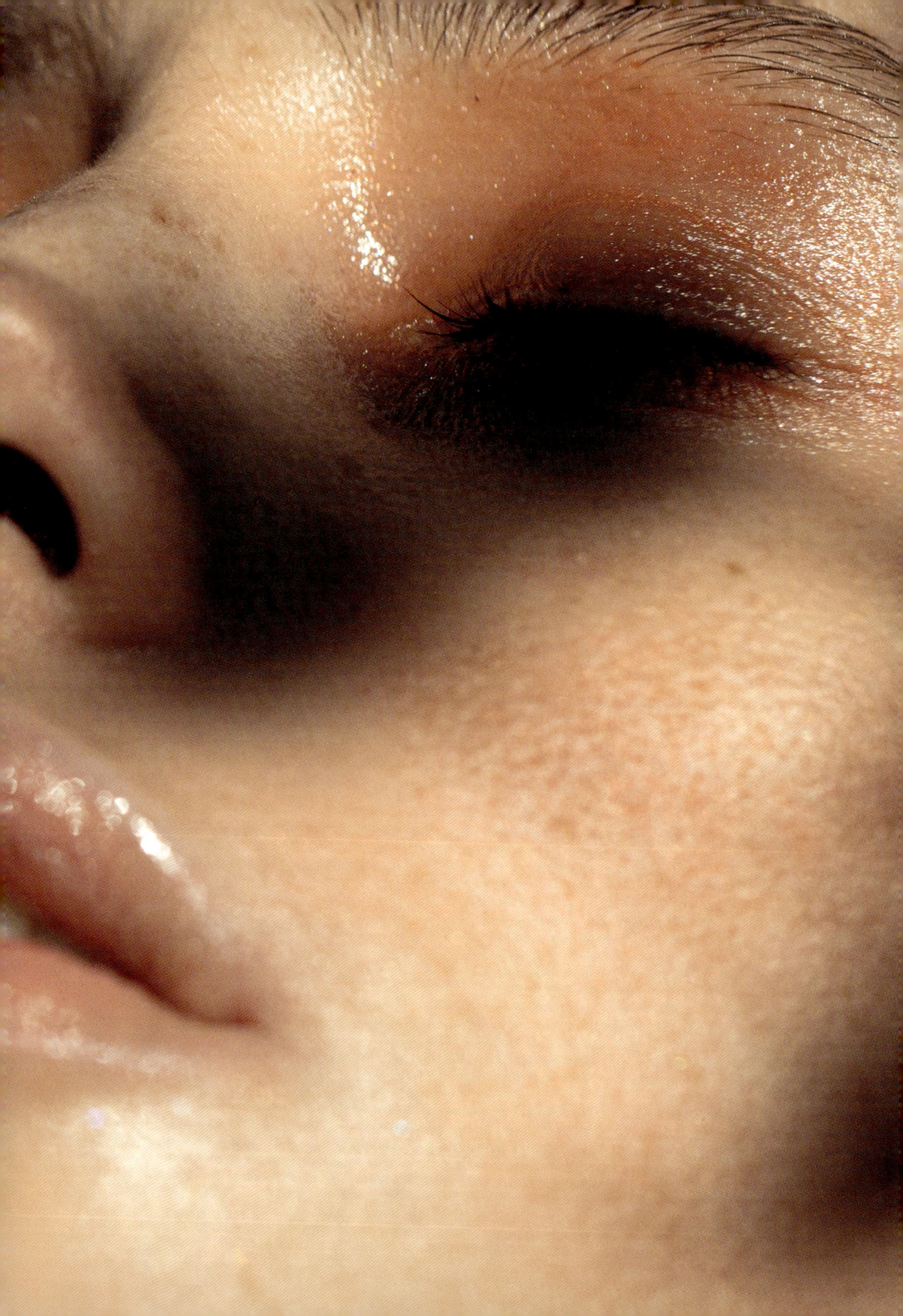

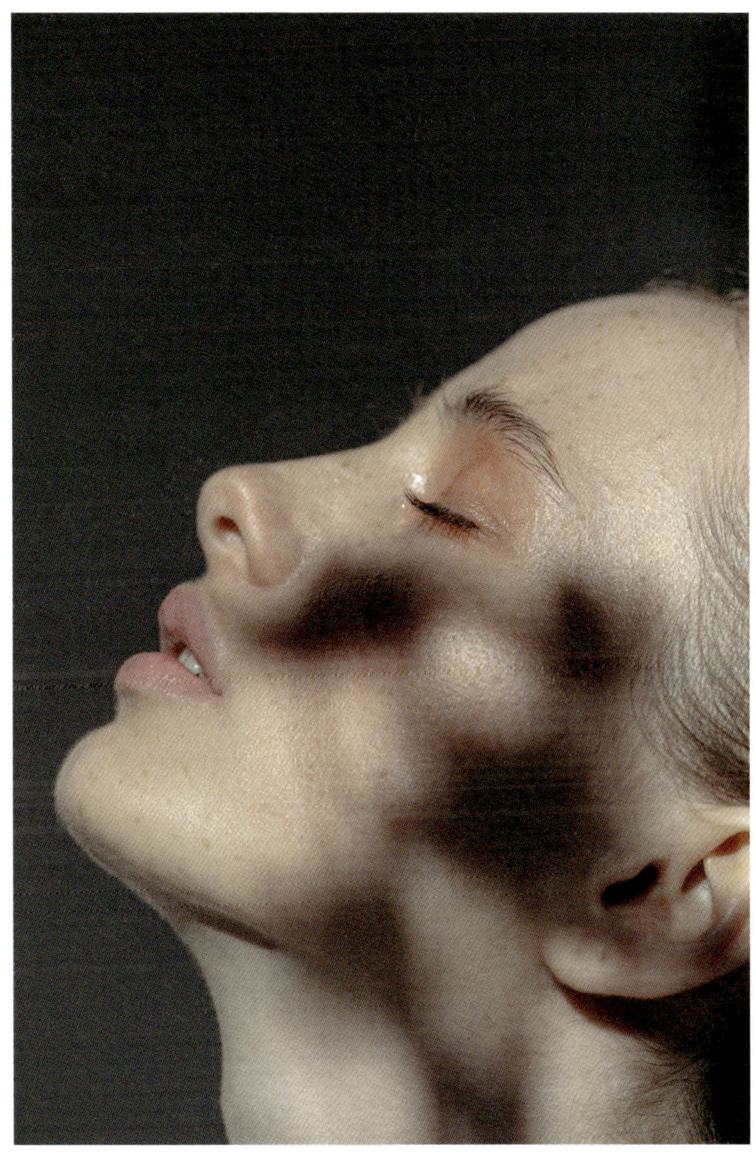

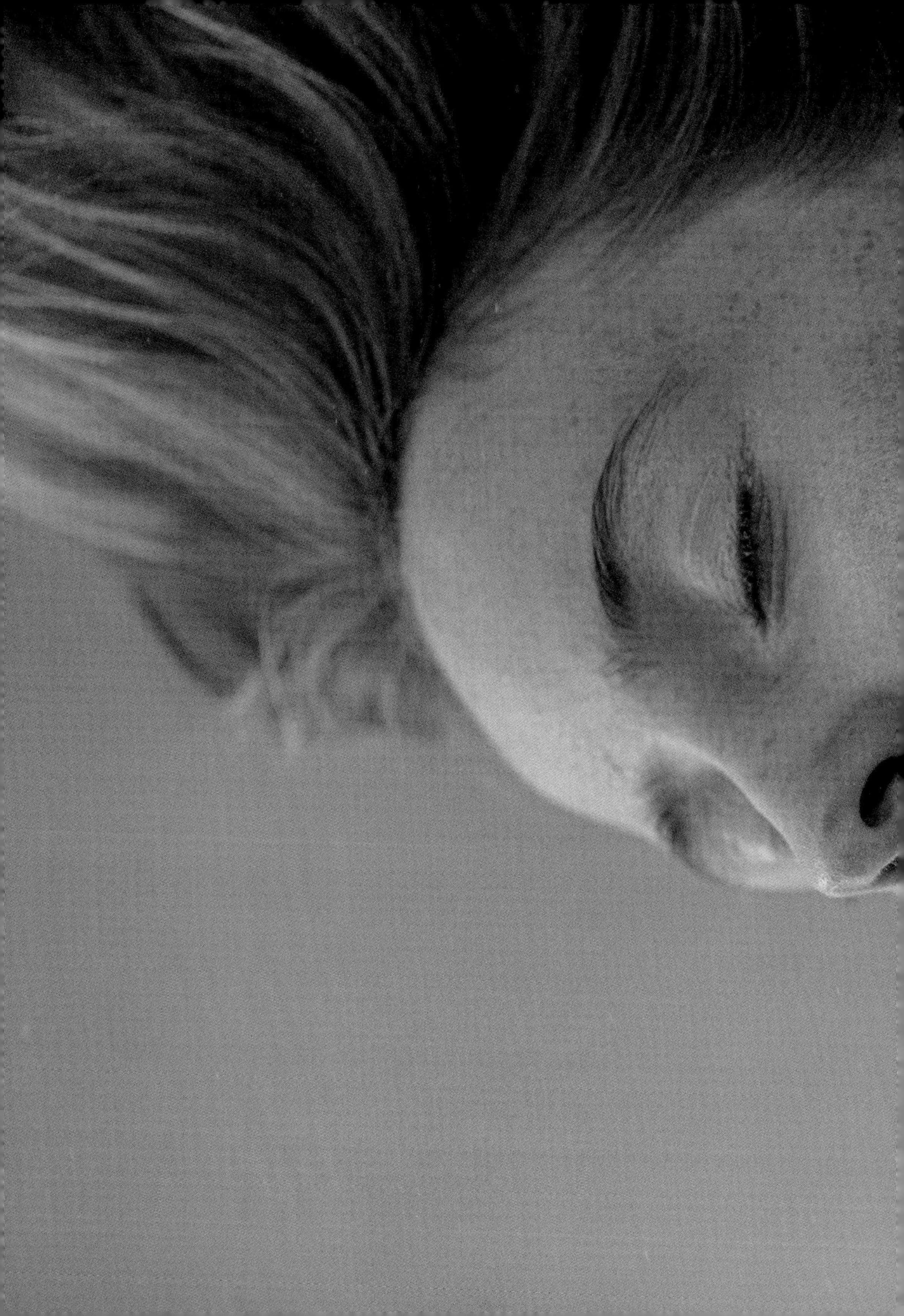

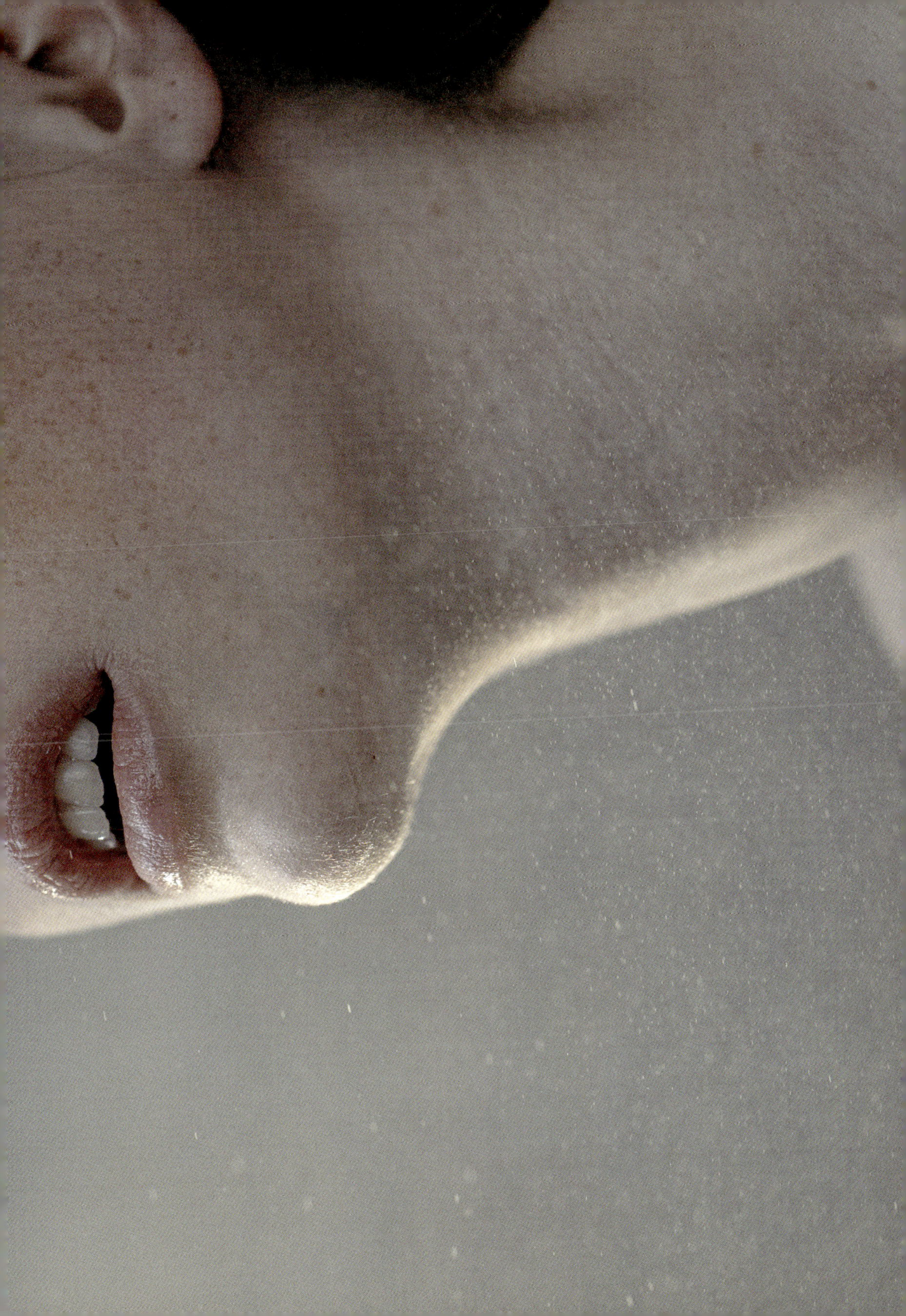

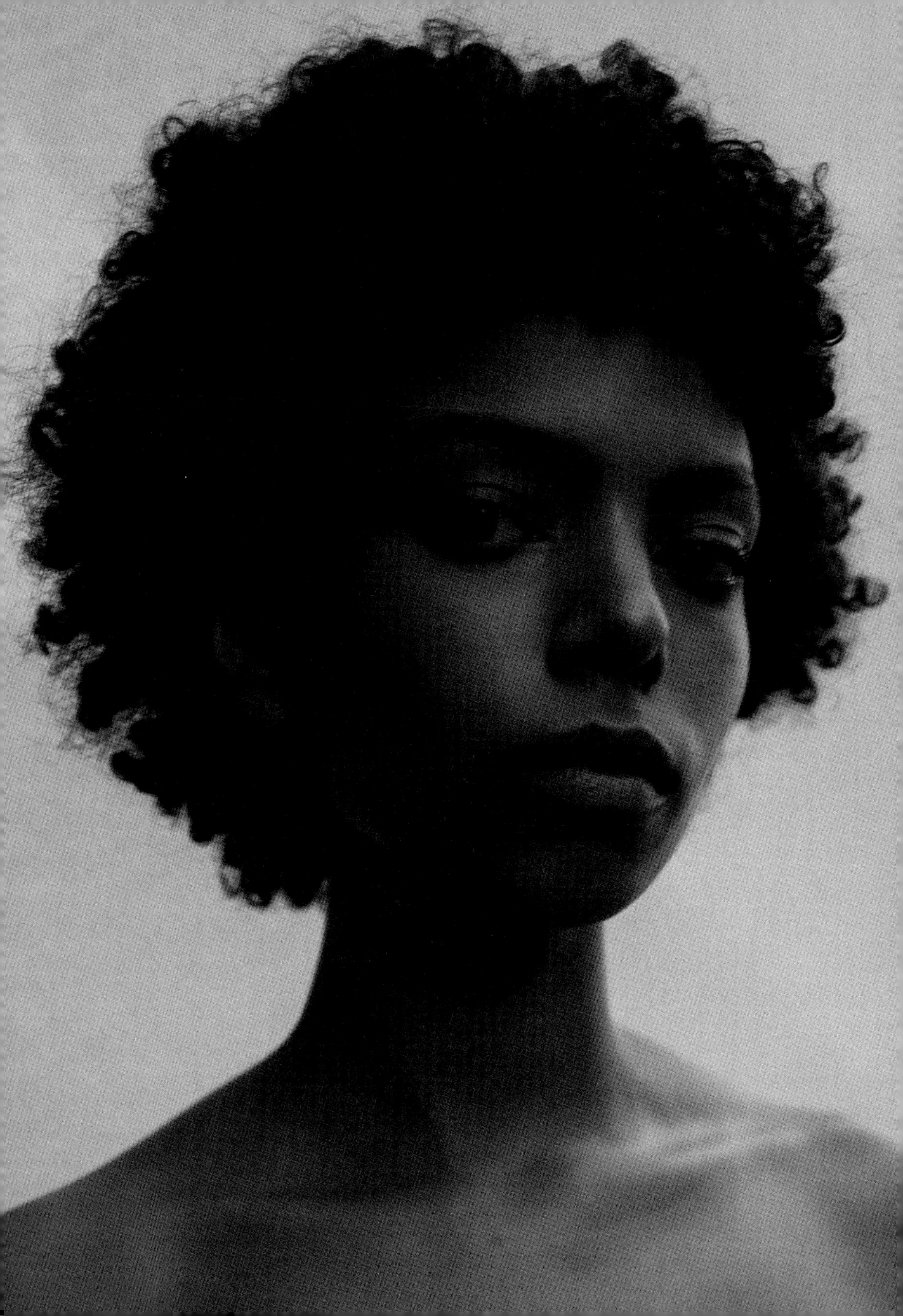

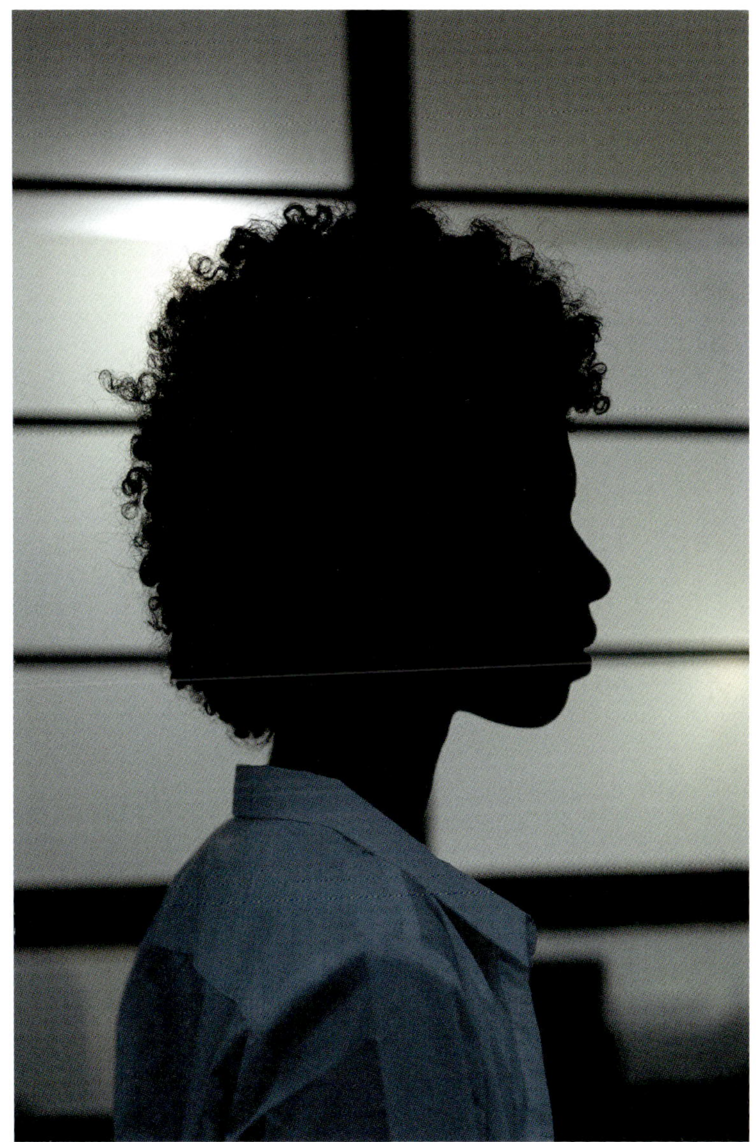

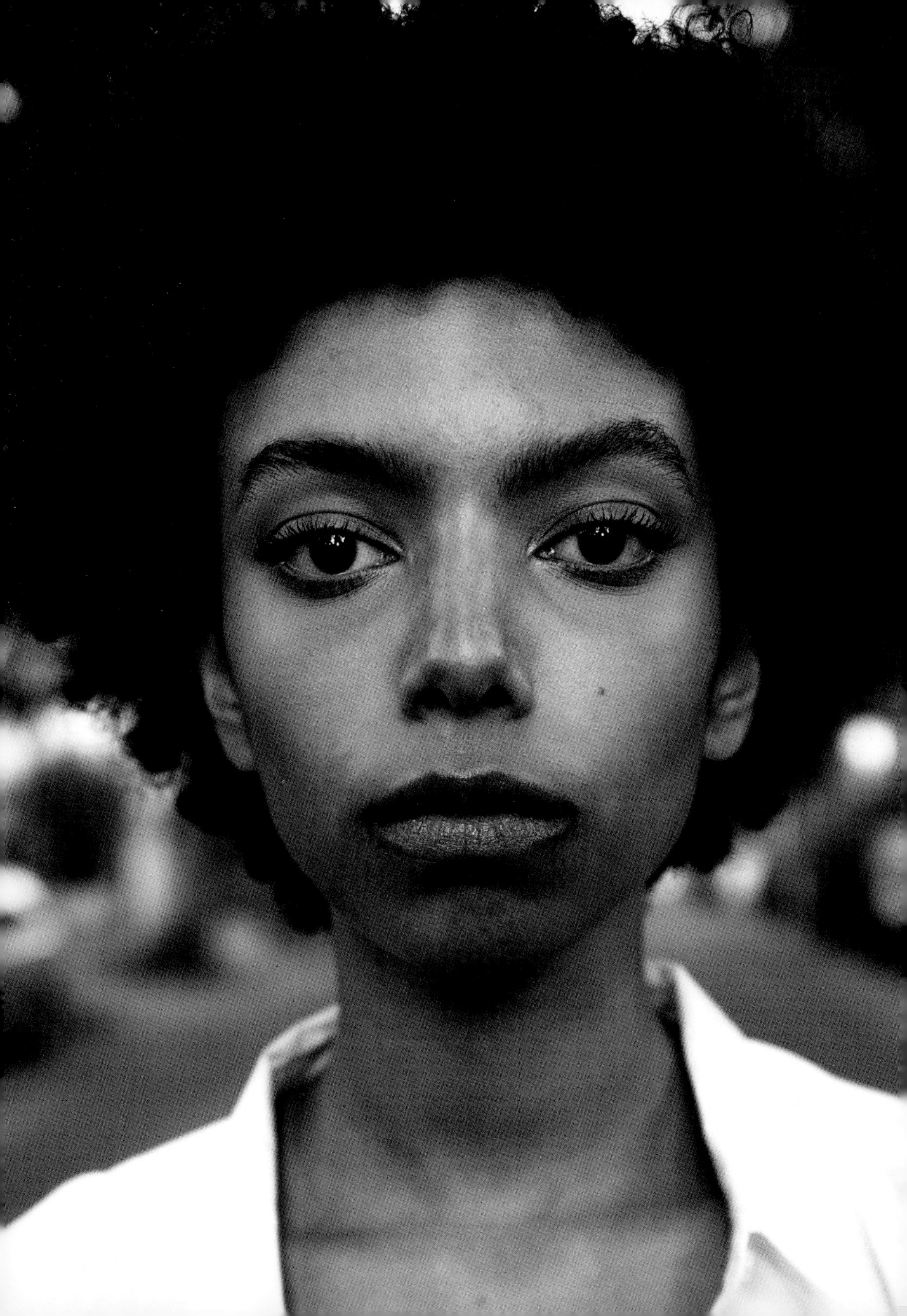

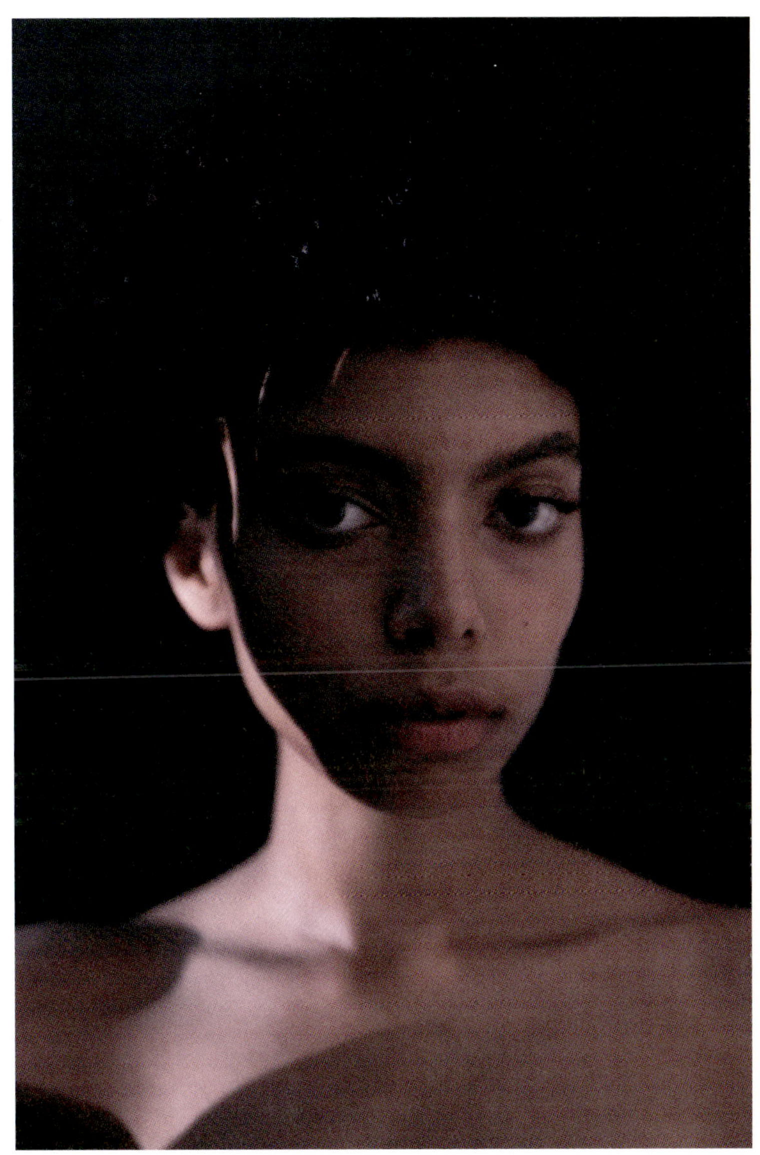

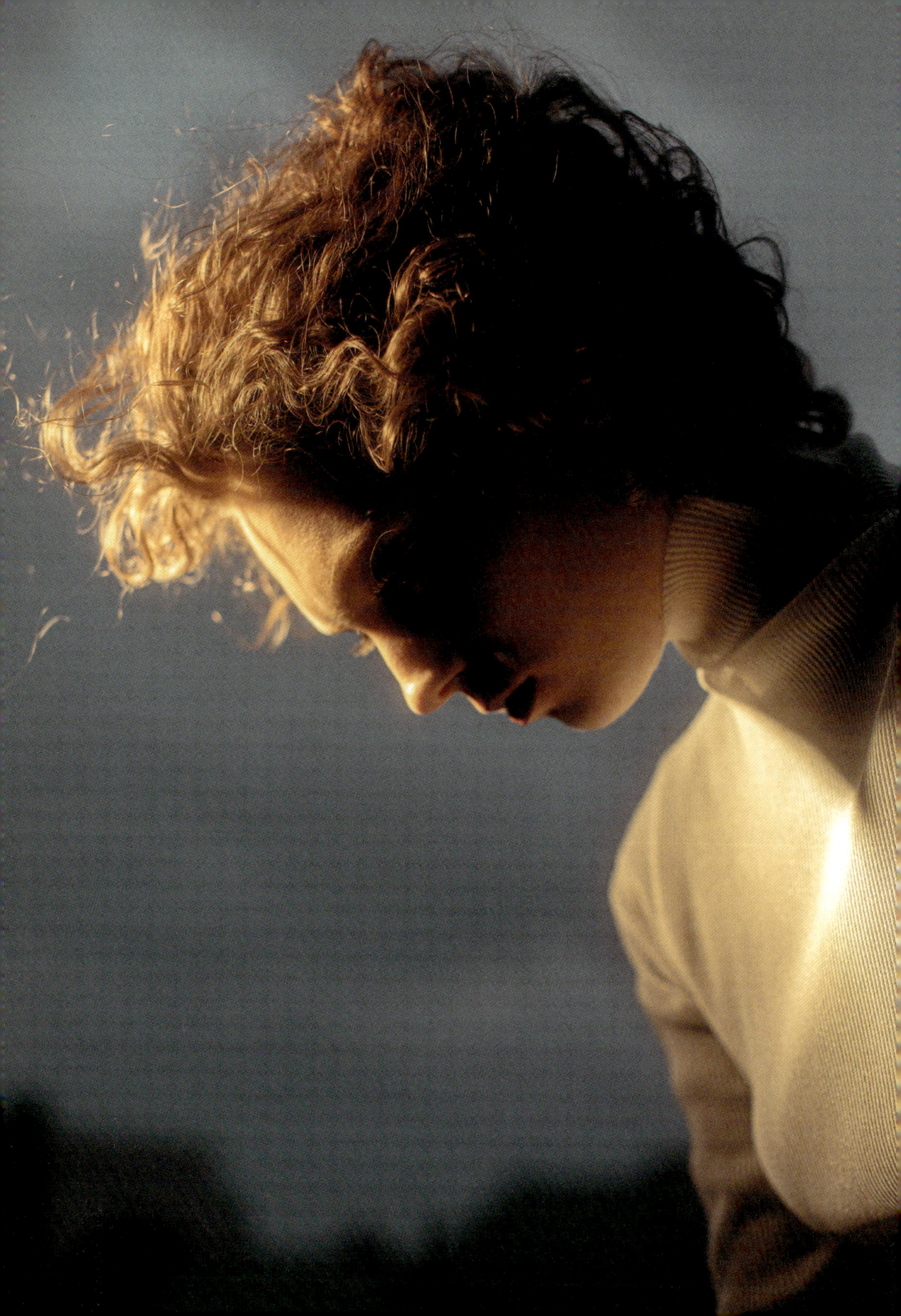

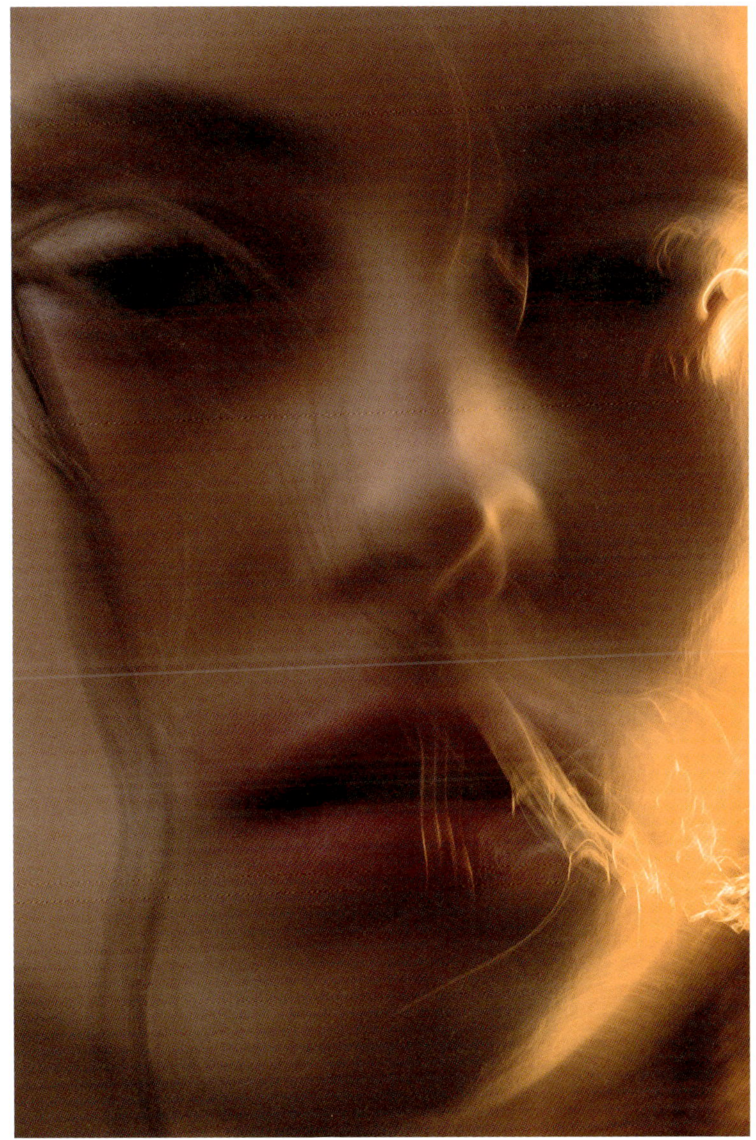

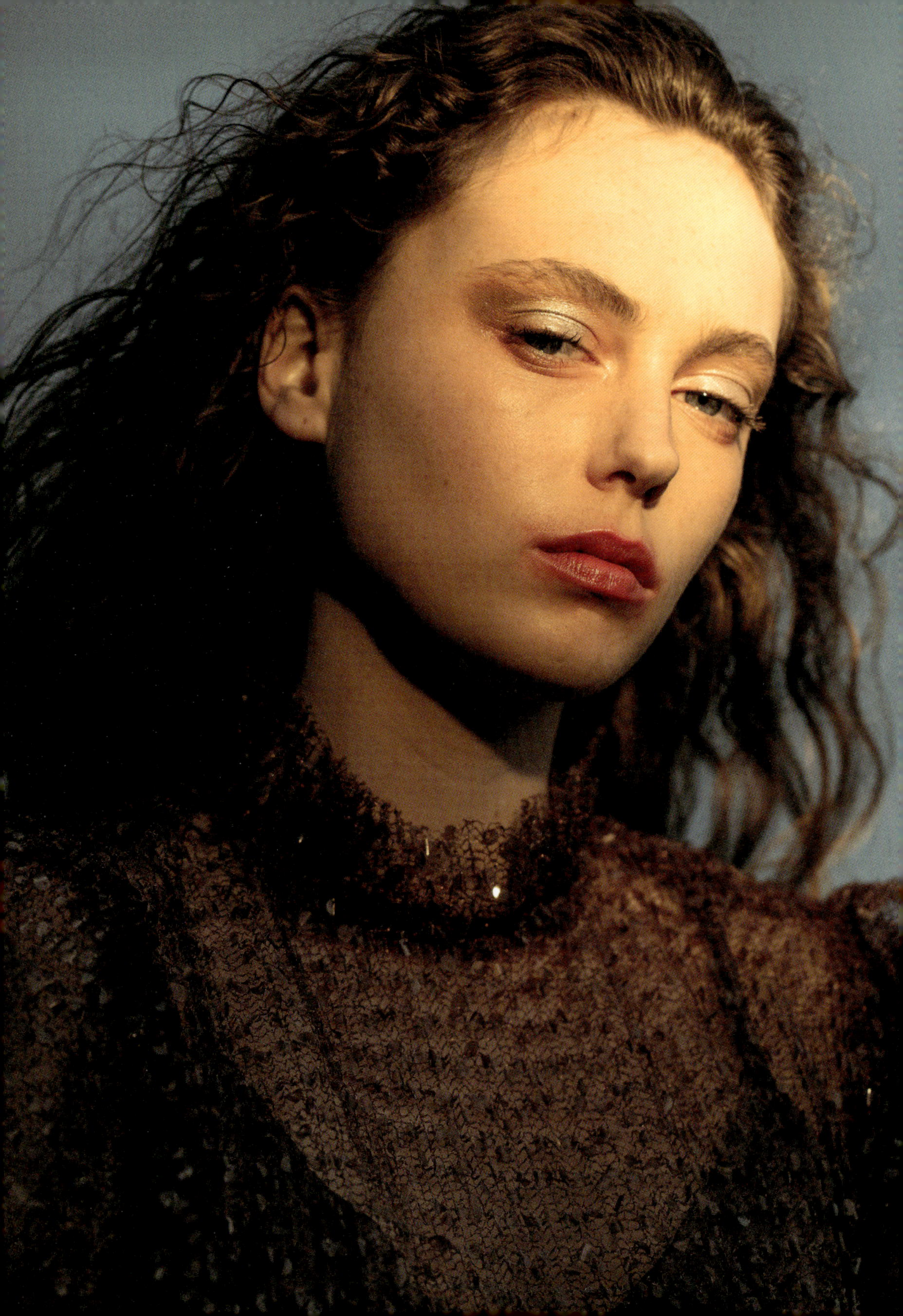

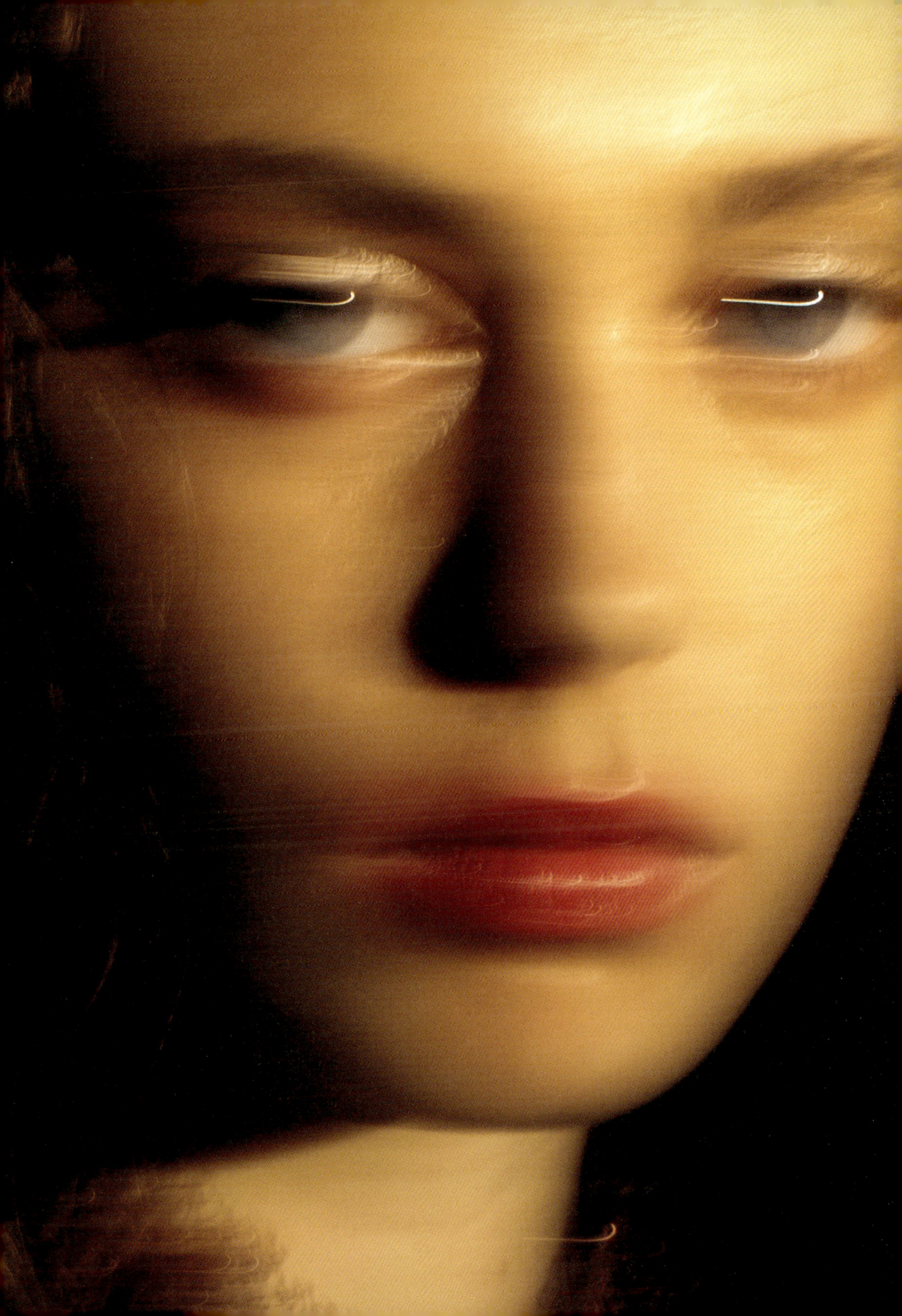

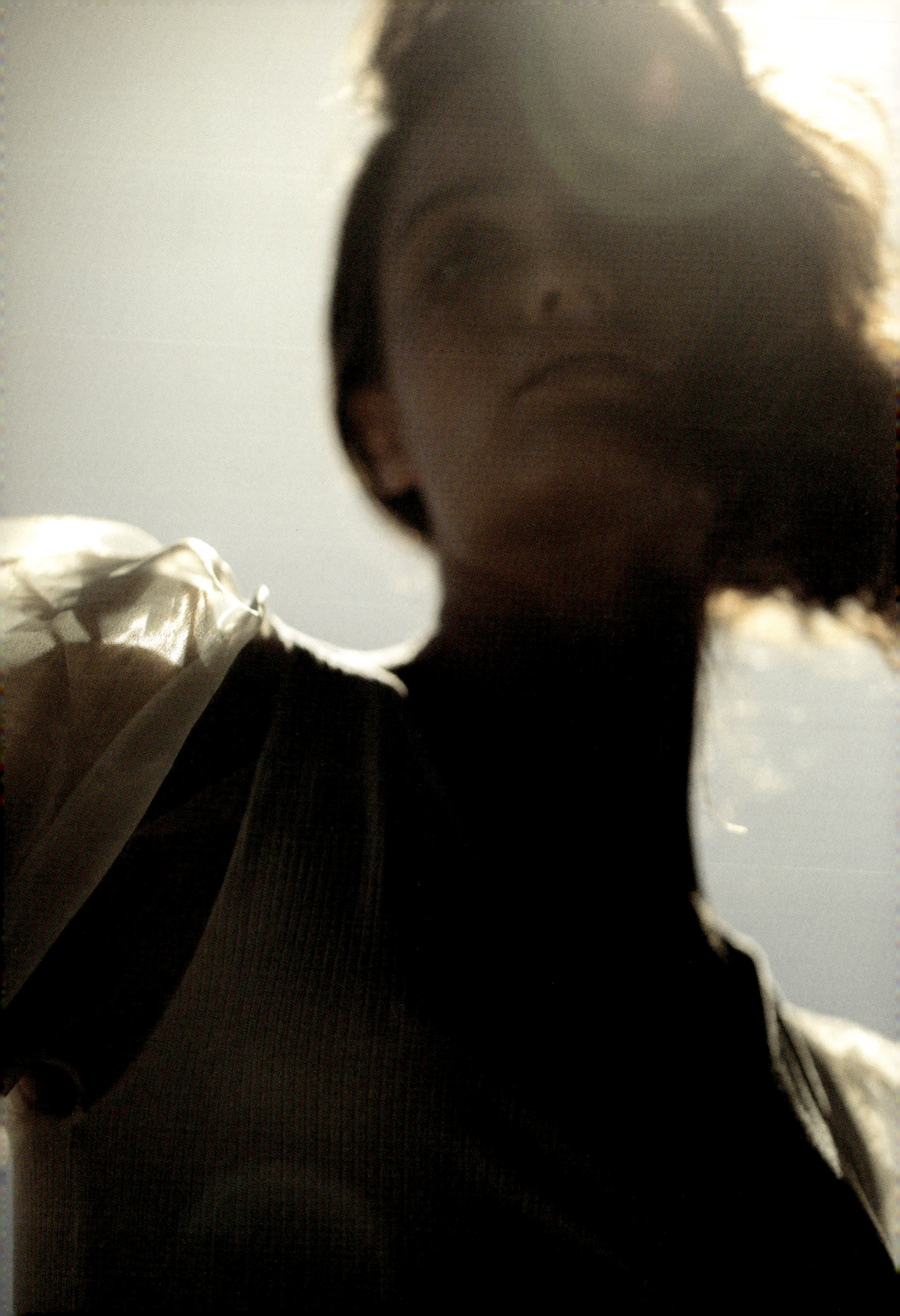

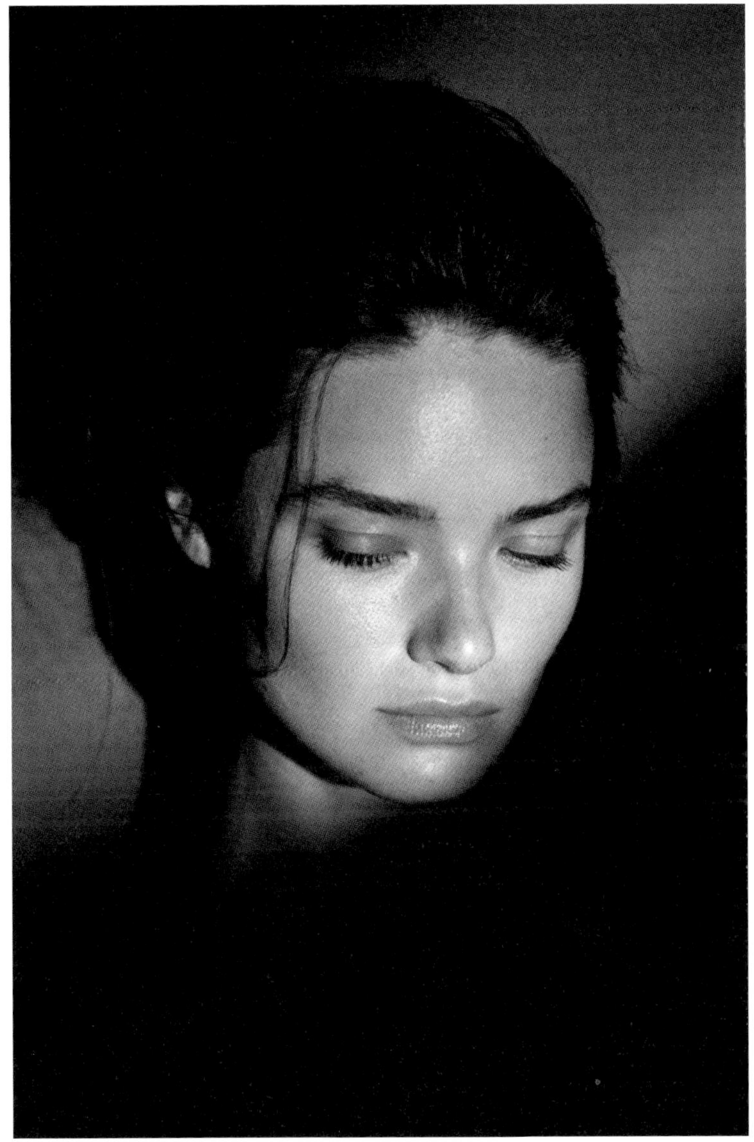

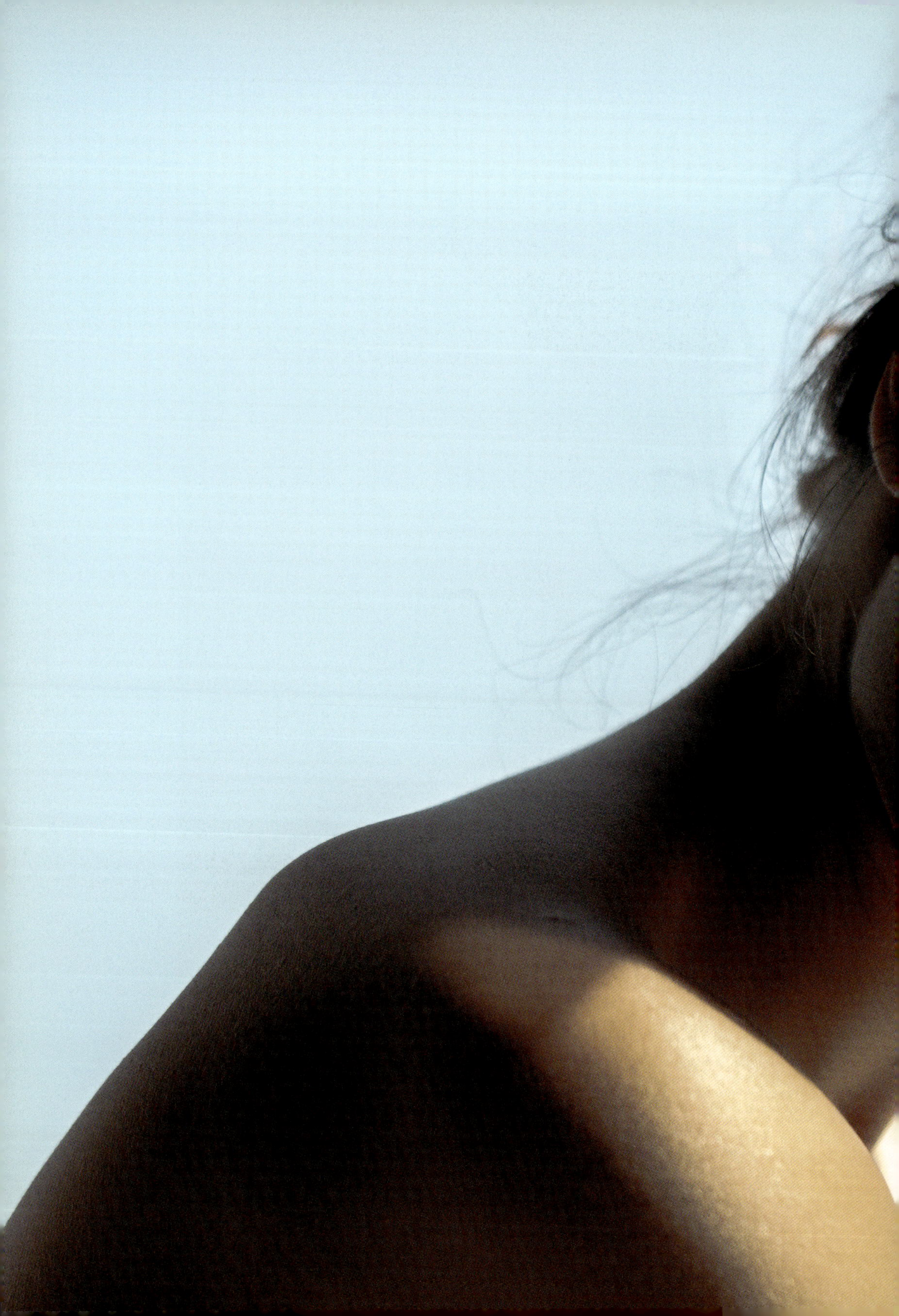

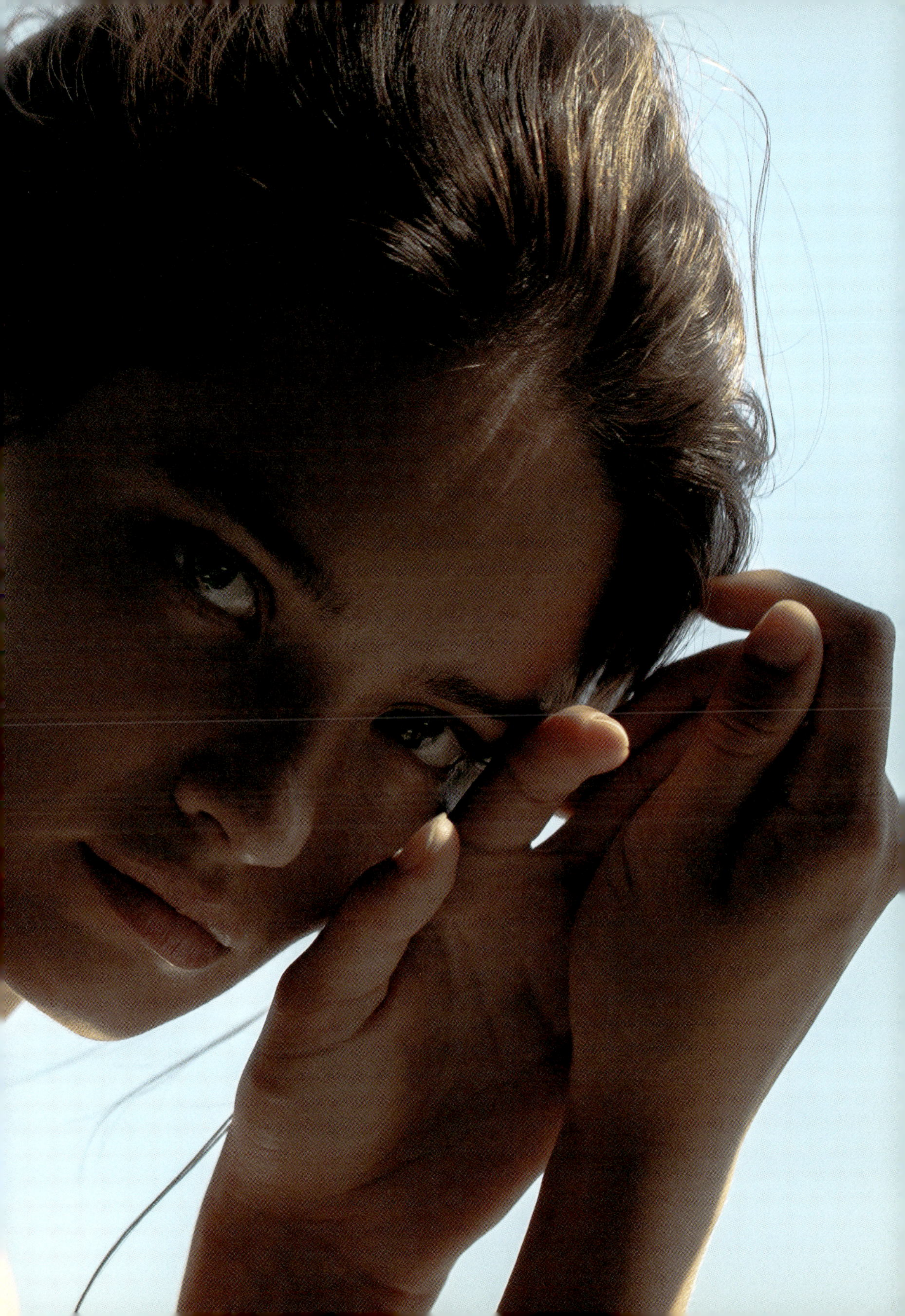

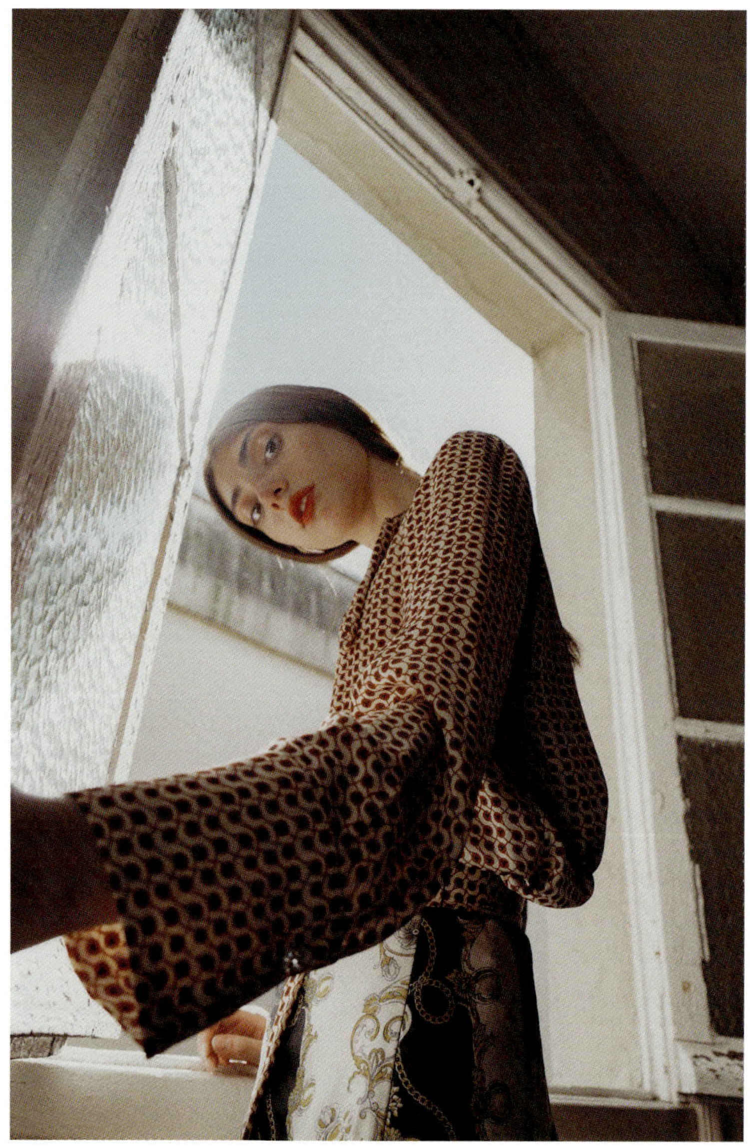

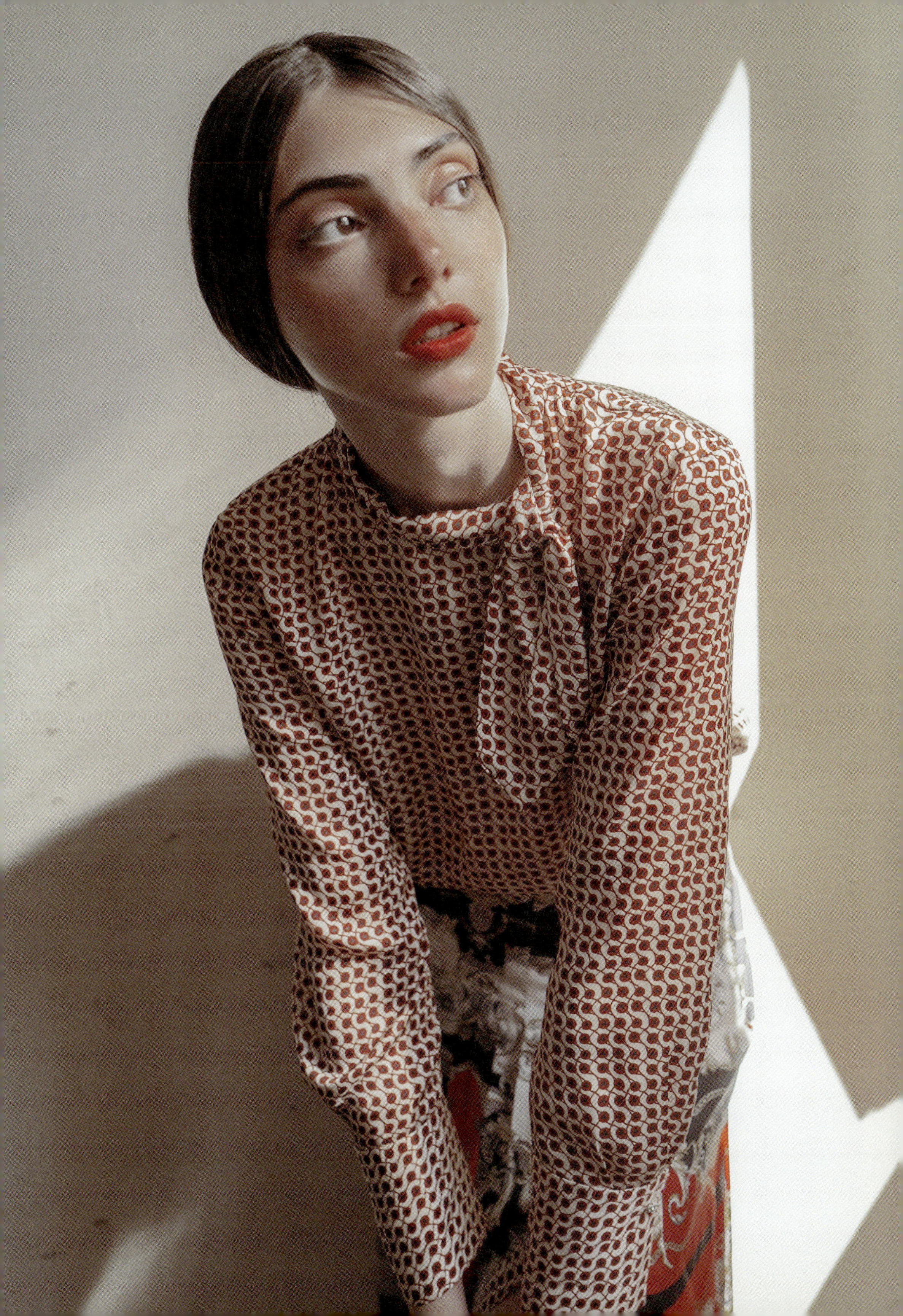

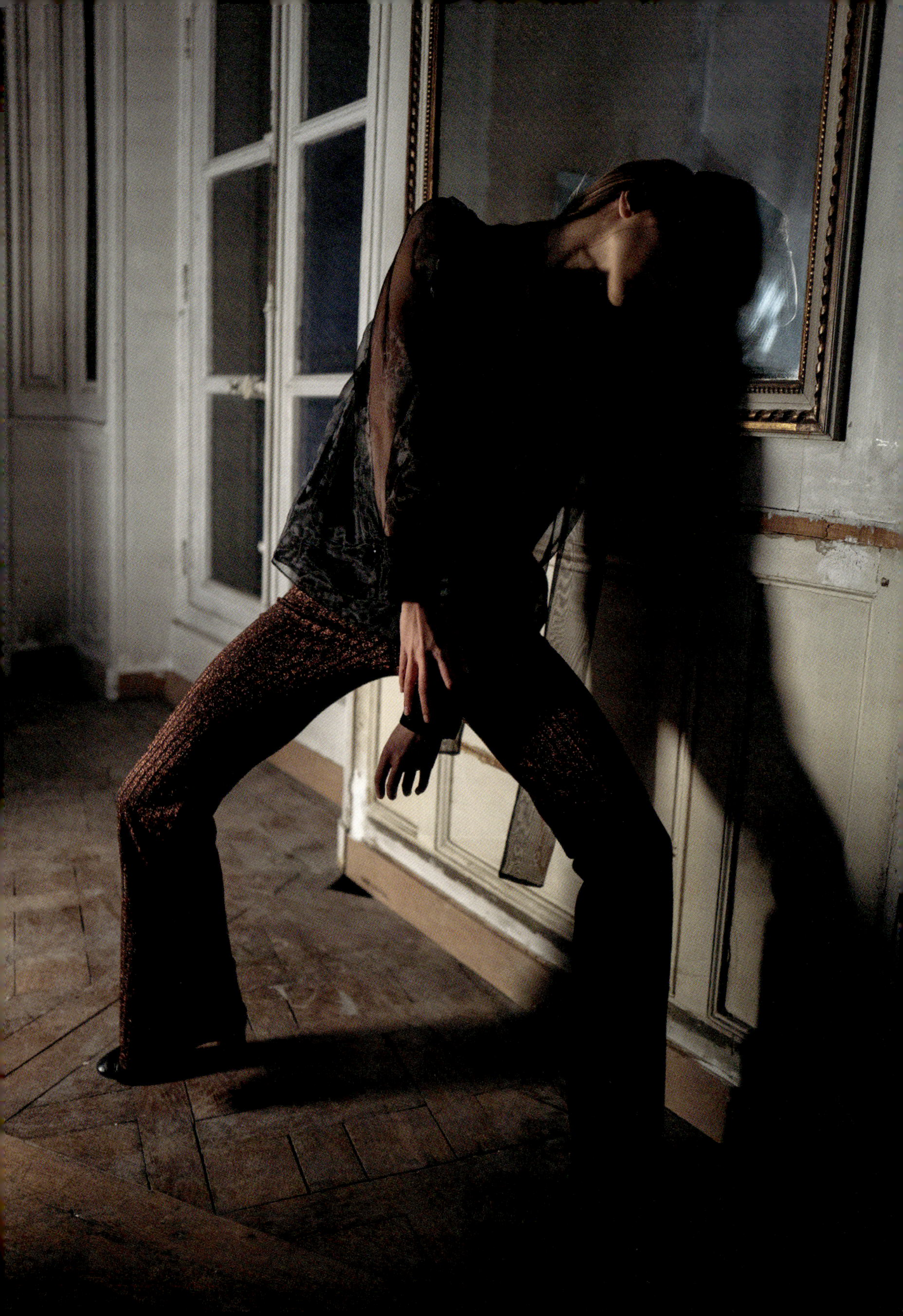

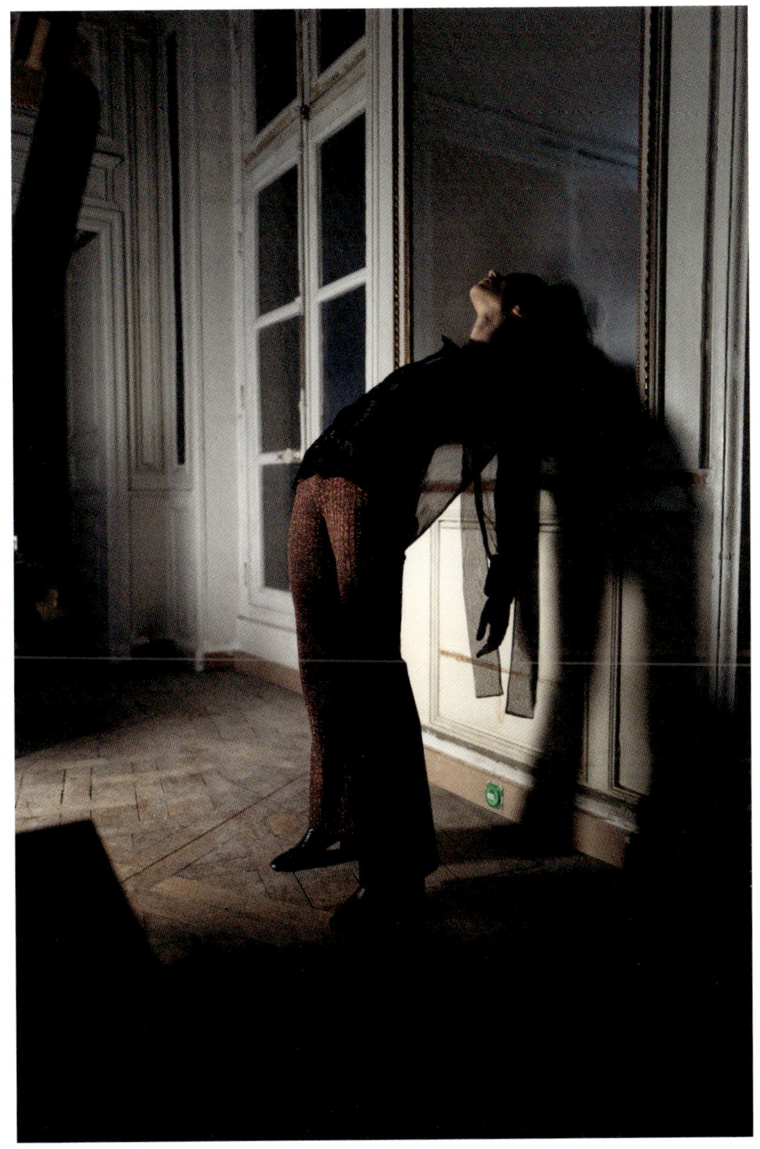

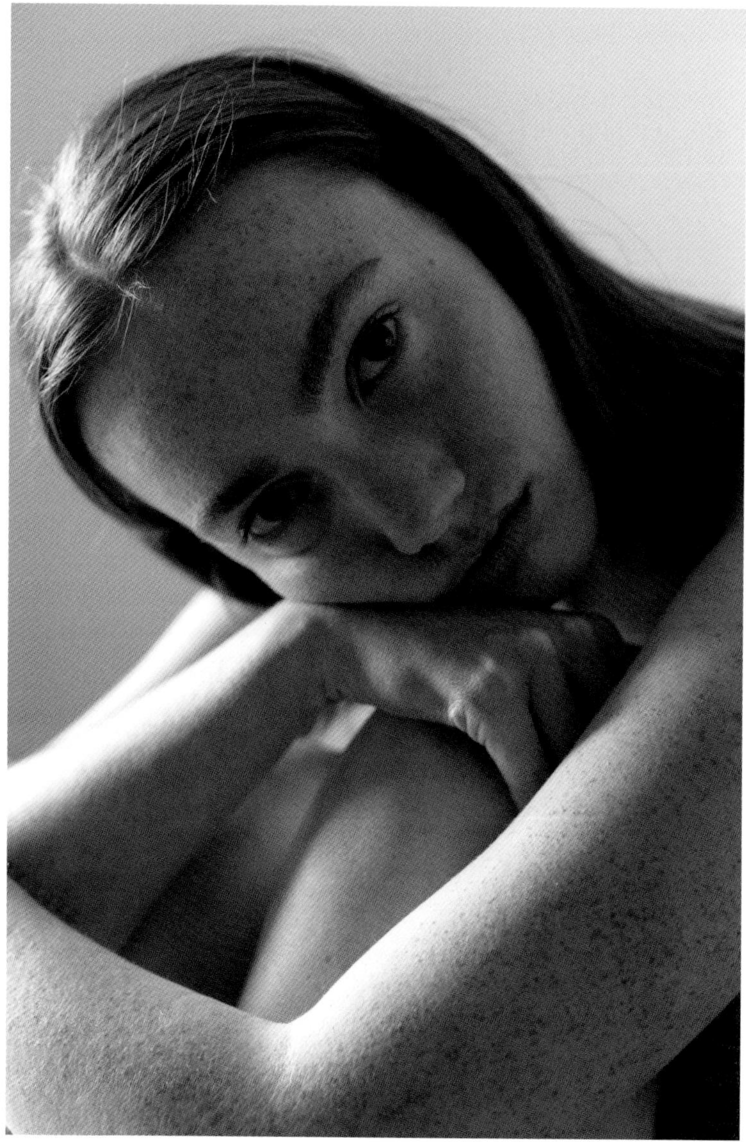

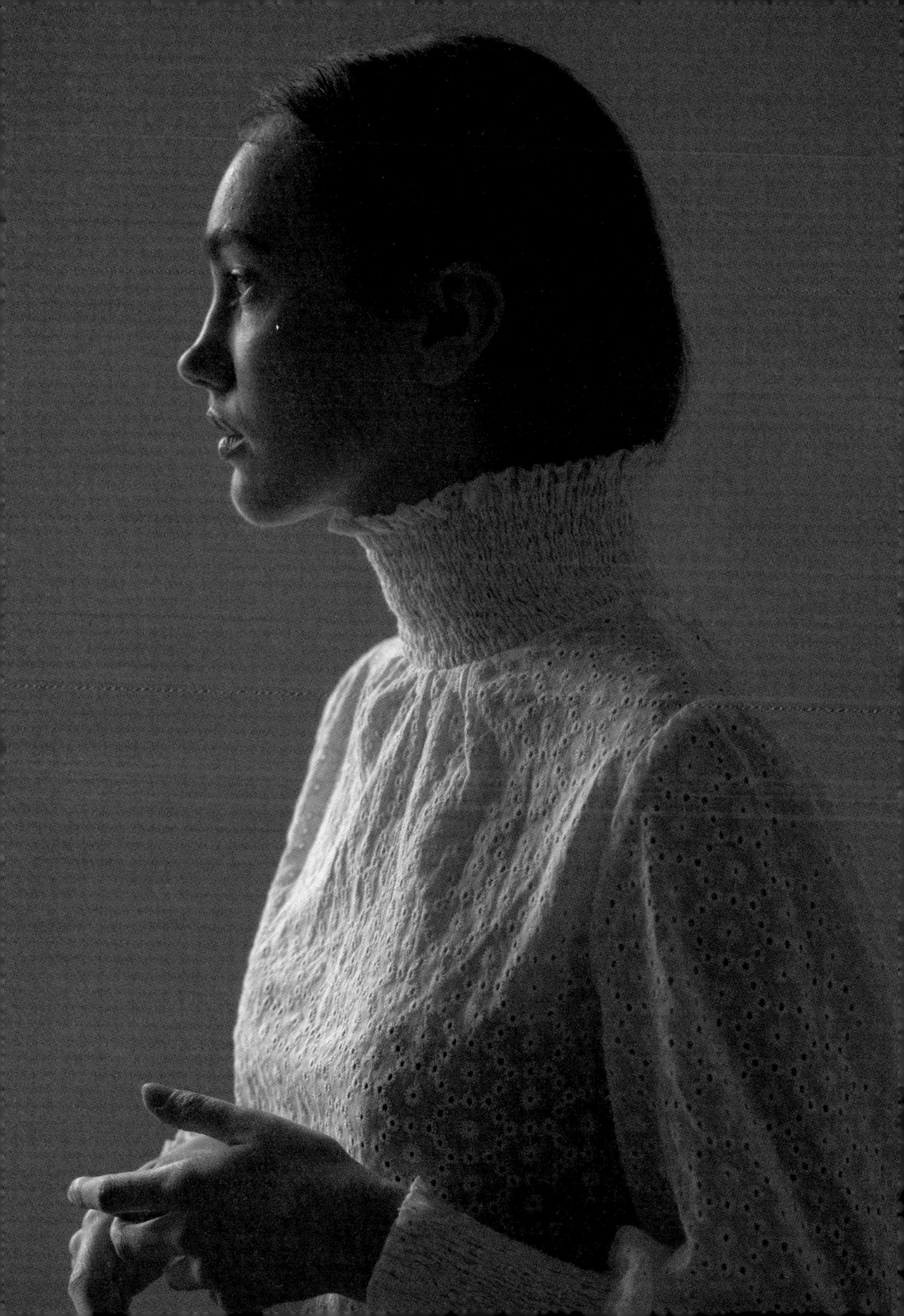

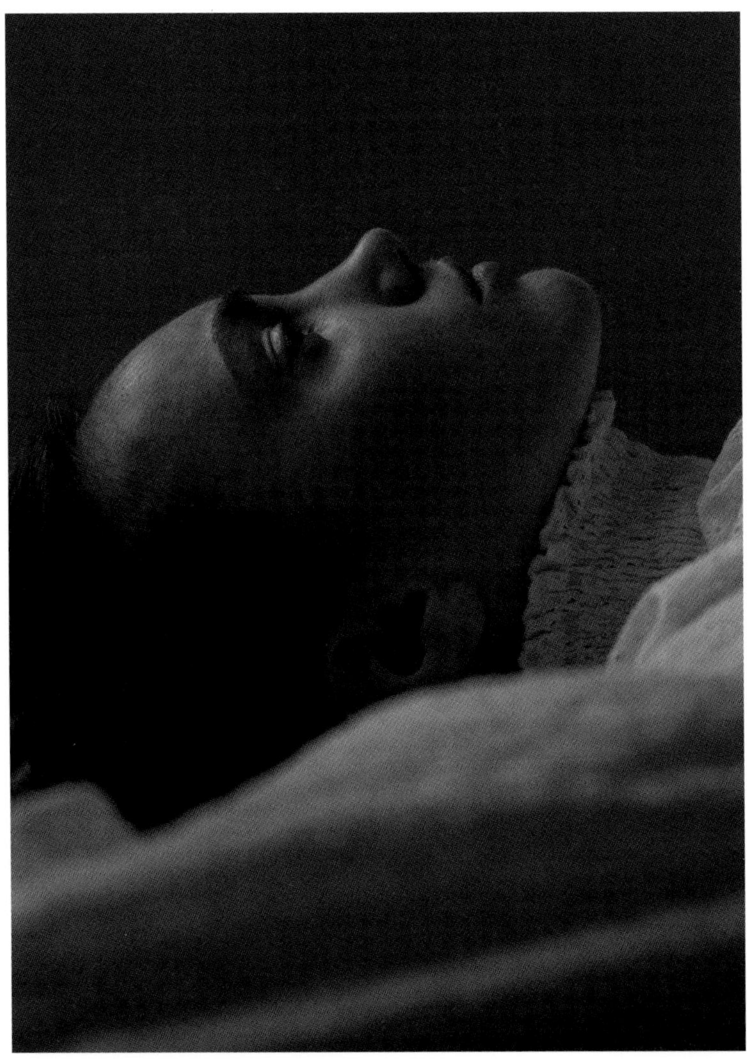

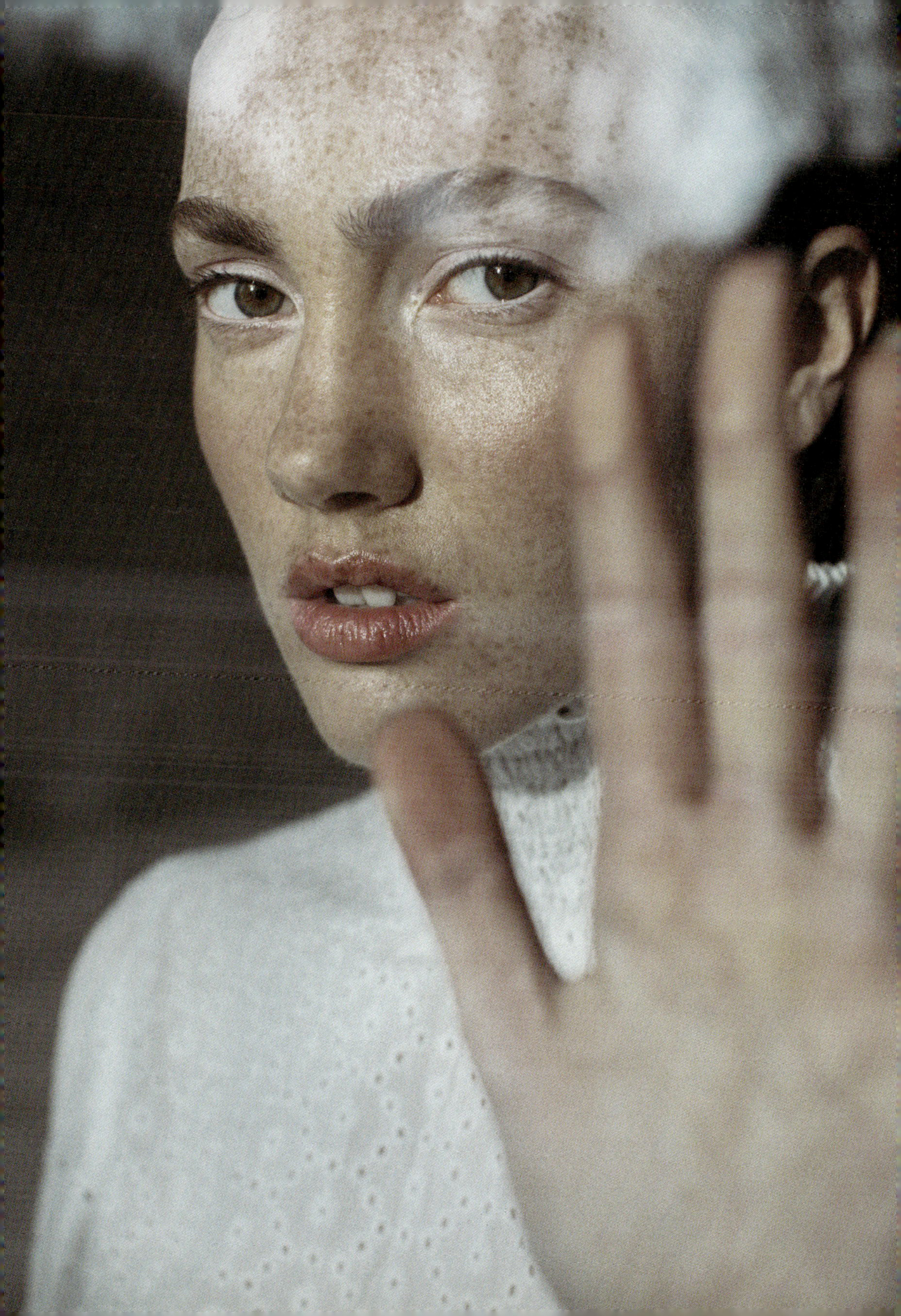

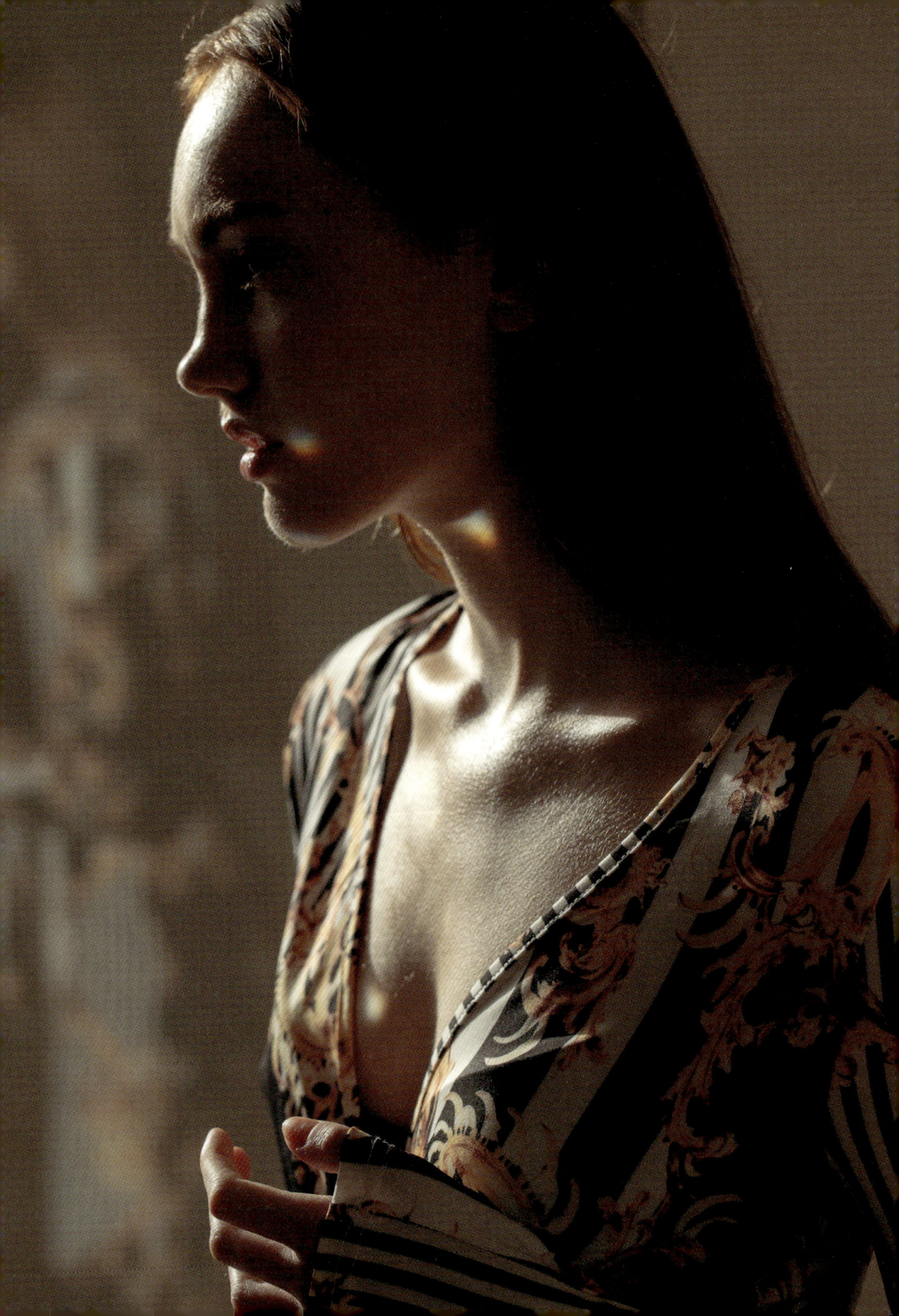

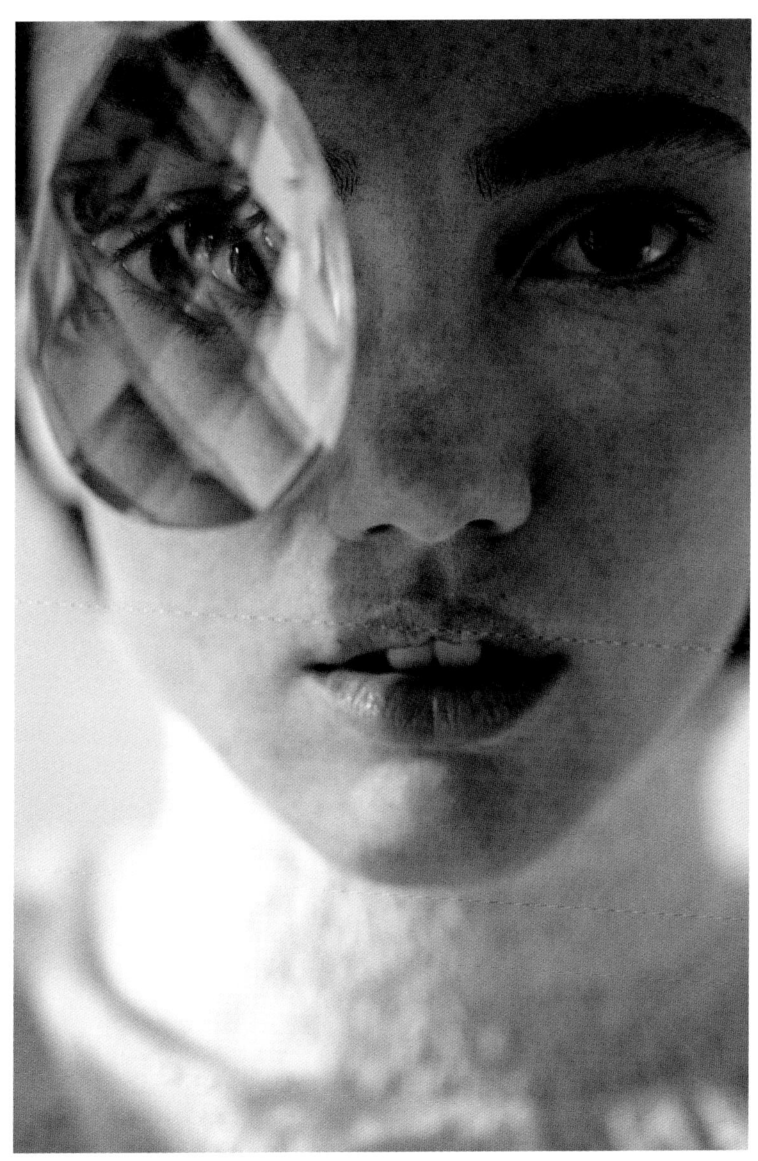

Mao

The role of the artist is not to create something
beautiful. His role is to be true.

– Malou Moulis, Artistologue

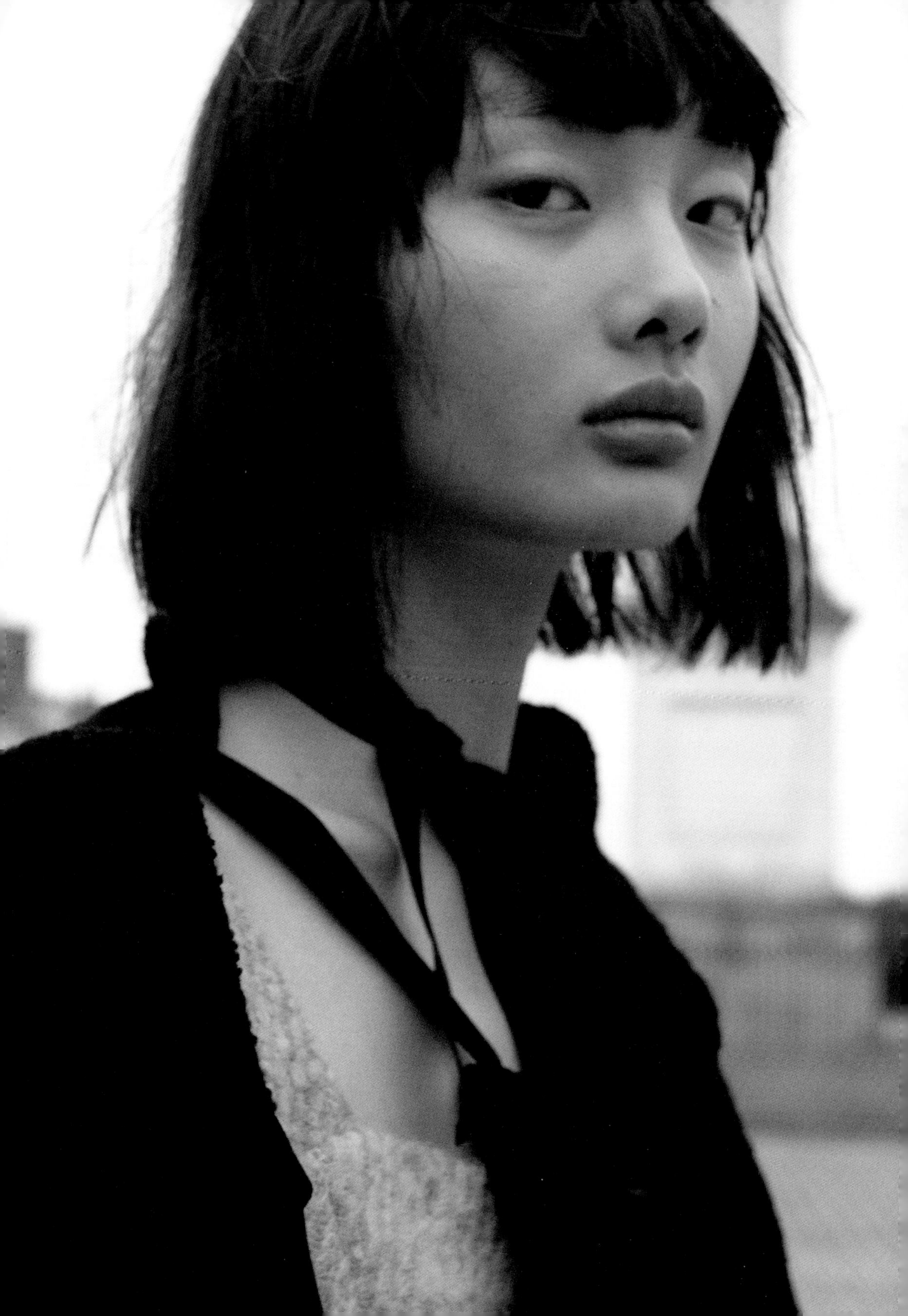

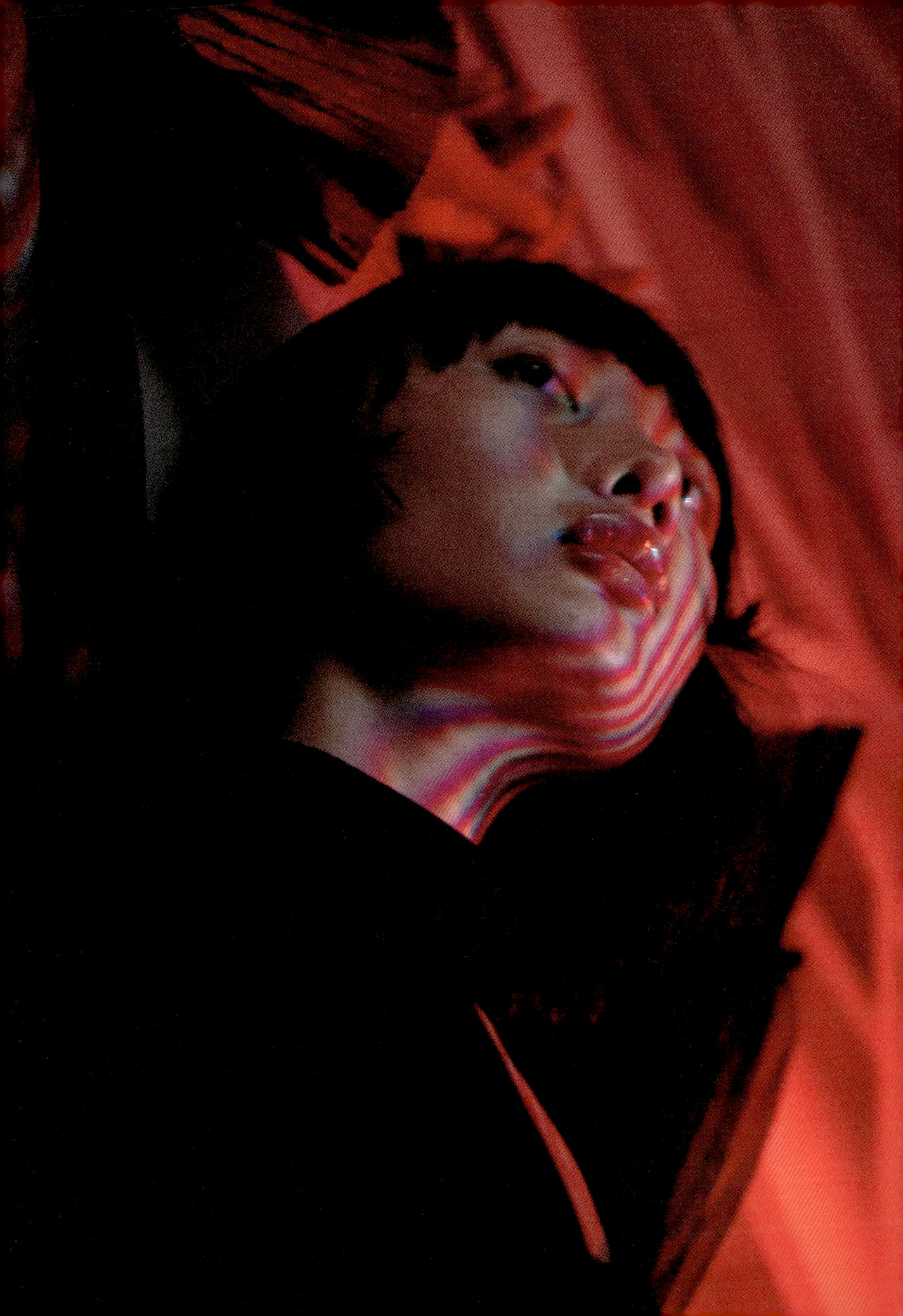

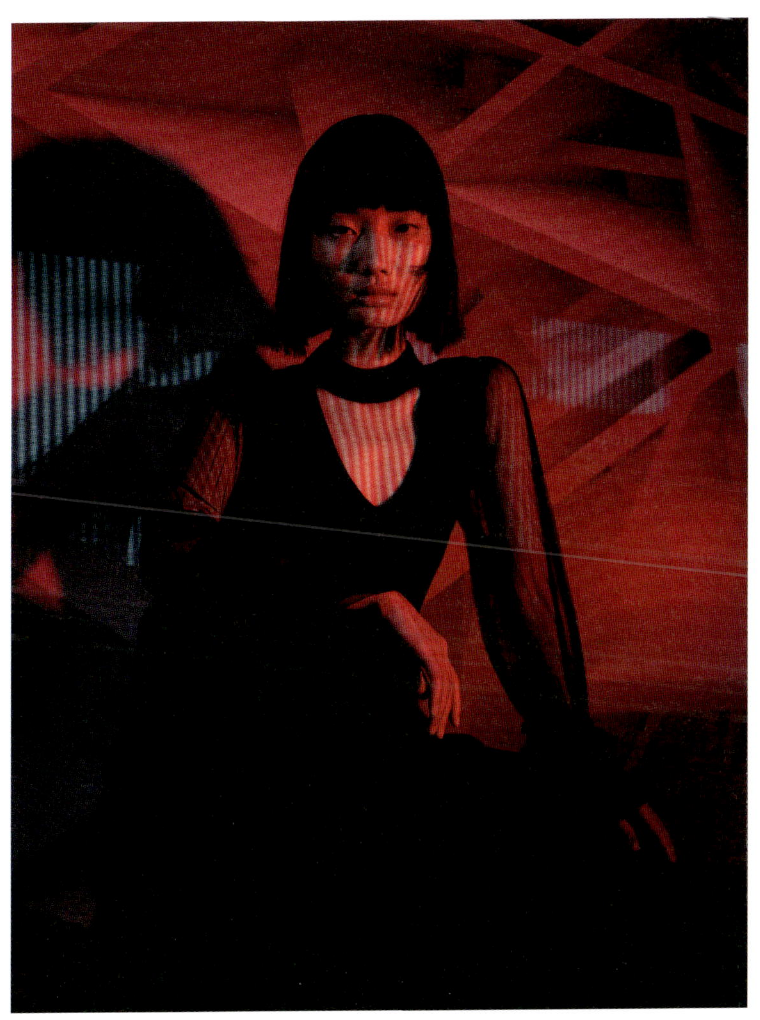

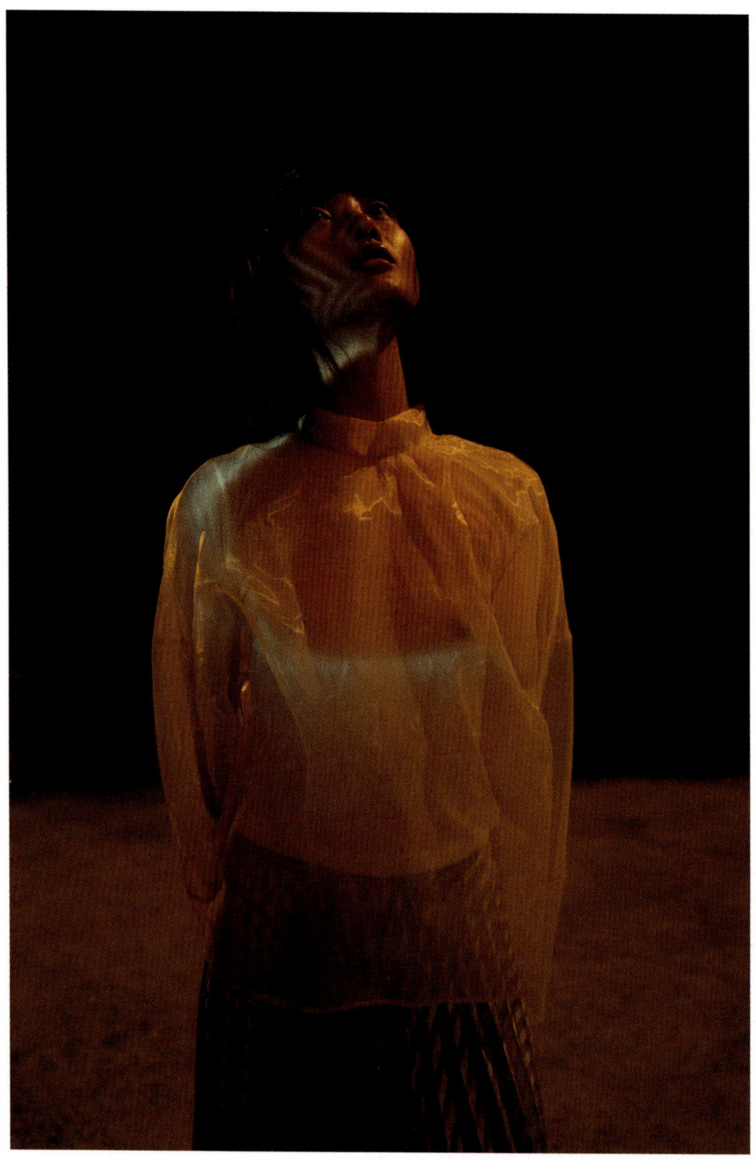

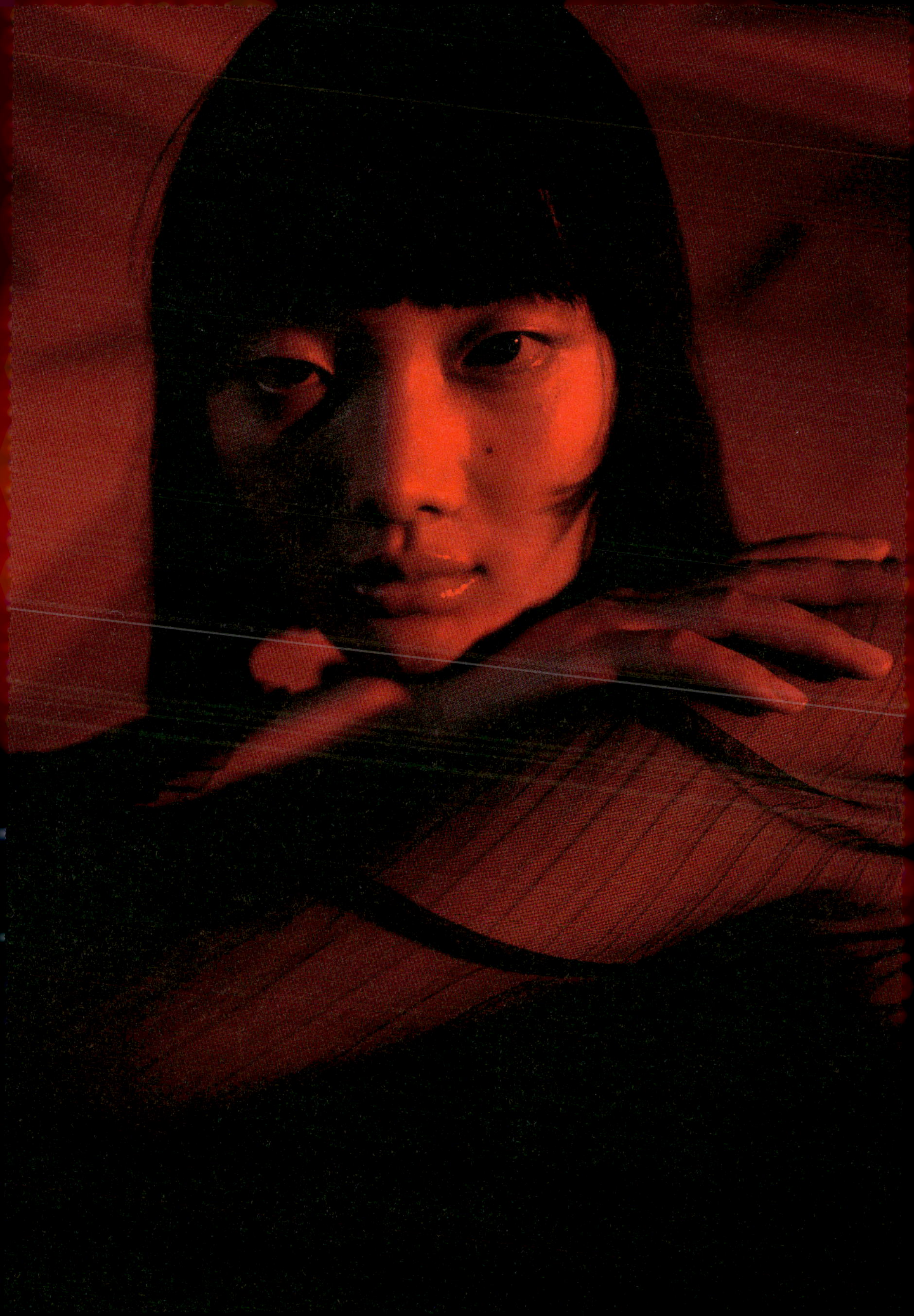

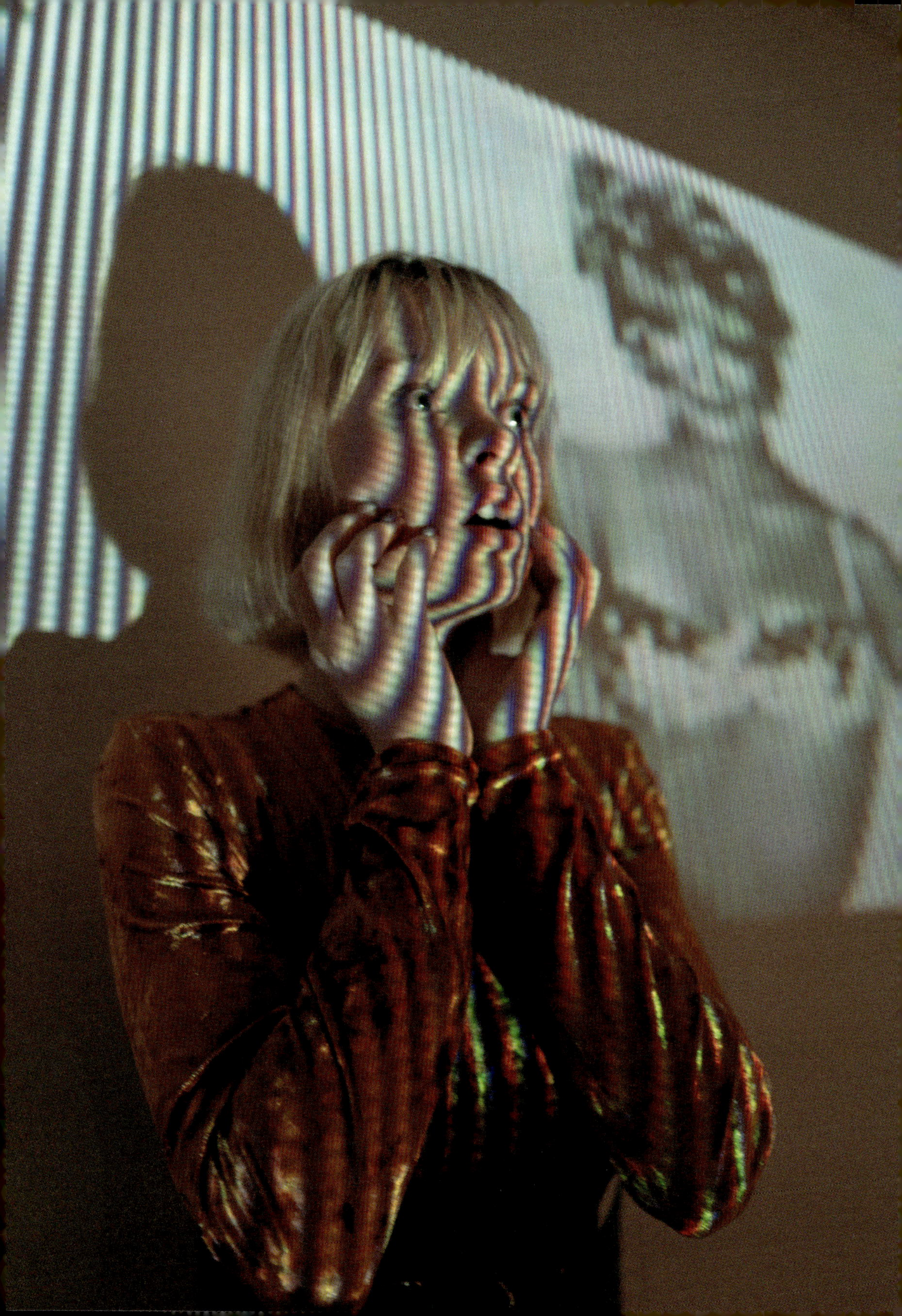

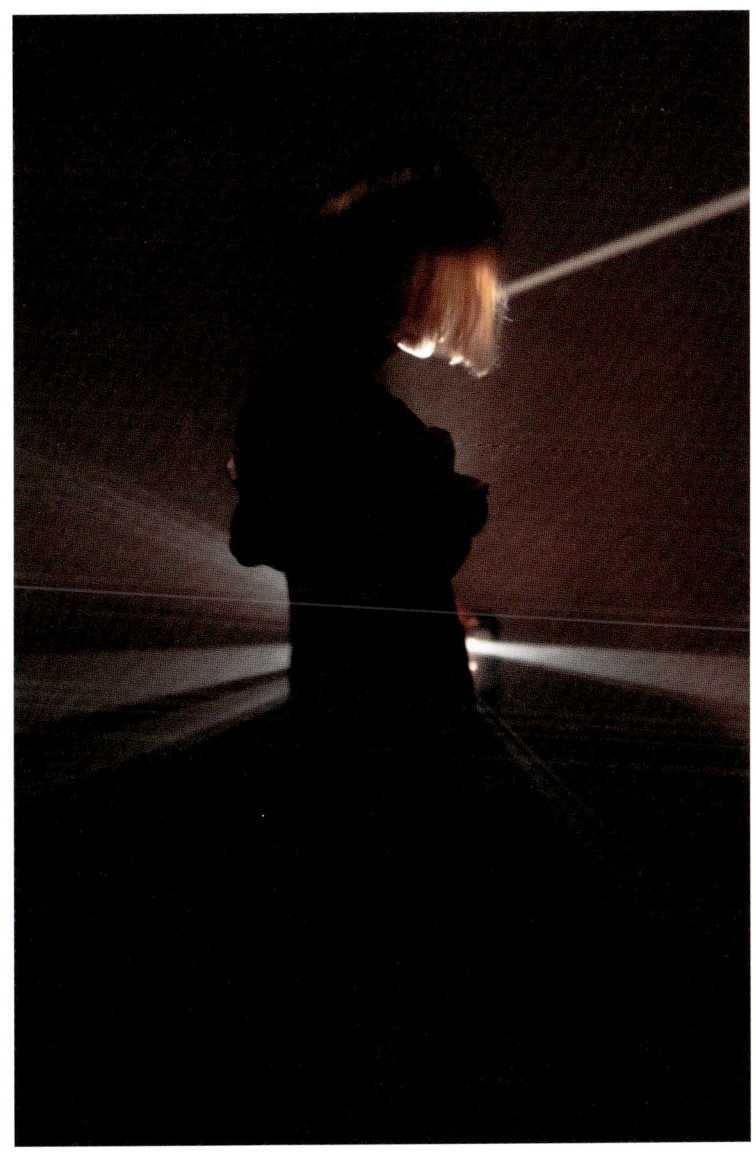

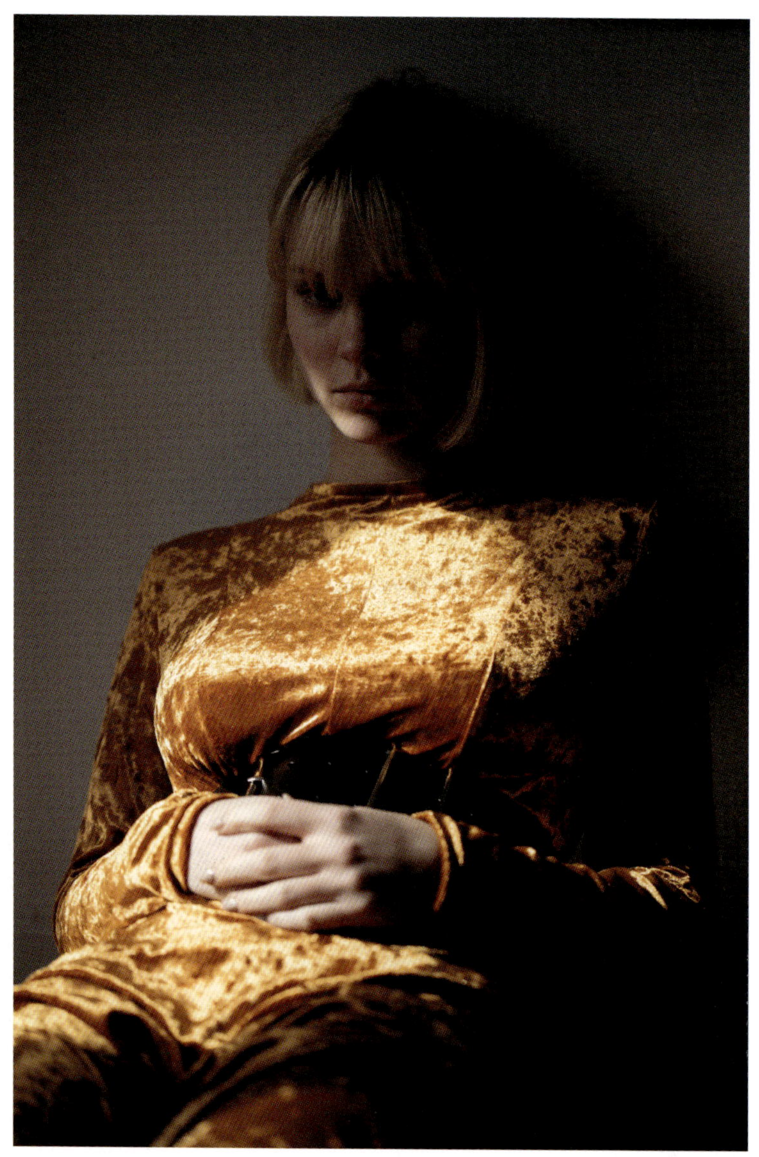

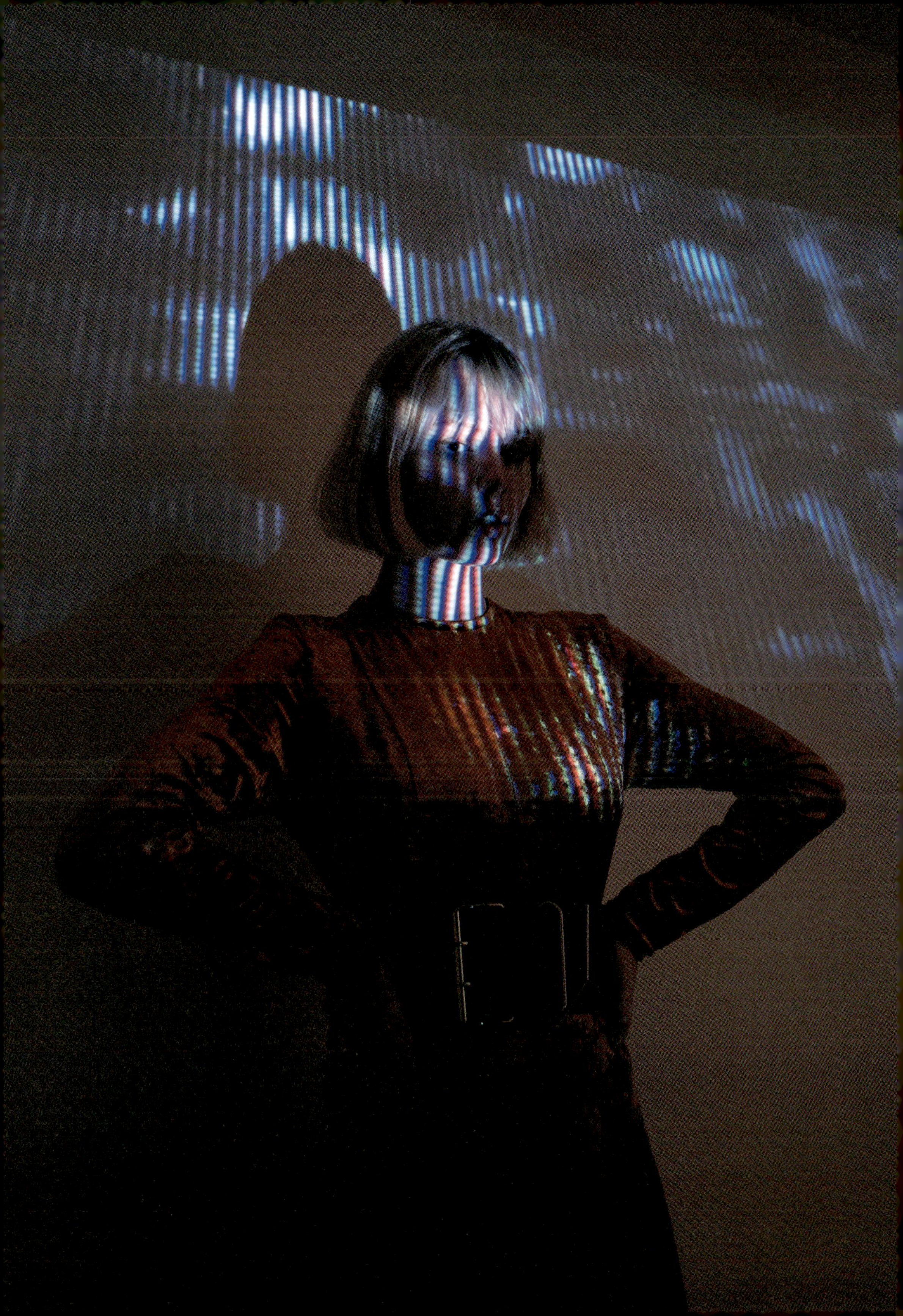

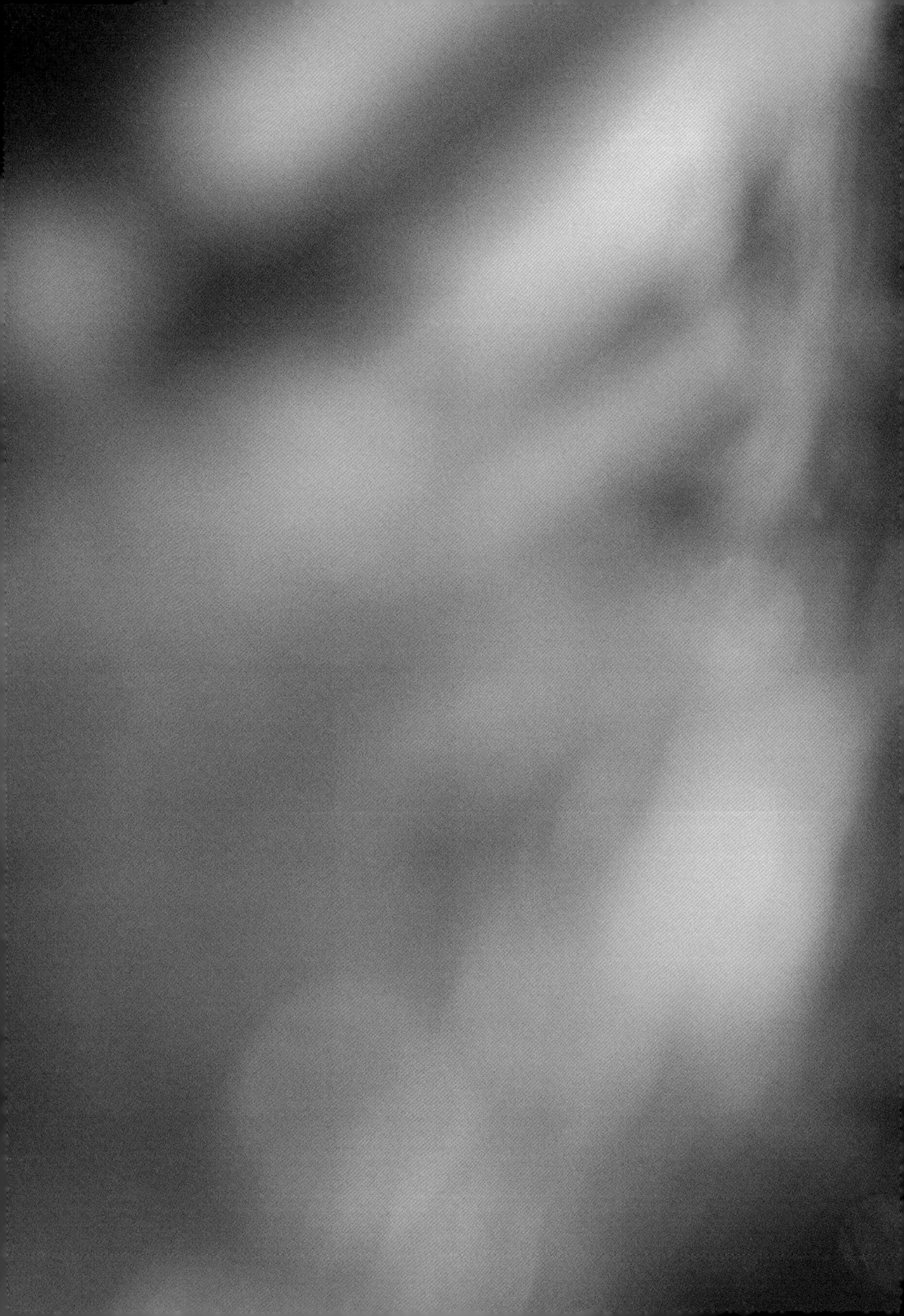

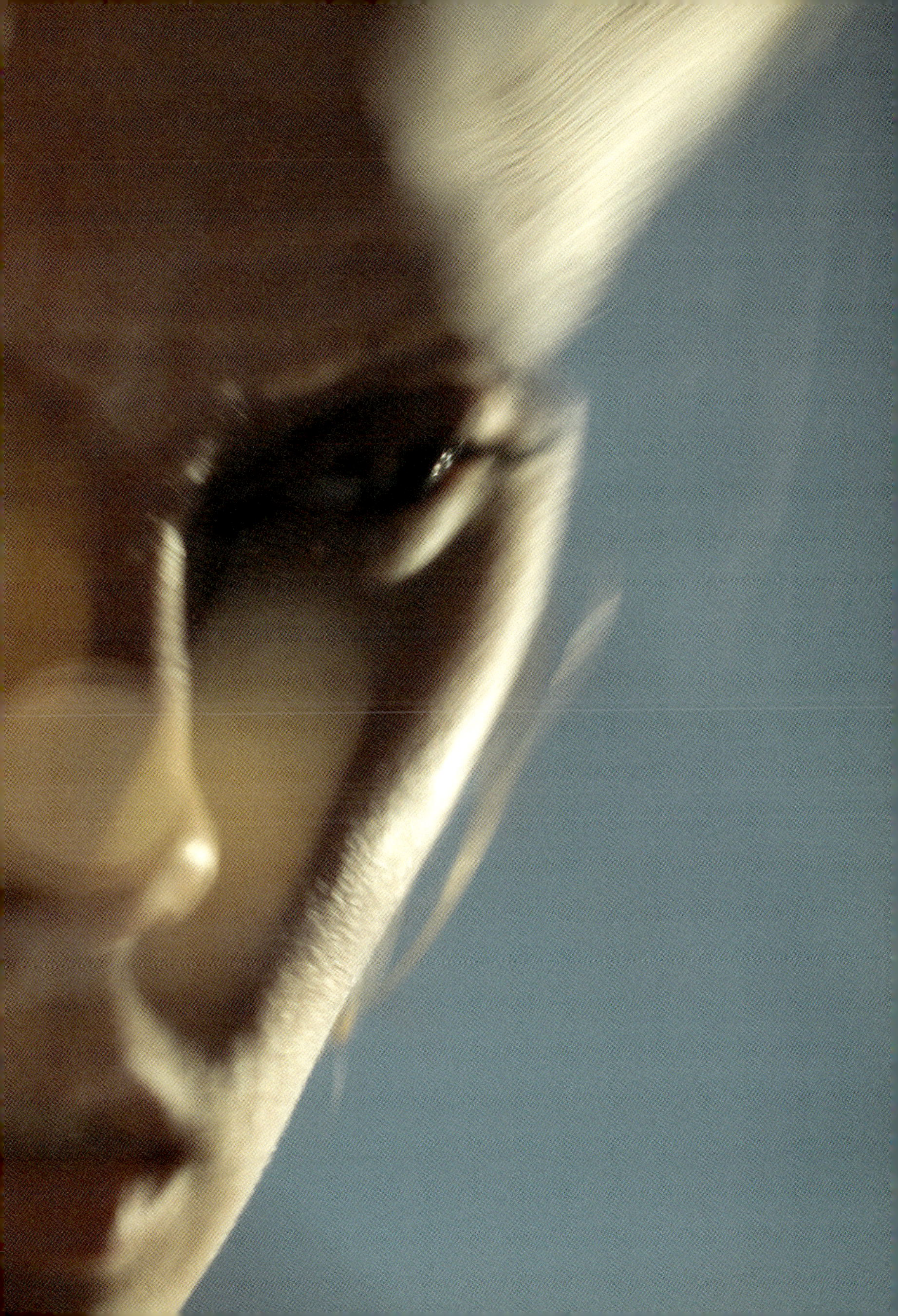

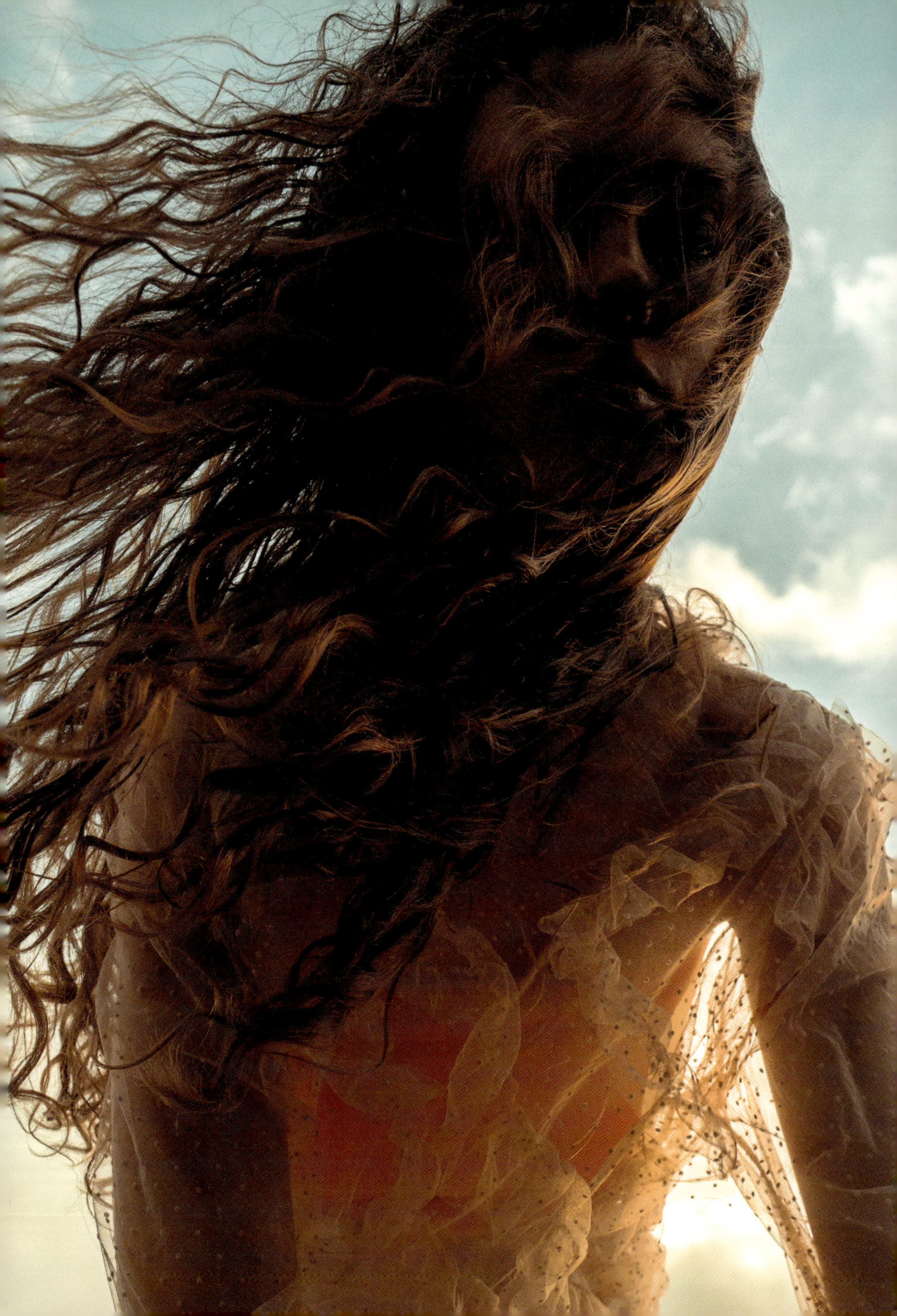

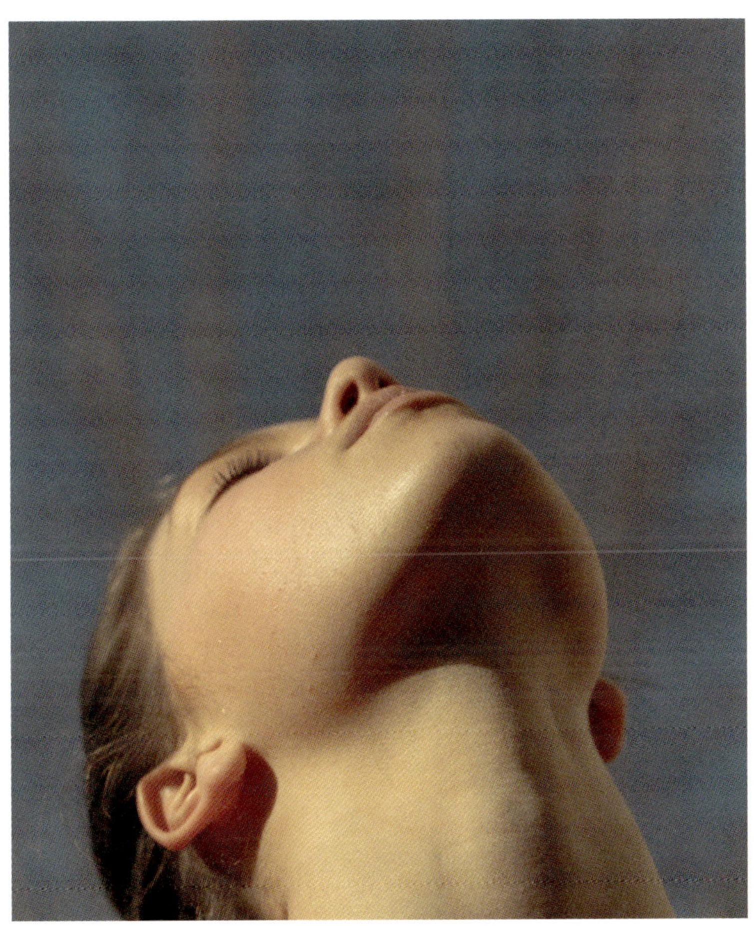

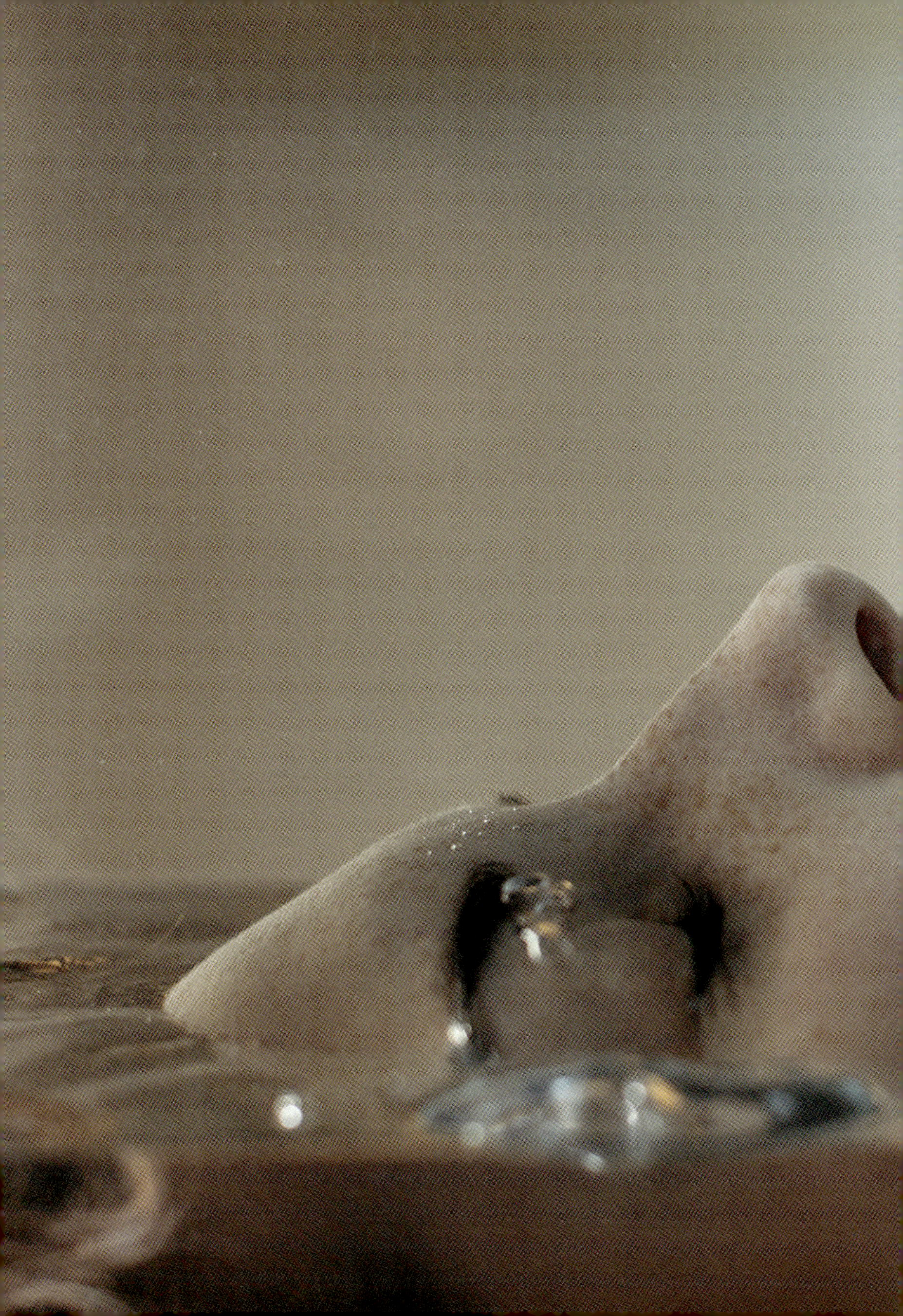

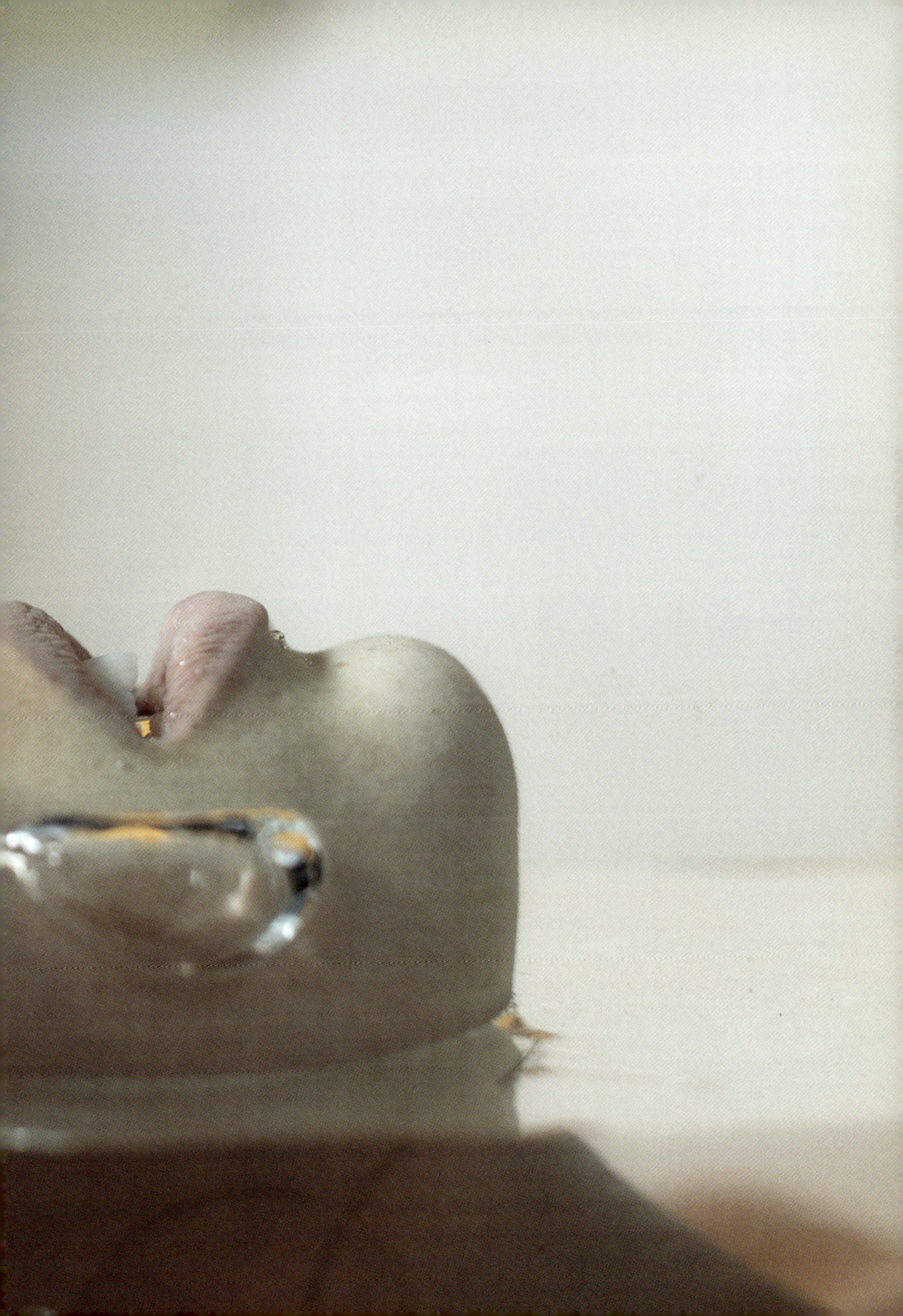

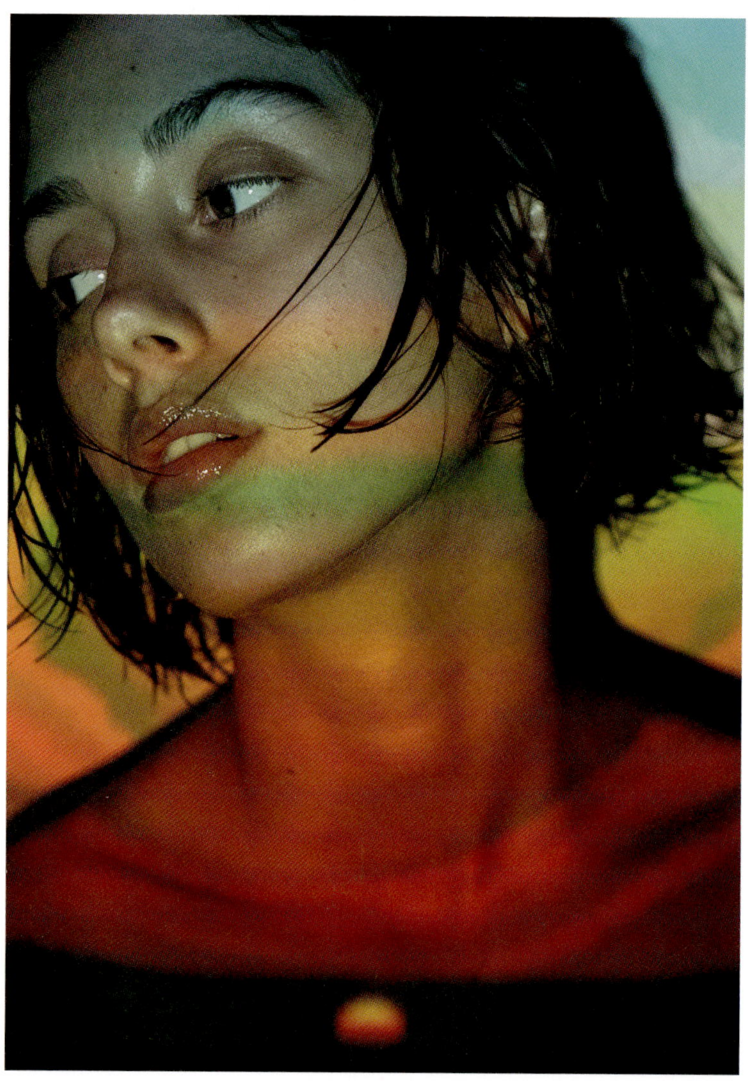

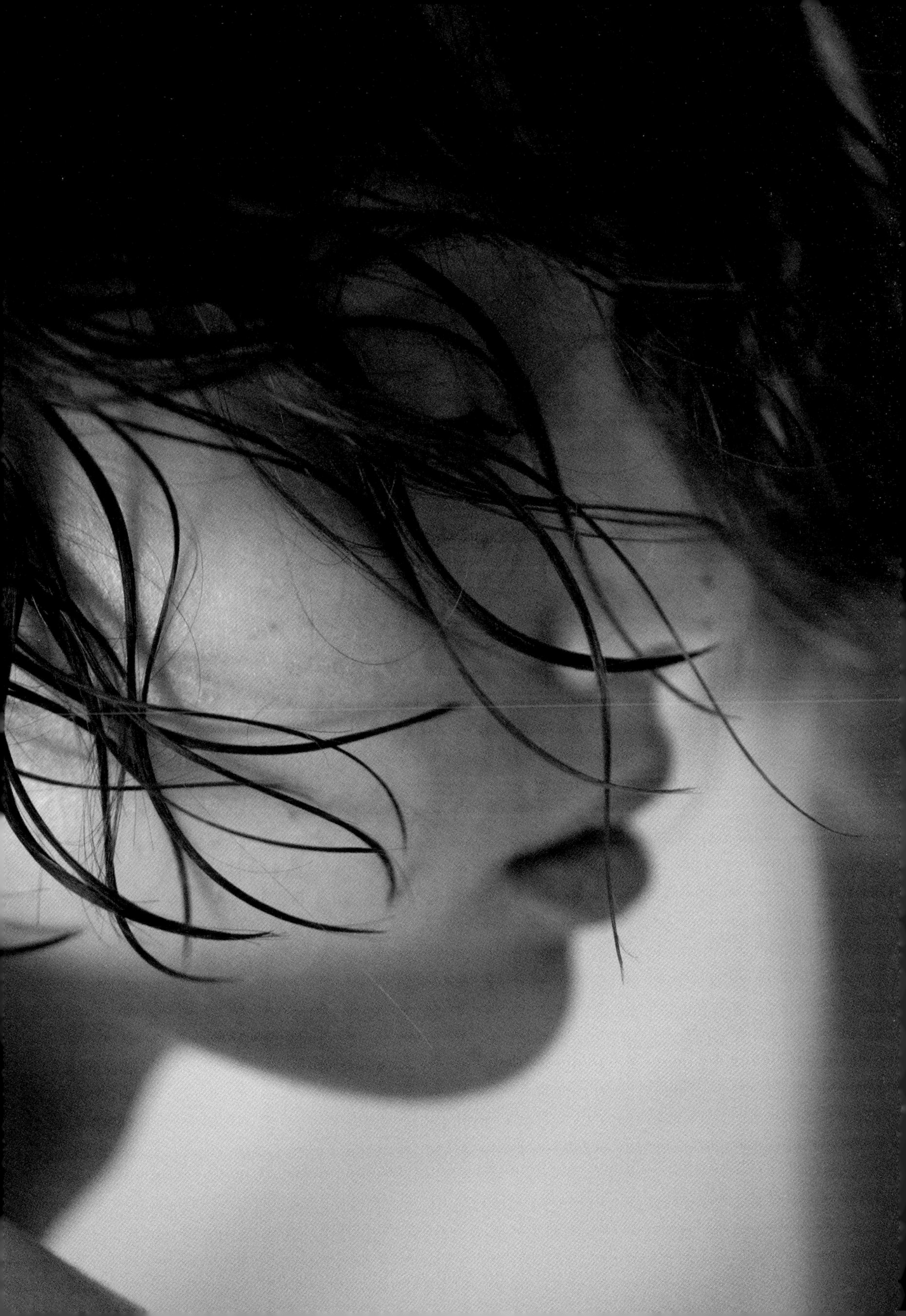

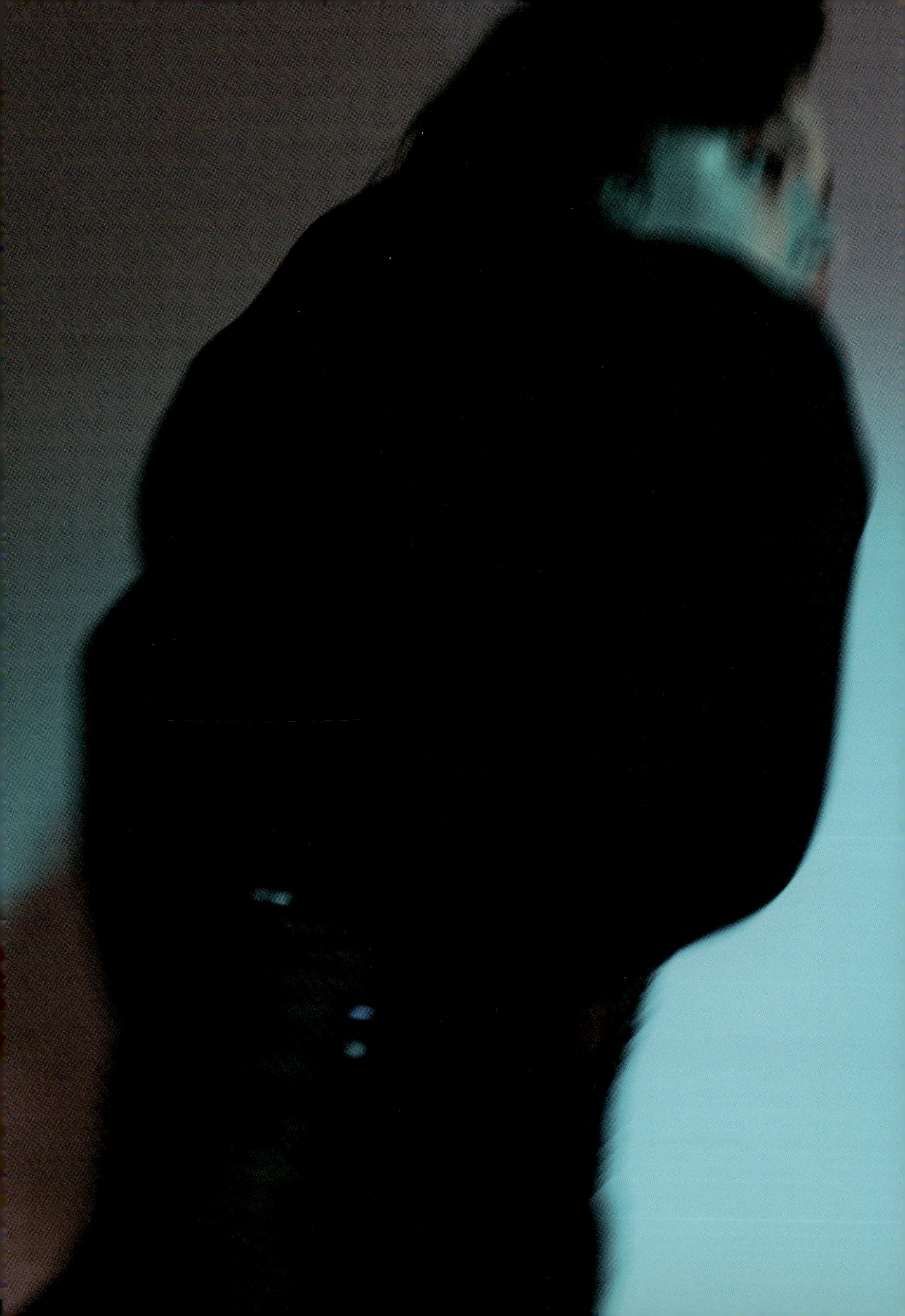

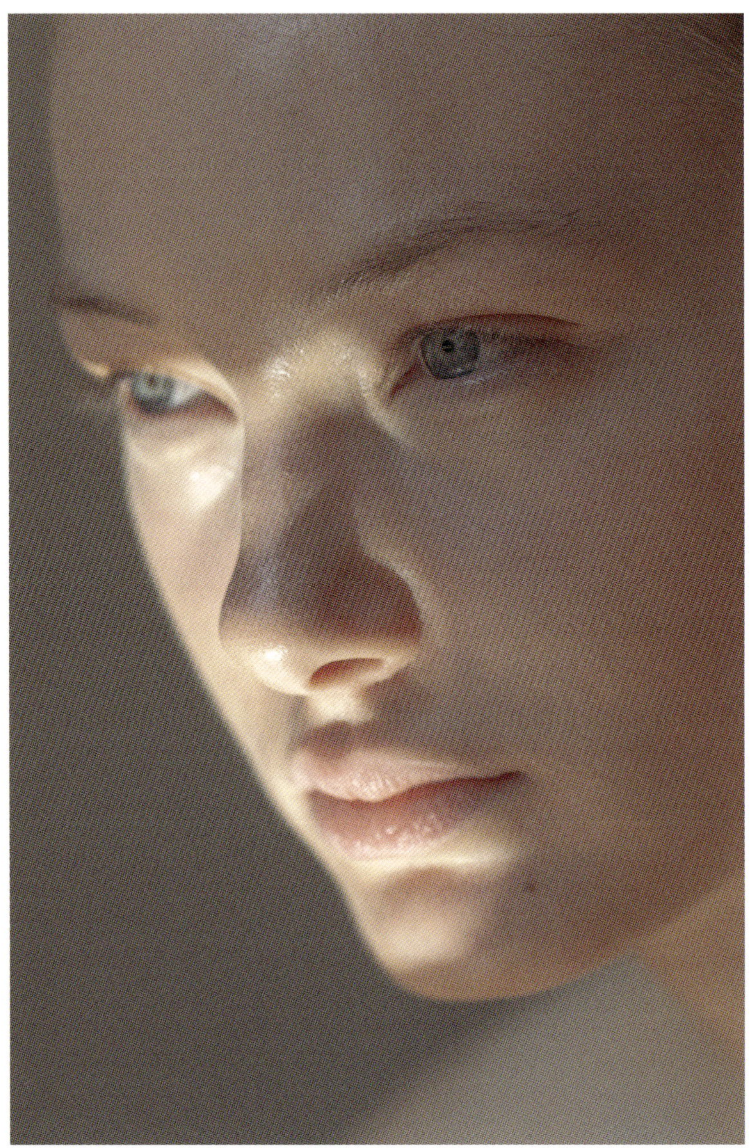

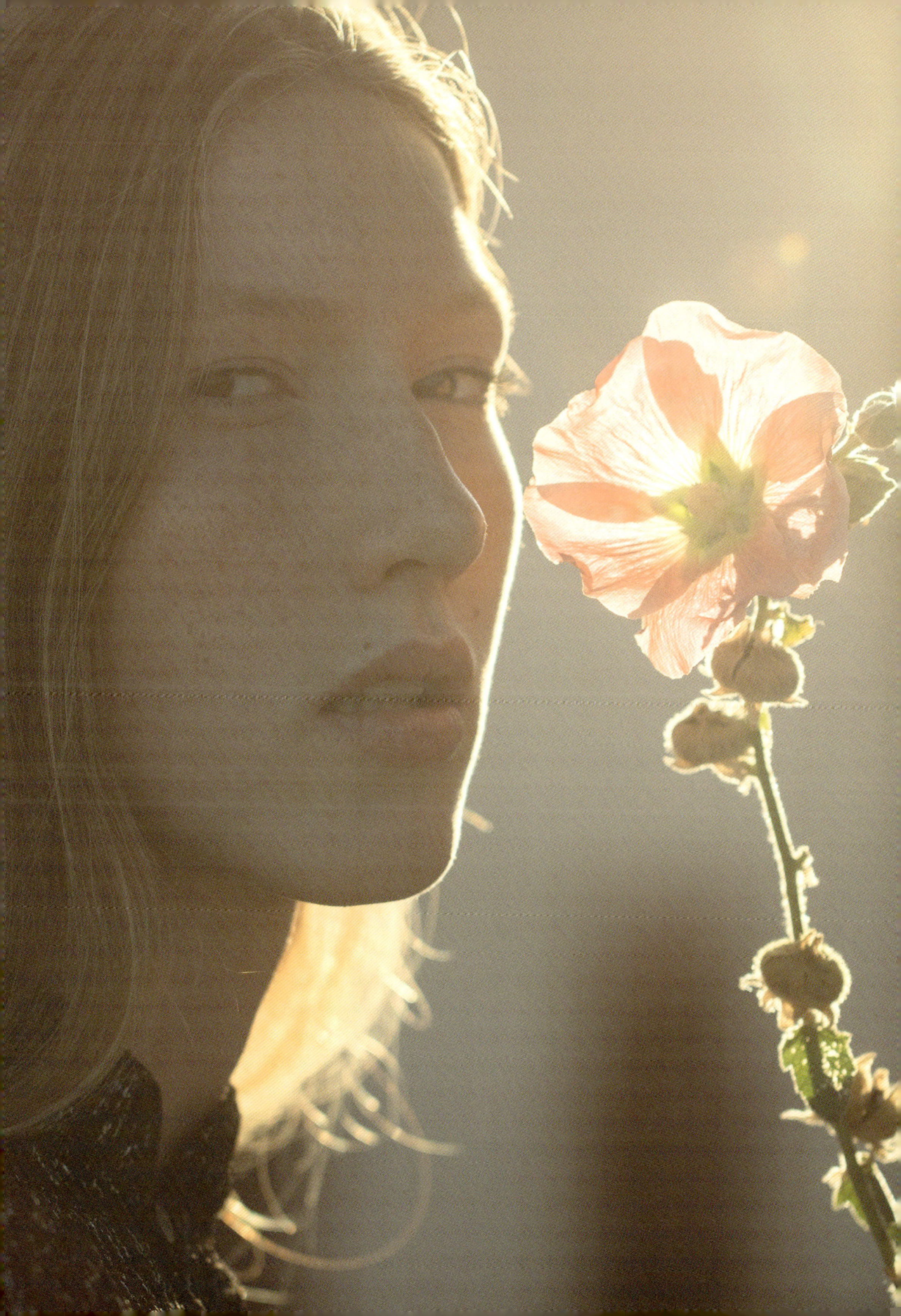

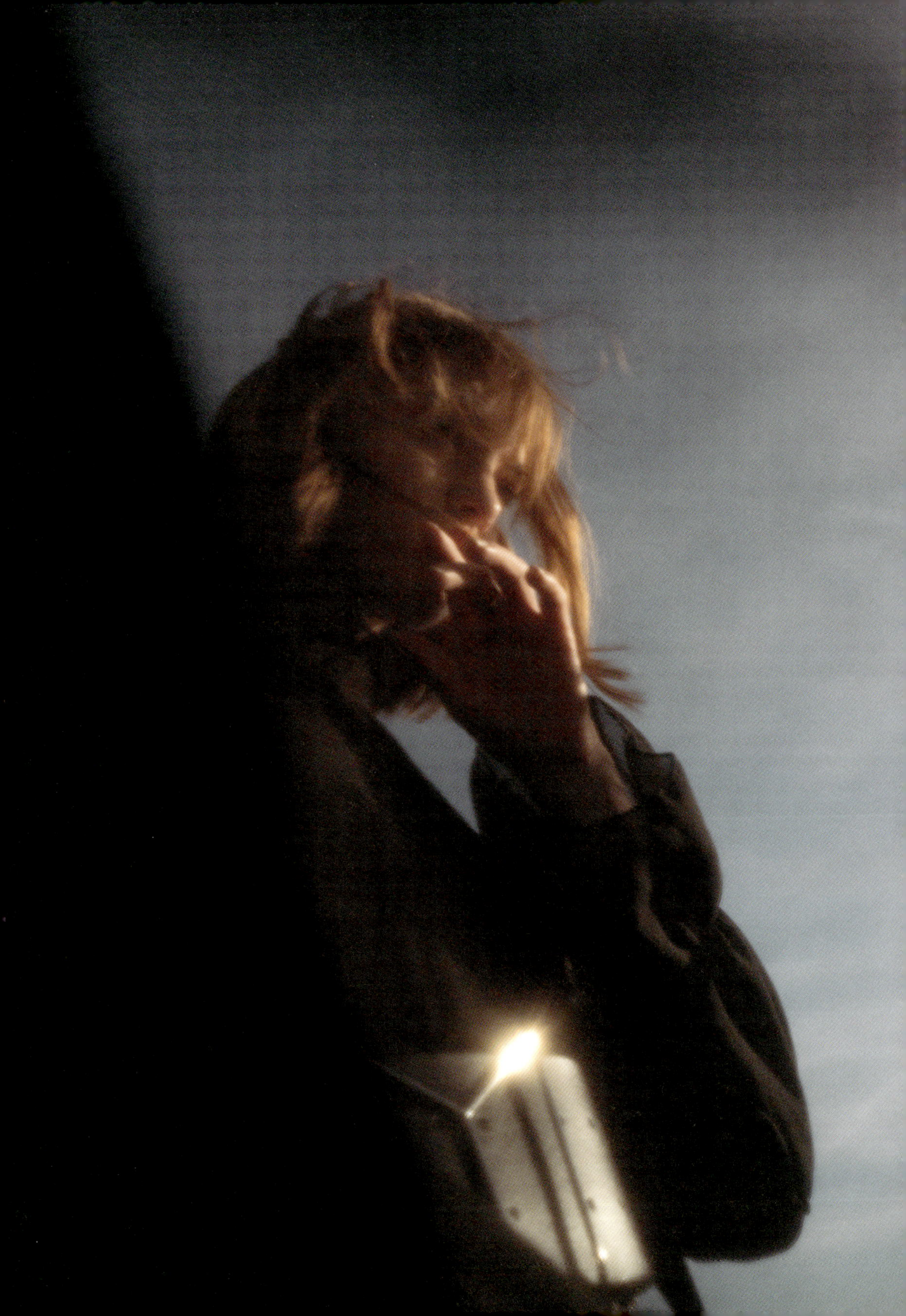

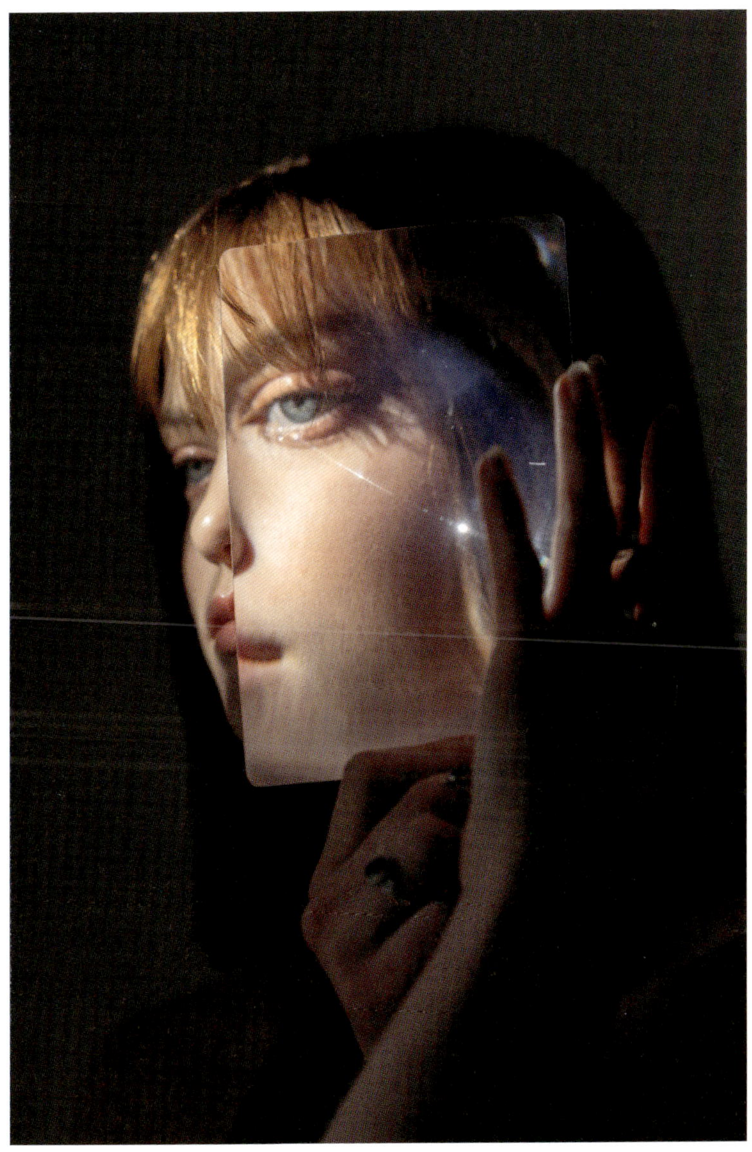

Glory Box

Pain is the poison of beauty.

– William Shakespeare

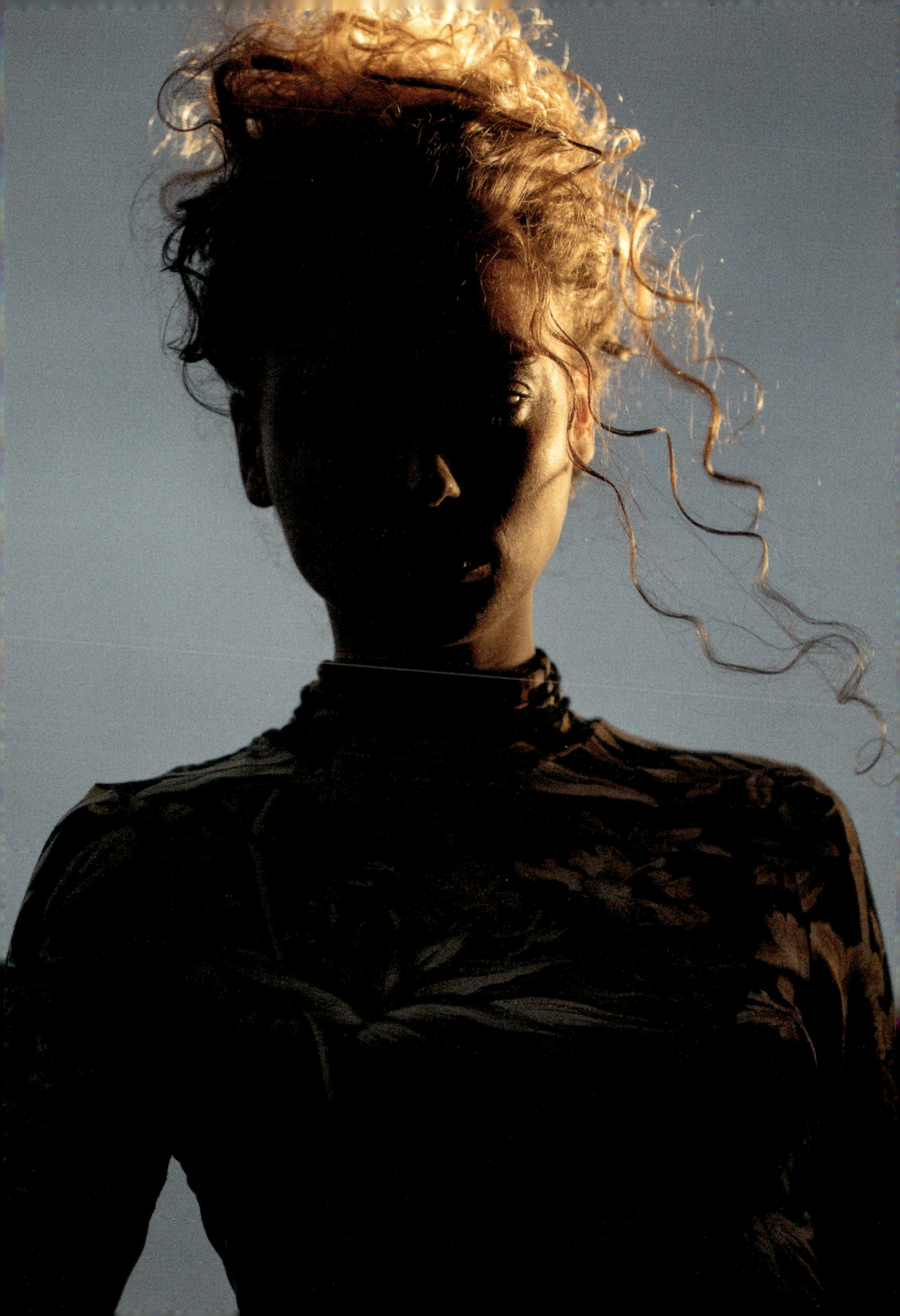

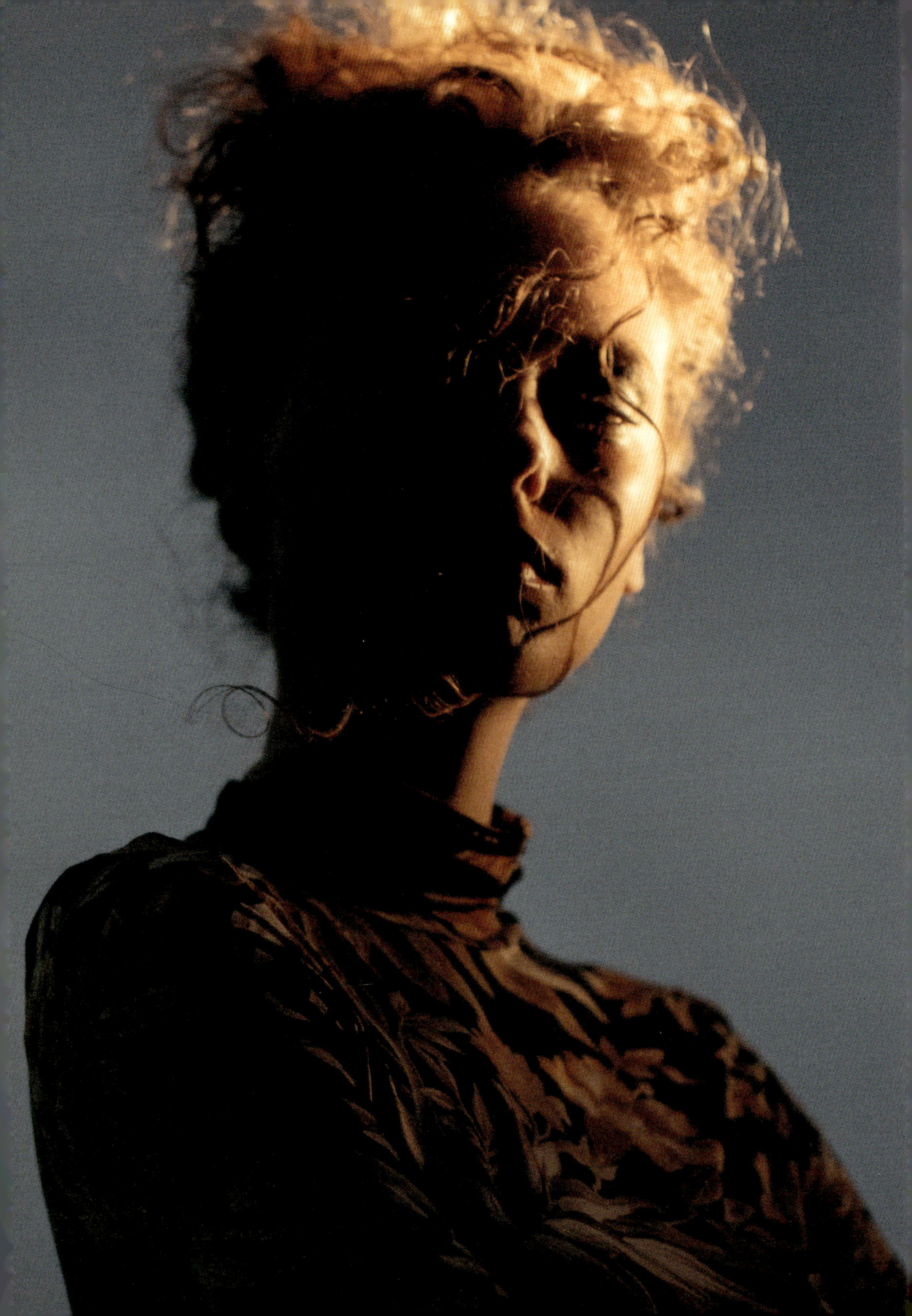

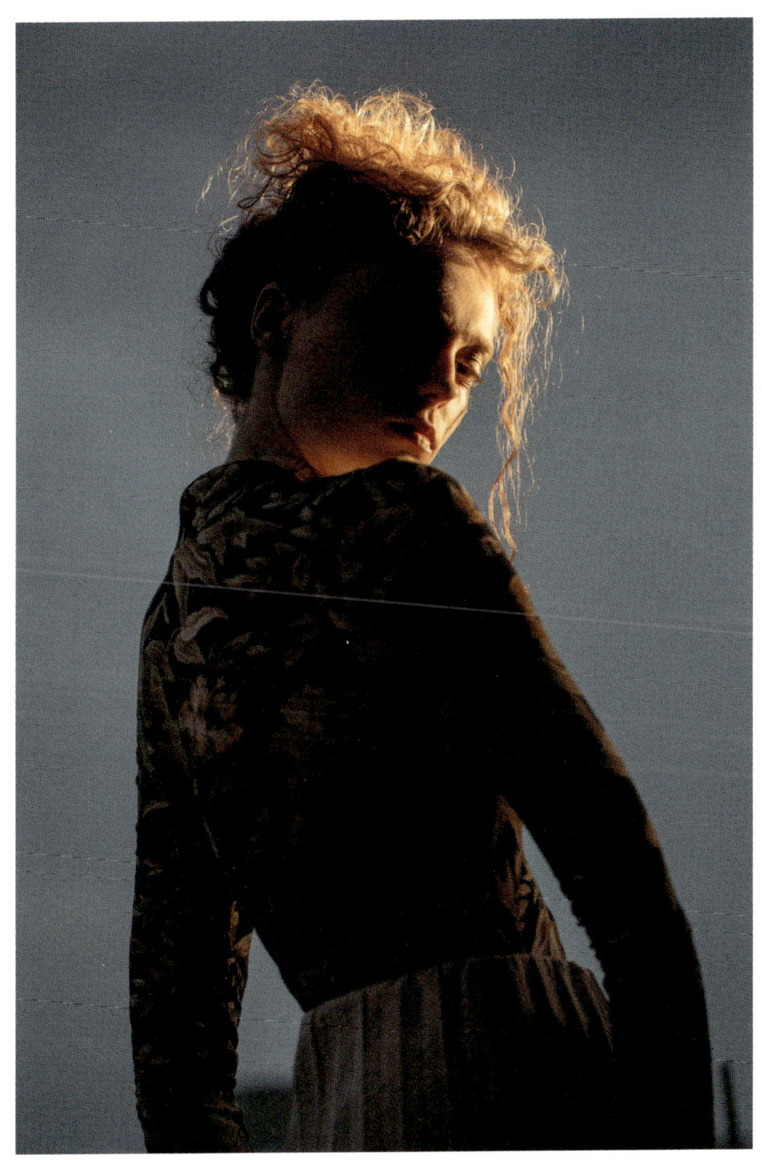

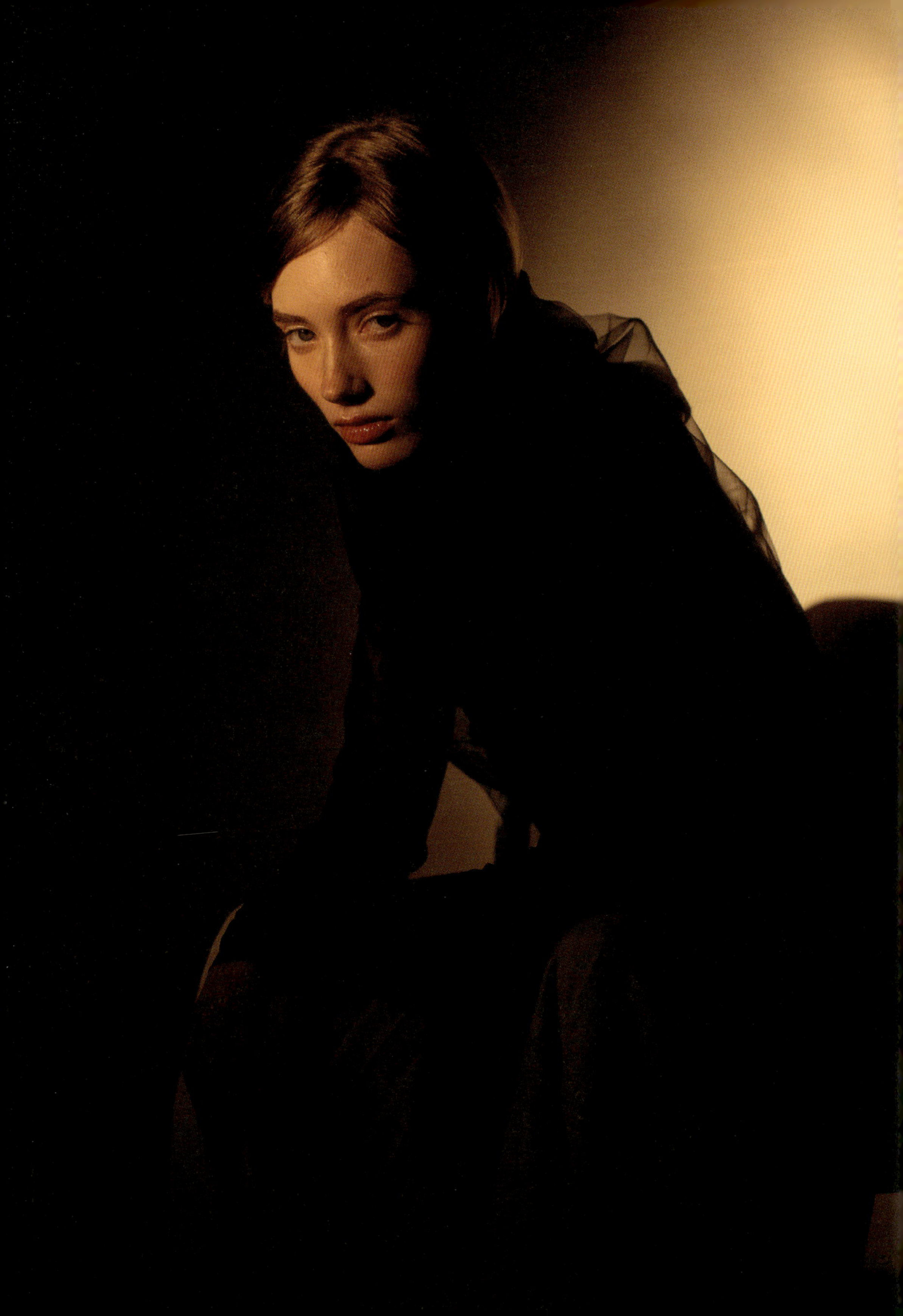

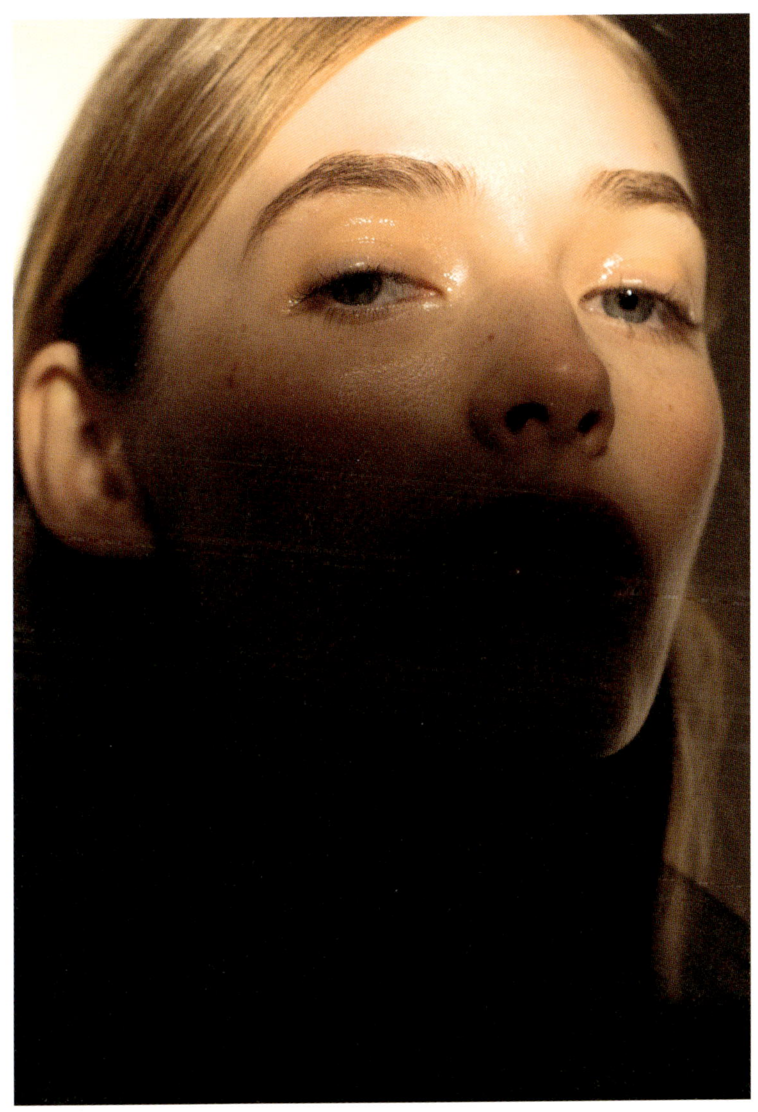

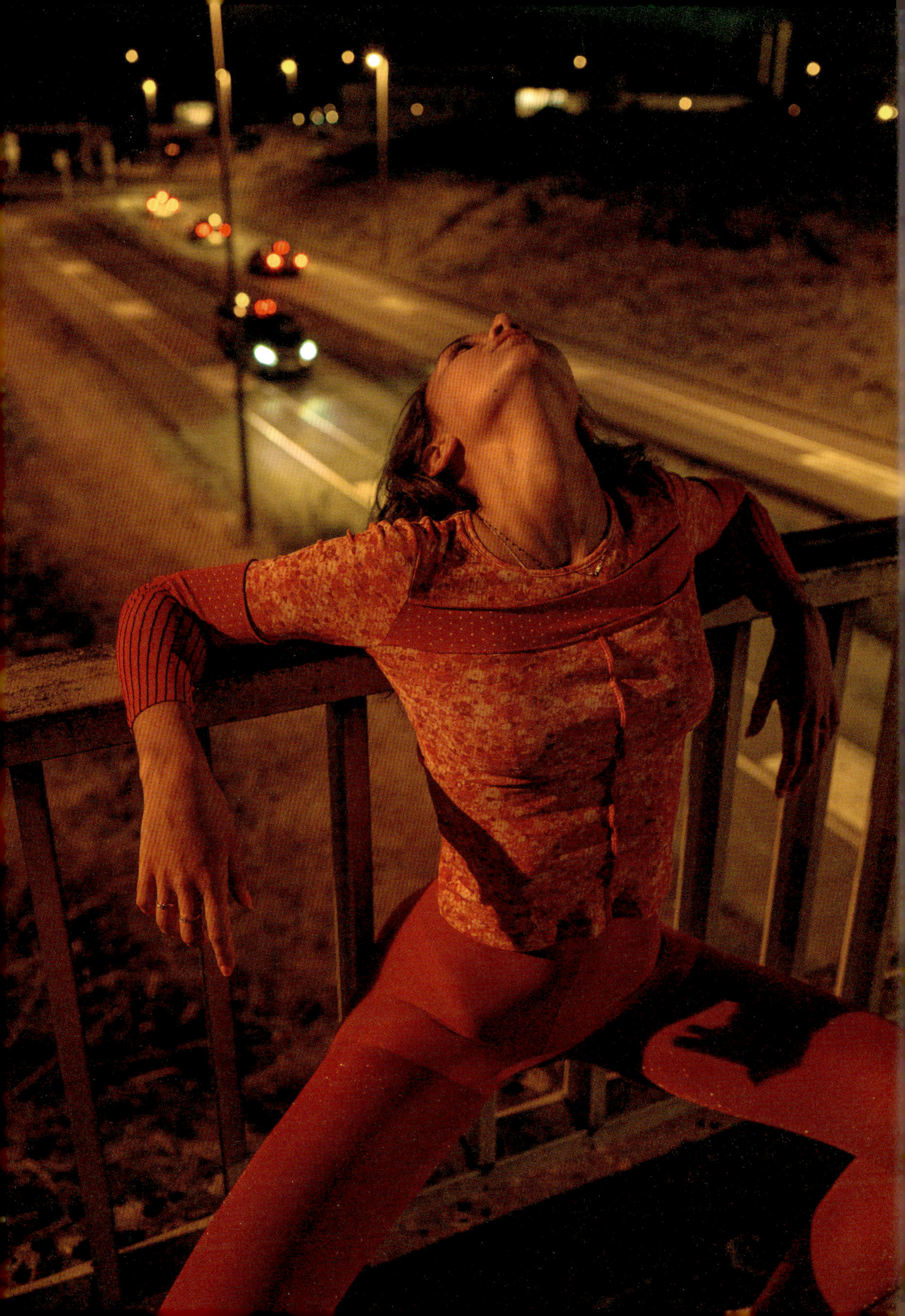

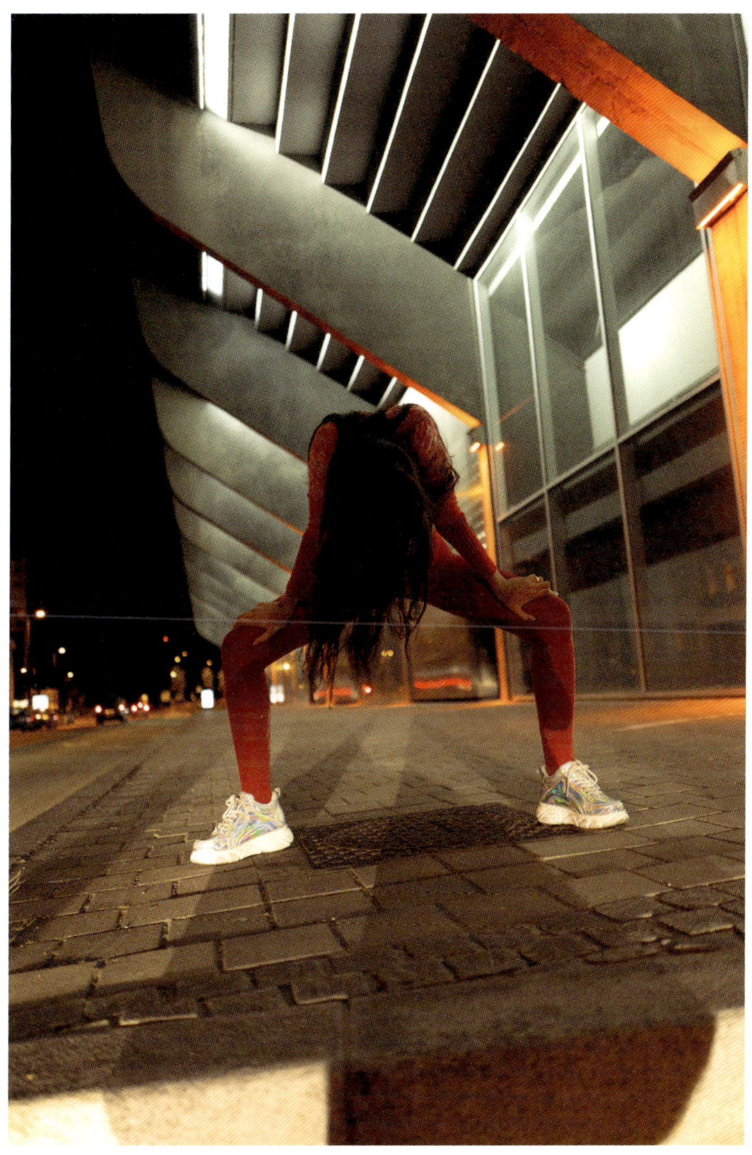

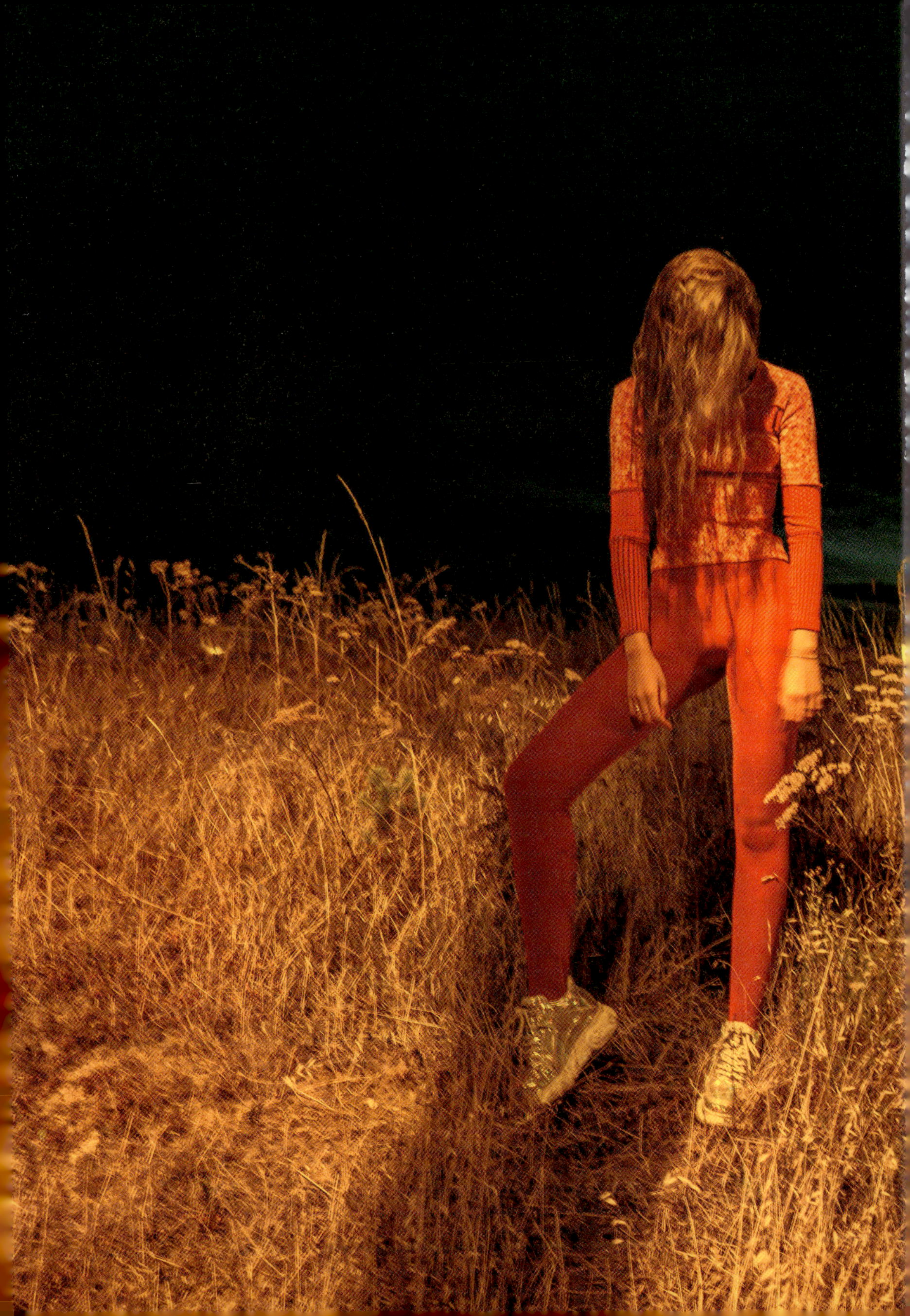

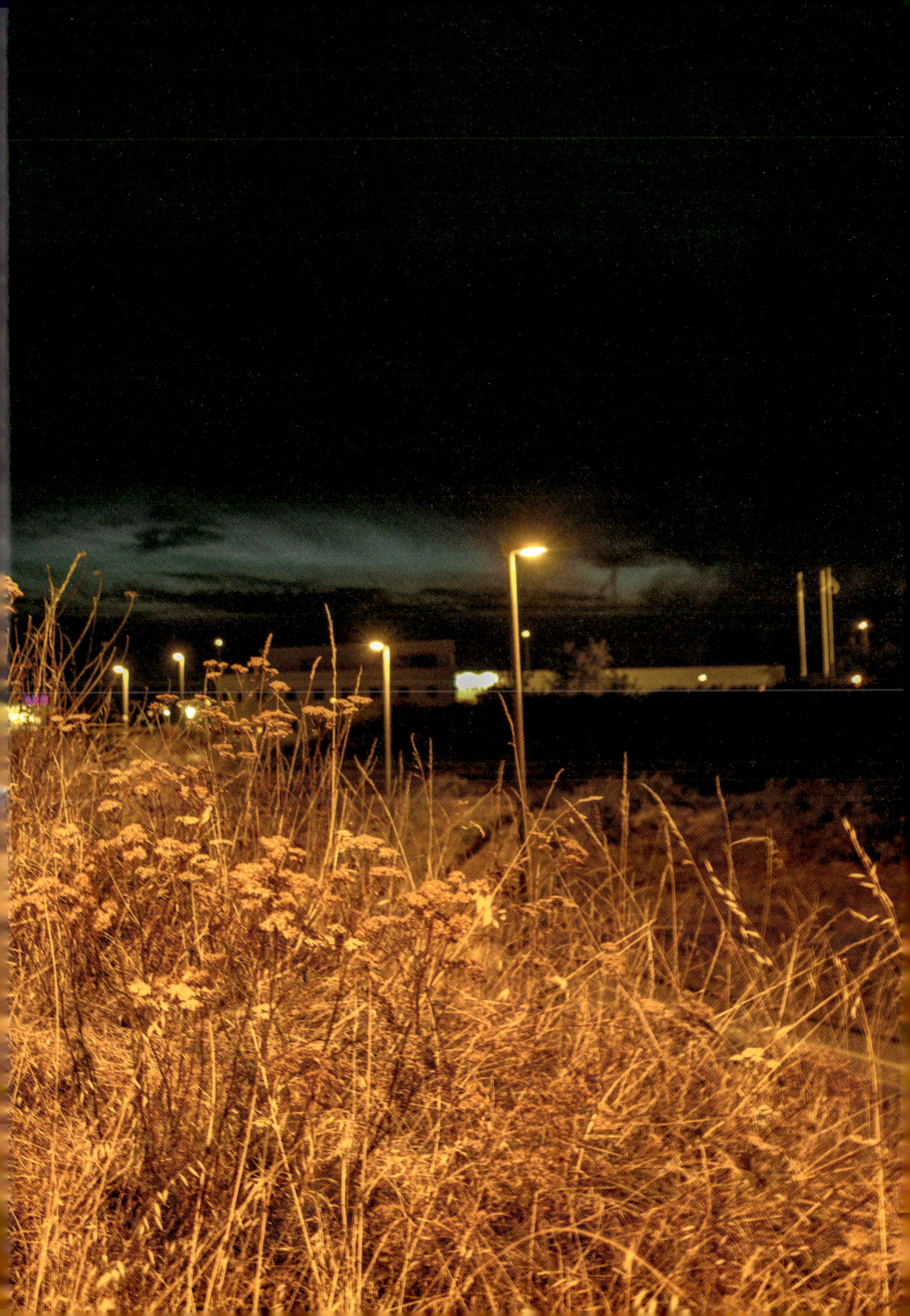

reverie

Published by New Heroes & Pioneers
Photography: Laurent Castellani
Creative Direction: Francois Le Bled
Book Design: Daniel Zachrisson

Print and bound by BALTO print (Lithuania)
Legal Deposit April 2021
ISBN 978-91-87815-79-9

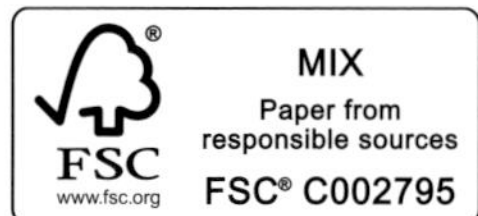

Thank you to François Le Bled for his trust, Madé Taounza, Olivier Berne, Rémy Badan, Anaïs Landet, Antoine Lermite, Sophie Edelin, Mathieu Marze, Marion Guénot, The "Docks du film" team and all the agencies, agents and models who contributed to this book.

– Laurent Castellani

Models by order of first appearance in the book:

Elise Lamarche, Heloïse Challet, Bertille Pinon Botté, Alizée Guillot, Lisa Louis Fratani, Juliette Jambon (via l'agence Premium Models Paris, agent Charlotte Stradere), Alma Durand, Veronika Vasilyeva, Laura Yumi Lambert, Léa Baxerres, Romane Martin, Noemie Porotti, Camille Maillé, Lola Bouchareb, Lotka Lakwijk (via l'agence Silent Paris, agent Samir Zouine), Elisabeth Schumacher, Lucie Poissonnier, Alice Bidelogne, Myrtille Rêvemont, Laura Tserkovna, Hortense Quentin de Gromard, Lou-Ann Pinel, Mao Xiaoing, Doria Poulain, Annah Pont, Ines Yahiaoui, Juliette Robin, Lise Augonnet, Loohan Herisson Arnal.

COLLECTIVE SHORTS
by NHP PUBLISHING